ALASKA
Reflections
on Land
and Spirit

ALASKA

**Reflections
on Land
and Spirit**

EDITED BY
ROBERT HEDIN AND
GARY HOLTHAUS

The University of Arizona Press   Tucson

THE UNIVERSITY OF ARIZONA PRESS

This book was set in 9/13 Linotron 202 Pilgrim.
Manufactured in the United States of America.

93 92 91 90 89   5 4 3 2 1

Library of Congress Cataloging-in-Publication Data

Alaska: reflections on land and spirit.

 1. Alaska–Description and travel.
2. Landscape–Alaska.
3. Man–Influence on nature–Alaska.
I. Hedin, Robert, 1949–   .
II. Holthaus, Gary H., 1932–   .
F904.A493   1989   979.8   88-27803
ISBN 0-8165-1093-8   .

British Library Cataloguing in Publication
data are available.

This Alaska is a great country. If they
can just keep from being taken over
by the U.S. they got a great future.

—WILL ROGERS

Contents

Introduction

Alaska: Reflections on Land and Spirit presents the scope and variety of nonfiction written about Alaska by Alaskans and non-Alaskans alike in the last one hundred years. In collecting these twenty-two essays, we have worked to gather what we feel is the best writing on Alaska by North America's finest writers, many of whom have been recipients of high literary awards—Guggenheims, Pulitzers, National Book Awards —as well as of honors from such organizations as the Sierra Club, the Wilderness Society, and the National Geographic Society for lifetime achievements in conservation and exploration.

On one level, *Alaska: Reflections on Land and Spirit* can be read as a collection of individual adventures with a land that has captured our culture's imagination for generations. Gathered are travelogues, diaries, meditations, and narratives by homesteaders, missionaries, anthropologists, psychologists, ornithologists, poets, teachers, and conservationists, all of whom go beyond the typical clichés and advertising slogans about Alaska to provide an authentic record of a given time and place.

On another level, the book is about recovery and reconciliation. Though set in various parts of Alaska, these essays go well beyond their local geographies to recover the mysterious and oftentimes terrifying intimacy that comes about when the old psychic links between humanity and the natural world are reestablished. Ultimately, *Alaska: Reflections on Land and Spirit* devotes itself to the retrieval of what John Haines calls "our native ground, the original and hardly comprehended thing under our feet, the actual and historical ground, compounded of rock and slime, of animal stench and human use."

The collection also offers glimpses into Alaska's history, its native populations, its current cultural and economic problems, as well as some terse reminders of the gross injustices we have done to the land, to our cultural dreams, and, by extension, to ourselves.

Size is often the first thing that comes to mind about Alaska. It is indeed large, a region so dramatic that it tends to defy the imagination. With a population of only half a million people, the state is larger than Texas, California, and Montana combined, a land so vast that one glacier alone is larger than Rhode Island, and a school district in the northwestern section of the state is larger than Ohio. Barrow, the northernmost community in North America, is roughly 1,300 miles from the North Pole; Ketchikan, on the southern tip of the Alaskan Panhandle, is about 400 miles from Seattle. Fairbanks and Anchorage are the only two cities of any size in the state, though they are separated by the highest mountain range in North America, by long stretches of tundra and taiga, and by a 400-mile stretch of frost-broken pavement. The distance from Fairbanks to Juneau is similar to that of Washington, D.C., to Chicago, and until recently included two time zones. Barrow to Point Hope is comparable to Des Moines to Denver. And Nome to Juneau is similar to that of Oklahoma City to Baltimore. It should be remembered that all these distances are "similar to" the distances in the continental United States, for in Alaska no roads exist between the points just mentioned. All total, the state comprises 586,000 square miles and contains six major geographical regions—Southeast, South-Central, Interior, Arctic, Bering, and Aleutian—each with a distinct climate and ecology.

Despite the fact that Alaska is one of the most recent entrants into the Union, having become a state in 1959, it is the oldest in terms of human history. The earliest of North America's settlers migrated to Alaska first, crossing the Bering Land Bridge some 25,000 years ago during the second stage of Wisconsin glaciation, and traveled down the ice-free valleys of Alaska and Canada into the American Southwest and Mexico. Some eventually returned to the region and settled in the Yukon Territory of Canada and in Alaska's Interior. Known as the Athapascans, they are linguistically related to the Navajos and Apaches of the American Southwest. The second major group to migrate to the New World were the Eskimos who settled along the Arctic coast of Alaska, except for a small enclave of hunters who moved inland.

Another group, now known as the Aleuts, settled in Alaska's Aleutian Chain. The Tlingit, Haida, and Tsimshian of Southeastern Alaska each have a distinctive language and set of traditions but are part of the Northwest Coast Indian culture that extends through British Columbia, Washington, and Oregon. Together, Alaskan Natives comprise 20 percent of the state's current population and speak over twenty distinct languages; many of their village histories are older than those of the city-states of ancient Greece.

Add to this history the Russian occupation of the region, the rise of the fur, fishing, and logging industries, the Klondike gold rush, and the construction of the Alaskan oil pipeline, and the result is a regional history of grand proportions, several intricate and overlapping plots that resonate with stunning complexity.

Though the state is a long way from the rest of the country and its people often speak in terms of distance and alienation, regularly referring to the continental United States as the "Outside," the "Lower 48," and even "America," ultimately the history of Alaska cannot be viewed in isolation from the rest of the country's. The economic, environmental, and cultural problems that are found in Alaska and that are reflected in these essays are, in their essence, nothing more than further acts in a persistent and seemingly unresolvable American drama whose plot centers around the exploitation of the land, its resources, and its native peoples.

For roughly two centuries, the adventurers who came to the state — trappers, traders, Klondike gold seekers, oil pipeline workers—all came with essentially one thing in mind: material gain. Alaska, in other words, was a land to be taken from. And almost every imaginable resource— fur, fish, lumber, gold, oil, human labor, scholarly information, sacred articles and artifacts—was extracted to build industrial profits and scholarly careers, often with little or no expense to the conscience. The prevailing view centered in and around the notion that the land could be endlessly mined and modified to accommodate a culture that stood squarely behind industrialization and urbanization. In the process, little real or intimate knowledge of the land and the deep cultural heritage of its native peoples was ever gained. No wonder, then, that Harry Crews, in writing about the construction of the Alaska oil pipeline in "Going Down in Valdeez," captures the mounting cynicism of many in the post-frontier era: "If Alaska is not our young whore, what is she? She is rich, but who can live with her? She is full of all that will pleasure us, but she is hard and cold to the bone. And if we scar her, leave her with pestilence and corrupted with infection, irrefutably marked with our own private design, who can blame us? Didn't we buy her for a trifling sum to start with?"

The essayists in *Alaska: Reflections on Land and Spirit* represent a different kind of adventurers. Their essays signal a dramatic departure from such an exploitative mentality, suggesting that the era of reckless free-will is over. Possessing a deep and fundamental regard for the natural world, and for its human inhabitants, they venture out not in opposition to this world but with the desire to stand squarely within it, to experience its elemental strength, magnificence, and beauty firsthand, on its own terms. At the heart of each of their quests lies a certain "communality of spirit" with the land, and they carry out into the solitude and wildness a desire to rediscover an appreciation for the land's value that goes well beyond its ability to produce fish and game, oil and gold. Though products of a western culture that believes its wilderness is present for the taking, most are in search of a healthy alternative, striving for what anthropologist Richard Nelson calls "a separate kind of conscience," one founded on an "older and more tested wisdom" that says the environment should be sustained and not debased.

Several of the essayists in *Alaska: Reflections on Land and Spirit* simply journey out to experience the landscape. Traveling by foot, boat, or plane, they allow themselves to be absorbed by the land, offering portraits of the sublime, rugged panoramas of the Alaskan wilderness such as those in John Muir's "In Camp at Glacier Bay," Robert Marshall's "Toward Doonerak," and William O. Douglas's "Brooks Range." Other depictions are more intimate and personal, such as those in John Haines' "Ice" and Billie Wright's "Four Seasons North." A surprising number—Margaret Murie's "Geese," Roger Tory Peterson's "Tundra of

the Emperors," Barry Lopez's "Borders," and Peter Matthiessen's "Oomingmak"—deal, in part, with expeditions into remote areas of Alaska
to study resident animal populations. Being patient and experienced
observers, the essayists offer many remarkable observational nuggets
of the land and its inhabitants, reminding us again of the vast singu-
larity of things as well as of our place in the natural world with all its
seasonal turnings and yearly migrations.

In addition, the authors provide portraits of Alaska's people, native
and non-native alike. Through them the land and its resonant history
are given a strong and articulate voice. There are the two old Eskimo
whalers, Oovi and Irrigoo, in David Boeri's "Grandfathers of Gambell,
Grandsons of the Stone Age," who recall a time when "the universe
was full of spirits" and the villagers of Gambell freely moved between
Alaska and Siberia to trade and wrestle. Or Helge Boquist in John
McPhee's "Riding the Boom Extension" who remembers a time when
"a telephone line ran from Circle a hundred and sixty-five miles" out
to the miners panning for gold along the creeks, a communal network
in which "everybody heard everybody else, from Circle to Ferry Roadhouse to Central to Miller House, and on Birch and Independence,
Deadwood and Ketchum, Mammoth and Mastodon Creeks." Or the
fourteen-year-old Eskimo girl in Robert Coles's "Distances" whose life
on the flat coastal plains of the Arctic is "a matter of balancing horizons—that of the water, that of the land, that of the air"—and who
remembers well her wise grandmother telling her that we are all "guests
of the land." Indeed, throughout much of *Alaska: Reflections on Land
and Spirit*, the lines dividing the people from their histories and from
the land they inhabit are erased, and a change in one means a change
in the other.

For many of the writers, Alaska is not only a region of extensive
and peculiar geography. It is also a land where the prehistoric, the
out-of-date, and the world of high technology come together to form
a place where time is warped and anomalies abound. In Sigurd Olson's
"Alaskan Wilderness," John Hildebrand's "Fables," and John Morgan's
"Letter From Wales (Alaska)," the thin tenuous surface of the present

continually gives way to reveal the intricate grains and cross-grains of human and nonhuman history. Indeed, every imaginable form of time can be heard ticking away, often creating intoxicating and bewildering effects. Other essayists punctuate their landscapes with exotic artifacts —bone awls, ivory arrowheads, beartooth pendants—or the remains of old dwellings, all suggesting a long and varied human occupation of the land. Along with all the incongruities of twentieth century living, Alaska is a place, we are reminded, where one can still glimpse something of the original grandeur and mystery of the universe.

From the time of the earliest explorers to the droves of modern back-packers, the wilderness has provided an abundance of things unknown and unimaginable as well as those challenges against which the American spirit has tested and retested itself. From its very inception, our culture has turned to the wilderness to define and to sustain itself physically and spiritually. Its presence, in short, lies at the very marrow of our cultural bones. Without it our nation would lack an essential spiritual direction that has helped make the American experience unique. Some areas of Alaska are already lost, having slipped quietly away into the mainstream of colorless American urbanity. Anchorage, for example, a city of 220,000 residents, has the nation's highest rates of venereal disease and divorce as well as a homicide rate that is three times greater than that of Los Angeles. The rest of the state remains much as it has been for generations. To preserve it in fact and in spirit means, in part, to preserve some of the original convictions, which we have long held as a culture, in the essential goodness and stalwart nature of the land and of ourselves. As several essayists in *Alaska: Reflections on Land and Spirit* suggest, the Alaskan wilderness should be saved at all costs because, quite simply, nothing else like it exists any longer; it is all that remains to us of what naturalist John Burroughs called "the great, shaggy barbarian earth."

Alaska: Reflections on Land and Spirit offers twenty-two pieces of a highly intricate puzzle that, when put together, form an effective and accurate portrait of Alaska in the post-frontier era. Some of the essays have been previously published in small regional magazines or in large nationally circulated journals. Others are reprinted from texts long out of print. However, several have been written specifically for the book and appear in print for the first time. All evoke the land and spirit of Alaska in a particular, palpable way. The result, we think, is a book that is both haunting and memorable, one that speaks from a great depth of time as well as from the immediacy of our own moment.

ROBERT HEDIN

GARY HOLTHAUS

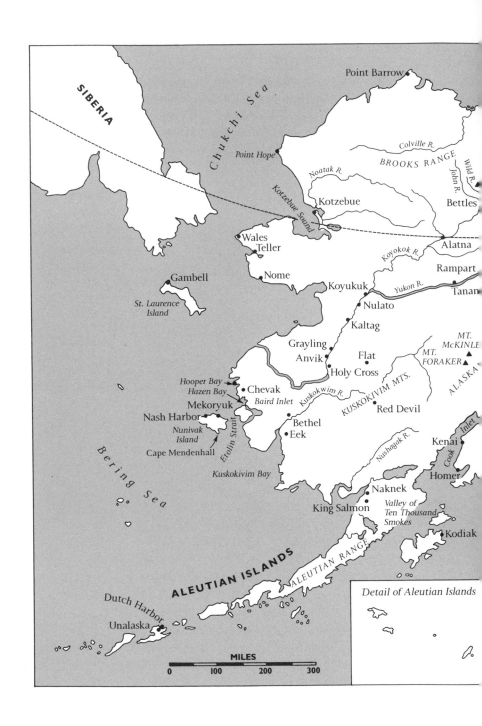

SIBERIA

Chukchi Sea

Point Barrow

Colville R.

BROOKS RANGE

Noatak R.

Wild R.

John R.

Point Hope

Kotzebue Sound

Kotzebue

Bettles

Wales

Teller

Alatna

Koyokok R.

Rampart

Nome

Koyukuk

Yukon R.

Tanan

Gambell

Nulato

St. Laurence Island

Kaltag

Grayling

Flat

MT. McKINLE

Anvik

MT. FORAKER▲

Holy Cross

Kuskokwim R.

KUSKOKIVIM MTS.

ALASKA

Hooper Bay

Hazen Bay

Chevak

Baird Inlet

Red Devil

Mekoryuk

Nash Harbor

Etolin Strait

Bethel

Eek

Nunivak Island

Nushagak R.

Kenai

Cook Inlet

Cape Mendenhall

Homer

Kuskokivim Bay

Naknek

Bering Sea

King Salmon

Valley of Ten Thousand Smokes

Kodiak

ALEUTIAN ISLANDS

ALEUTIAN RANGE

Detail of Aleutian Islands

Dutch Harbor

Unalaska

MILES

0   100   200   300

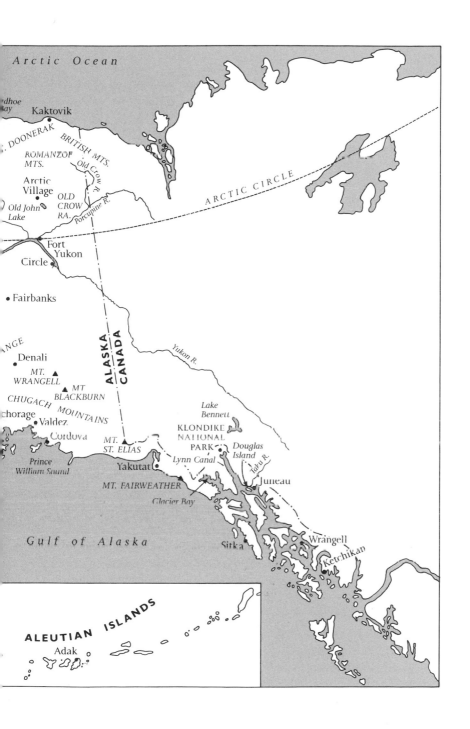

ALASKA
**Reflections
on Land
and Spirit**

Alaskan
Wilderness

Sigurd Olson is the author of *The
Singing Wilderness, Listening Point,
The Lonely Land, Open Horizons,
Wilderness Days, Reflections from the
North Country, Of Time and Place,* and
Runes of the North. Born in Chicago
in 1899, he was educated at Northern
College, the University of Wisconsin,
and the University of Illinois. He
was at one time the president of
the Wilderness Society, as well as
the National Parks Association. He
also served as a consultant to the
Department of the Interior and to
numerous conservation groups.

Alaska holds within itself some of the finest wilderness scenery on the continent. An enormous peninsula a thousand miles from end to end, even its boundaries are dramatic: the rolling Pacific, the Bering Sea, the Arctic Ocean, and Canada's Territory of the Yukon.

The Brooks Range is a towering rampart against the north, the Aleutian and Alaskan Ranges a matching bulwark to the south, between them a complex of many other ranges, peaks, and valleys that are still relatively unknown and some unnamed. Along its rugged, beetling coasts are fiords, living glaciers, and ice fields which remind one of an age that is past. Down the very center of this wild northwest extension of the continent, crossing and recrossing the Arctic Circle itself, flows the Yukon, one of the earth's mightiest rivers, twisting and turning for almost two thousand miles until it disgorges its silt in a vast delta of tangled waterways.

In the warm, rainswept archipelago of the southeast are lush, rain forests along the coastal beaches, spruce, cedar, and hemlock, huge trees festooned with mosses in yellow-green. Quiet always reigns there for the cushion of moss underneath is soft and deep. In the north are tundras and muskegs matched only by the barren lands of Canada. As though this were not enough, Alaska's stormy Aleutian Islands extend in an unbroken chain almost halfway to Japan.

It is a land of big bears and moose, of walrus and seal, of whales and salmon. Caribou herds roam the tundras of their ancient range, goats and sheep climb the cliffs and slopes of its mountains, polar bears hunt the ice floes. Eskimos live along its western and northern coasts, Indians in the interior and the south. This was the pathway of migration of Asiatic tribes across the Bering Strait from Siberia.

Here is a land of immensity and contrasts seldom found in such extravagant profusion. No wonder then, that, in my search for wilderness, I found it there in a majesty and grandeur I had never known before. True, like all the north, Alaska has changed, but because of its size and remoteness there is still much of the wild as it used to be. It was in this region that I found the wilderness at its best, scenes so vivid and full of meaning they will never be forgotten.

John Hopkins Inlet of Glacier Bay in the southeast was such a place. As the little ship *Nunatak* pushed its careful way up into the fiord, bergs and floes became more numerous, blocks of ice so transparently green-blue they might have been dropped from the skies themselves. On the left a whale blew, turned over on its side, a flipper striking the water with a resounding smack. Then there were two lying side by side and whirling as though on a spit. Again and again they turned, and each time there was a silver spout as flippers crashed against the surface.

Porpoises were keeping steady pace with the ship; the floes grew denser and many had seals upon them. The mountainous shores were without life, for they had emerged from the glacier at the head of the inlet within the memory of man, their summits mirrored in the still waters. The boat seemed small and fragile as it threaded its way up the passage and through the reflections. Rivers of ice filled the valleys on either side, remnants of the dying glacier that once filled the entire bay.

We were within half a mile of the ice front. Seals were everywhere now, and unafraid, they swam close, their eyes large and luminous. Guillemots, murrelets, and scoters rested all around, while sea gulls convoyed us in. There was a constant rustling as the floes moved past. Sometimes they turned over, but as they steadied, the seals climbed back on them, slipping and sliding on the smooth, unstable surfaces.

The air was colder now, for we were close enough to the great mass of ice to feel its breath. Suddenly there was a muffled roar as a column of brown water and mud surged skyward, the sound reverberating from mountain to mountain. The column subsided, water heaved and the huge blocks moved up and down; the boat rode with them as though on a tidal wave. We watched the wave as it sped down the inlet, seals riding their cakes of ice as nonchalantly as though nothing had happened.

It was still once more and, had it not been for the uneasy whispering and movement of the water, we would not have known new bergs were being spawned. No sooner had the quiet descended, however, than we were conscious again of a soft rushing at the forefront of the glacier, a rushing punctuated by a succession of detonations as from artillery barrage. Again the sense of movement, the column of spray, mud, and water, then in slow motion a huge block of ice broke away and sank into the sea.

The scene has never left me. Because of this living remnant of the past, I had returned to the glacial age at a time when with the recession of the ice, such spawnings took place all over the north. I had spanned ten thousand years of continental history in the short space of a day, had lived along the edge of the great glacier and watched its retreat.

The McNeil is a typical Alaskan river with a sand bar and a broad alluvial flat where it enters the sea. As we approached, we saw its mouth was very much alive. Salmon were running, the rapids full of them heading upstream to spawn. Brown bears were feeding, hooking the fish with their claws, grasping them with their teeth, wading in the shallows and over the rocks, gorging on the harvest as they have for uncounted centuries. One enormous old bear sat half-submerged in the water and caught the salmon as they ran against him. A bite or two and he would catch another without moving, the bloody carcasses floating downstream. This bear was great and fat; he had learned the secret of taking fish the easy way without pursuit. Leaner, hungrier bears wallowed around the slippery boulders, rushed frantically into pools, cornered their prey between the rocks or against the ledges. We counted many that morning, the far-famed brownies of Alaska.

Back of the bears were eagles, feeding on half-eaten salmon washed up on the bank. There was a constant screaming and movement of wings as the big birds hovered over their feast. Flocks of sea gulls completed the picture, and over all was the silver canopy of wings and the sound of their incessant mewing. The scene was the same when the Russians established colonies along the coast almost two centuries ago, an ecological balance not yet disturbed by man.

As I watched, it was not hard to imagine a primitive man crouched behind one of those boulders waiting to move in and get his share. Knowing a spear was no protection, he would bide his time and wait for the fish that would be his when the animals, their hunger appeased, left for the dense alder brush on either side of the river. Then like the eagles and the gulls, he would run in and scavenge with them. Carcasses lay everywhere, but still he dared not move. He was hungry, had waited long, and watched with envy. A fish drifted close and tempted, he grasped his spear, grew cautious, settled down once more.

That summer one of the dormant volcanoes in the Valley of Ten Thousand Smokes exploded, spewing smoke, gases, and ash some thirty thousand feet into the air over an area of fifty square miles, blotting out the sun in some places a hundred miles away. Shortly afterward, I flew into the region, our little plane following a valley that led toward the volcano. As we approached the interior, I was conscious of a yellowish cloud different from fog or ordinary dust. Thicker and thicker grew the haze. There was a smell of sulphur in the air and visibility dropped until it was difficult to judge altitude or direction.

I looked down and below was a bed of cinders and ash. Not a tree, a bush, or any living thing was there. Smoke and gas issued from fumeroles, evidence that volcanic forces were still alive. This, I thought, was how the earth looked several billions of years ago before its crust had cooled enough for waters to form, a span devoid of life until at last the rains formed pools and lakes and seas, and in their warm and stagnant backwaters, molecules combined to form the first organic structures.

Here was the primeval from which all life had come, including man. From such smoke and ash, molten lava and gas, had come the miracle of a creature who could turn back time, destroy all life and perhaps the planet itself. Out of that had emerged our culture, our consciousness of beauty, and a wisdom garnered over the ages which could keep the flame of spirit alive if only it willed. This was an elemental world: the expanding universe, exploding suns and meteorites, colliding nebulae, the beginning of all things and possibly their end.

Words from the Book of Revelations went through my mind:

And he opened the bottomless pit; and there smoke arose out of the pit, as the smoke of a great furnace; and the sun and the air were darkened by reason of the smoke of the pit.

One misty day I climbed a brush-grown plateau to a lookout point unparalleled even in Alaska, where unusual vistas are commonplace. A lake lay in the distance but its waters were dull; and the muskeg and tundra, with its scattered scrub spruce, dwarf birch, and willow, dripped with moisture. One might just as well have been in a protected back-country flat as far as view was concerned.

Then a miracle happened. The low-hanging mists lifted and the sun shone forth in an unclouded sky. The distant lake became a sparkling expanse of blue, and all around me for over a hundred miles was a panorama of shining, snow-capped mountains flanked by glistening ice fields and glaciers. To the north was the great arc of the Alaskan Range, to the south the Chugaches bordering the gulf, southeast in a gigantic cluster, Mounts Wrangell, Blackburn, and Sanford. But I knew Denali, the giant of them all loomed to the west and, though hidden by other summits, stood there brooding and alone.

I was breathless with the scene. No words could describe the sense of immensity, of almost limitless terrain before me. Instead of one mountain peak, there were groups and clusters; instead of one glacier, major continental ice fields with uncounted tributaries alive and flowing. Here was an overwhelming beauty that dwarfed all my preconceptions.

This had the permanence of high-mountain country everywhere, a certain feeling of stability and defiance of man's efforts to change. Such a land, I felt, should stay as it is, and fulfill its highest use for mankind as a reminder of a virgin continent. Men should be able to stand on this lookout a thousand years from now and, with such vistas around them, be at peace. No room here for little thoughts; this was a place for expansiveness of the soul and cosmic perception.

The clouds were moving in again and with their constant shifting and shadows the mountain ranges seemed like floating mirages over the horizons. Within half an hour the peaks began to disappear, each one in a final flash of light. Then the mists descended over the plateau and the scene vanished, only the dripping spruce and scrubby bush remained.

In the far north lies the Brooks Range, one of the most formidable and unknown mountain expanses of the continent. We left Fort Yukon and flew low over the mouth of the Porcupine, the river that reaches so far east it almost touches the Mackenzie. Below us lay the vast flats of the Yukon River with its thousands of ponds and bogs. To the northeast were rising foothills with the Coleen and the Sheenjek rivers which we would follow. We glimpsed the distant ranges flanking the Brooks toward the east. To the west was the Chandalar country and beyond it nothing but mountains as far as the Chukchi Sea.

The foothills dropped behind us and the Sheenjek, now laded with silt, was white and turbulent as it tumbled down the slopes. We climbed steadily, hurtled a few lesser peaks, and then were over the crest of the range itself, one of such primordial savagery, it seemed utterly presumptuous to challenge its heights in a small seaplane.

Below were precipitious peaks, jagged, black, and sharp. Naked valleys and gorges lay between them. Only when flying over the Alps had I seen such stark and threatening pinnacles, but they were friendly compared to these. There, green and verdant meadows held picturesque chalets, while villages with white church spires nestled in among them, and, connecting all the valleys, were ribbons of roads and trails. Here was nothing but rock, limitless, barren reaches, and talus slopes with no signs of man or of any living thing.

To me they looked new, as though recently emerged from some gigantic cataclysm within the earth, without time enough to have been softened by erosion. Squalls and steamers of mist swirled around knife-edged cliffs, and the little plane bounced and fought its way through them toward the headwaters of the Chandalar. To the south lay the foothills and the broad valley of the Yukon, to the north, down a slope of a hundred miles, the misty fog-shrouded shores of the Arctic Ocean.

At last we caught the gleam of the river, turned and flew down it as far as Old John Lake where the Koness River leaves to find the Sheenjek, our highway going in. We landed there and looked back at the mighty rampart we had left. At that distance, it was softened and blue, not so terribly cold and unfriendly as it seemed when we were flying above it. I knew then that what I had felt up there was an illusion, that over its brown and seemingly empty stretches, flowers bloom in exotic colors, and mosses and lichens paint rocks and hillsides, that birds sing and many other creatures are at home there.

All Alaska has an early morning freshness for me. While it is not

young, and some of its ranges are as ancient as any on earth, I cannot
help but feel when I see such mountains as the Brooks, that this is
how the Appalachians, the Rockies, and the Laurentians once were.
With that realization I somehow see, with greater understanding, the
long road over which not only mountains, but all life has come. Such
places answer a question for me that has reverberated down through
the centuries:

When I consider thy heavens, the work of thy fingers, the moon and the stars,
which thou has ordained; What is man that thou are mindful of him?

JOHN MUIR

In Camp at Glacier Bay

Naturalist and explorer John Muir
was born in Scotland in 1838 and
was educated at the University of
Wisconsin in Madison. The author
of *A Thousand Mile Walk to the Gulf,*
The Story of My Boyhood and Youth,
The Mountains of California, Our
National Parks, Stickeen, My First
Summer in the Sierra, The Yosemite,
Travels in Alaska, and *Steep Trails,*
Mr. Muir was a leader in the forest
conservation movement and was
president of the Sierra Club from 1902,
the year of its formation, until his
death in 1914.

I left San Francisco for Glacier Bay on the steamer City of Pueblo, June 14, 1890, at 10 A.M., this being my third trip to southeastern Alaska and fourth to Alaska, including northern and western Alaska as far as Unalaska and Pt. Barrow and the northeastern coast of Siberia. The bar at the Golden Gate was smooth, the weather cool and pleasant. The redwoods in sheltered coves approach the shore closely, their dwarfed and shorn tops appearing here and there in ravines along the coast up to Oregon. The wind-swept hills, beaten with scud, are of course bare of trees. Along the Oregon and Washington coast the trees get nearer the sea, for spruce and contorted pine endure the briny winds better than the redwoods. We took the inside passage between the shore and Race Rocks, a long range of islets on which many a good ship has been wrecked. The breakers from the deep Pacific, driven by the gale, made a glorious display of foam on the bald islet rocks, sending spray over the tops of some of them a hundred feet high or more in sublime, curving, jagged-edged and flame-shaped sheets. The gestures of these up-springing, purple-tinged waves as they dashed and broke were sublime and serene, combining displays of graceful beauty of motion and form with tremendous power—a truly glorious show. I noticed several small villages on the green slopes between the timbered mountains and the shore. Long Branch made quite a display of new houses along the beach, north of the mouth of the Columbia.

I had pleasant company on the Pueblo and sat at the chief engineer's table, who was a good and merry talker. An old San Francisco lawyer, rather stiff and dignified, knew my father-in-law, Dr. Strentzel. Three ladies, opposed to the pitching of the ship, were absent from table the greater part of the way. My best talker was an old Scandinavian sea-captain, who was having a new bark built at Port Blakely,—an interesting old salt, every sentence of his conversation flavored with sea-brine, bluff and hearty as a sea-wave, keen-eyed, courageous, self-reliant, and so stubbornly skeptical he refused to believe even in glaciers.

"After you see your bark," I said, "and find everything being done to your mind, you had better go on to Alaska and see the glaciers."

"Oh, I haf seen many glaciers already."

"But are you sure that you know what a glacier is?" I asked.

"Vell, a glacier is a big mountain all covered up with ice."

"Then a river," said I, "must be a big mountain all covered up with water."

I explained what a glacier was and succeeded in exciting his interest. I told him he must reform, for a man who neither believed in God nor glaciers must be very bad, indeed the worst of all unbelievers.

At Port Townsend I met Mr. Loomis, who had agreed to go with me as far as the Muir Glacier. We sailed from here on the steamer Queen. We touched again at Victoria, and I took a short walk into the adjacent woods and gardens and found the flowery vegetation in its glory, especially the large wild rose for which the region is famous, and the spiraea and English honeysuckle of the gardens.

June 18. We sailed from Victoria on the Queen at 10:30 A.M. The weather all the way to Fort Wrangell was cloudy and rainy, but the scenery is delightful even in the dullest weather. The marvelous wealth of forests, islands, and waterfalls, the cloud-wreathed heights, the many avalanche slopes and slips, the peral-gray tones of the sky, the browns of the woods, their purple flower edges and mist fringes, the endless combinations of water and land and ever-shifting clouds—none of these greatly interest the tourists. I noticed one of the small whales that frequent these channels and mentioned the fact, then called attention to a charming group of islands, but they turned their eyes from the islands, saying, "Yes, yes, they are very fine, but where did you see the whale?"

The timber is larger and apparently better every way as you go north from Victoria, that is on the islands, perhaps on account of fires from less rain to the southward. All the islands have been overswept by the ice-sheet and are but little changed as yet, save a few of the highest summits which have been sculptured by local residual glaciers. All have approximately the form of greatest strength with reference to the overflow of an ice-sheet, excepting those mentioned above, which have been more or less eroded by local residual glaciers. Every channel also has the form of greatest strength with reference to ice-action. Islands, as we have seen, are still being born in Glacier Bay and elsewhere to the northward.

I found many pleasant people aboard, but strangely ignorant on the subject of earth-sculpture and landscape-making. Professor Niles, of the Boston Institute of Technology, is aboard; also Mr. Russell and Mr. Kerr of the Geological Survey, who are now on their way to Mt. St. Elias, hoping to reach the summit; and a granddaughter of Peter Burnett, the first governor of California.

We arrived at Wrangell in the rain at 10:30 P.M. There was a grand rush on shore to buy curiosities and see totem poles. The shops were jammed and mobbed, high prices paid for shabby stuff manufactured expressly for tourist trade. Silver bracelets hammered out of dollars and half dollars by Indian smiths are the most popular articles, then baskets, yellow cedar toy canoes, paddles, etc. Most people who travel look only at what they are directed to look at. Great is the power of the guidebook-maker, however ignorant. I inquired for my old friends Tyeen and Shakes, who were both absent.

June 20. We left Wrangell early this morning and passed through the Wrangell Narrows at high tide. I noticed a few bergs near Cape Fan-shawe from Wrangell Glacier. The water ten miles from Wrangell is colored with particles derived mostly from the Stickeen River glaciers and Le Conte Glacier. All the waters of the channels north of Wrangell are green or yellowish from glacier erosion. We had a good view of the glaciers all the way to Juneau, but not of their high, cloud-veiled fountains. The stranded bergs on the moraine bar at the mouth of Sum Dum Bay looked just as they did ten years ago.

Before reaching Juneau, the Queen proceeded up the Taku Inlet that the passengers might see the fine glacier at its head, and ventured to within half a mile of the berg-discharging front, which is about three quarters of a mile wide. Bergs fell but seldom, perhaps one in half an hour. The glacier makes a rapid descent near the front. The inlet, there-fore, will not be much extended beyond its present limit by the reces-sion of the glacier. The grand rocks on either side of its channel show ice-action in telling style. The Norris Glacier, about two miles below the Taku, is a good example of a glacier in the first stage of decadence. The Taku River enters the head of the inlet a little to the east of the glaciers, coming from beyond the main coast range. All the tourists are delighted at seeing a grand glacier in the flesh. The scenery is very fine here and in the channel at Juneau. On Douglas Island there is a large mill of 240 stamps, all run by one small water-wheel, which, however, is acted on by water at enormous pressure. The forests around the mill are being rapidly nibbled away. Wind is here said to be very violent at times, blowing away people and houses and sweeping scud far up the mountainside. Winter snow is seldom more than a foot or two deep.

June 21. We arrived at Douglas Island at five in the afternoon and went sight-seeing through the mill. Six hundred tons of low-grade quartz are crushed per day. Juneau, on the mainland opposite the Douglas Island mills, is quite a village, well supplied with stores, churches, etc. A dance-house in which Indians are supposed to show native dances of all sorts is perhaps the best-patronized of all the places of amusement. A Mr. Brooks, who prints a paper here, gave us some information on Mt. St. Elias, Mt. Wrangell, and the Cook Inlet and Prince William Sound region. He told Russell that he would never reach the summit of St. Elias, that it was inaccessible. He saw no glaciers that discharged bergs into the sea at Cook Inlet, but many in Prince William Sound.

June 22. Leaving Juneau at noon, we had a good view of the Auk Glacier at the mouth of the channel between Douglas Island and the mainland, and of Eagle Glacier a few miles north of the Auk on the east side of Lynn Canal. Then the Davidson Glacier came in sight, finely curved, striped with medial moraines, and girdled in front by its magnificent tree-fringed terminal moraine; and besides these many others of every size and pattern on the mountains bounding Lynn Canal, most of them comparatively small, completing their sculpture. The mountains on either hand and at the head of the canal are strikingly beautiful at any time of the year. The sky to-day is mostly clear, with just clouds enough hovering about the mountains to show them to best advantage as they stretch onward in sustained grandeur like two separate and distinct ranges, each mountain with its glaciers and clouds and fine sculpture glowing bright in smooth, graded light. Only a few of them exceed five thousand feet in height; but as one naturally associates great height with ice-and-snow-laden mountains and with glacial sculpture so pronounced, they seem much higher. There are now two canneries at the head of Lynn Canal. The Indians furnish some of the salmon at ten cents each. Everybody sits up to see the midnight sky. At this time of the year there is no night here, though the sun drops a degree or two below the horizon. One may read at twelve o'clock San Francisco time.

June 23. Early this morning we arrived in Glacier Bay. We passed through crowds of bergs at the mouth of the bay, though, owing to wind and tide, there were but few at the front of Muir Glacier. A fine, bright day, the last of a group of a week or two, as shown by the dryness of the sand along the shore and on the moraine—rare weather hereabouts. Most of the passengers went ashore and climbed the moraine on the east side to get a view of the glacier from a point a little higher than the top of the front wall. A few ventured on a mile or two farther. The day was delightful, and our one hundred and eighty passengers were happy, gazing at the beautiful blue of the bergs and the shattered pinnacled crystal wall, awed by the thunder and commotion of the falling and rising icebergs, which ever and anon sent spray flying several hundred feet into the air and raised swells that set all the fleet of bergs in motion and roared up the beach, telling the story of the birth of every iceberg far and near. The number discharged varies much, influenced in part no doubt by the tides of weather and seasons, sometimes one every five minutes for half a day at a time on the average, though intervals of twenty or thirty minutes may occur without any considerable fall, then three or four immense discharges will take place in as many minutes. The sound they make is like heavy thunder, with a prolonged roar after deep thudding sounds—a perpetual thunderstorm easily heard three or four miles away. The roar in our tent and the shaking of the ground one or two miles distant from points of discharge seems startlingly near.

I had to look after camp-supplies and left the ship late this morning, going with a crowd to the glacier; then, taking advantage of the fine weather, I pushed off alone into the silent icy prairie to the east, to Nunatak Island, about five hundred feet above the ice. I discovered a small lake on the larger of the two islands, and many battered and ground fragments of fossil wood, large and small. They seem to have come from trees that grew on the island perhaps centuries ago. I mean to use this island as a station in setting out stakes to measure the glacial flow. The top of Mt. Fairweather is in sight at a distance of perhaps thirty miles, the ice all smooth on the eastern border, wildly broken in the central portion. I reached the ship at 2:30 P.M. I had intended getting back at noon and sending letters and bidding friends good-bye, but could not resist this glacier saunter. The ship moved off as soon as I was seen on the moraine bluff, and Loomis and I waved our hats in farewell to the many wavings of handkerchiefs of acquaintances we had made on the trip.

Our goods—blankets, provisions, tent, etc.—lay in a rocky moraine hollow within a mile of the great terminal wall of the glacier, and the discharge of the rising and falling icebergs kept up an almost continuous thundering and echoing, while a few gulls flew about on easy wing or stood like specks of foam on the shore. These were our neighbors.

After my twelve-mile walk, I ate a cracker and planned the camp. I found that one of my boxes had been left on the steamer, but still we have more than enough of everything. We obtained two cords of dry wood at Juneau which Captain Carroll kindly had his men carry up the moraine to our camp-ground. We piled the wood as a wind-break, then laid a floor of lumber brought from Seattle for a square tent, nine feet by nine. We set the tent, stored our provisions in it, and made our beds. This work was done by 11:30 P.M., good daylight lasting to this time. We slept well in our roomy cotton house, dreaming of California home nests in the wilderness of ice.

June 25. A rainy day. For a few hours I kept count of the number of bergs discharged, then sauntered along the beach to the end of the crystal wall. A portion of the way is dangerous, the moraine bluff being capped by an overlying lobe of the glacier, which as it melts sends down boulders and fragments of ice, while the strip of sandy shore at high tide is only a few rods wide, leaving but little room to escape from the falling moraine material and the berg-waves. The view of the ice-cliffs, pinnacles, spires and ridges was very telling, a magnificent picture of nature's power and industry and love of beauty. About a hundred or a hundred and fifty feet from the shore a large stream issues from an arched, tunnel-like channel in the wall of the glacier, the blue of the ice hall being of an exquisite tone, contrasting with the strange, sooty, smoky, brown-colored stream. The front wall of the Muir Glacier is about two and a half or three miles wide. Only the central portion about two miles wide discharges icebergs. The two wings advanced over the washed and stratified moraine deposits have little or no motion, melting and receding as fast, or perhaps faster, than it advances. They have been advanced at least a mile over the old re-formed moraines, as is shown by the overlying, angular, recent moraine deposits, now being laid down, which are continuous with the medial moraines of the glacier.

In the old stratified moraine banks, trunks and branches of trees showing but little sign of decay occur at a height of about a hundred feet above tidewater. I have not yet compared this fossil wood with that of the opposite shore deposits. That the glacier was once withdrawn considerably back of its present limit seems plain. Immense torrents of water had filled in the inlet with stratified moraine-material, and for centuries favorable climatic conditions allowed forests to grow upon it. At length the glacier advanced, probably three or four miles, uprooting and burying the trees which had grown undisturbed for centuries. Then came a great thaw, which produced the flood that deposited the uprooted trees. Also the trees which grew around the shores above reach of floods were shed off, perhaps by the thawing of the soil that was resting on the buried margin of the glacier, left on its retreat and protected by a covering of moraine-material from melting as fast as the exposed surface of the glacier. What appear to be remnants of the margin of the glacier when it stood at a much higher level still exist on the left side and probably all along its banks on both sides just below its present terminus.

June 26. We fixed a mark on the left wing to measure the motion if any. It rained all day, but I had a grand tramp over mud, ice, and rock to the east wall of the inlet. Brown metamorphic slate, close-grained in places, dips away from the inlet, presenting edges to ice-action, which has given rise to a singularly beautiful and striking surface, polished and grooved and fluted.

All the next day it rained. The mountains were smothered in dull-colored mist and fog, the great glacier looming through the gloomy gray fog fringes with wonderful effect. The thunder of bergs booms and rumbles through the foggy atmosphere. It is bad weather for exploring but delightful nevertheless, making all the strange, mysterious region yet stranger and more mysterious.

June 28. A light rain. We were visited by two parties of Indians. A man from each canoe came ashore, leaving the women in the canoe to guard against the berg-waves. I tried my Chinook and made out to say that I wanted to hire two of them in a few days to go a little way back on the glacier and around the bay. They are seal-hunters and promised to come again with "Charley," who "hi yu kumtux wawa Boston" -knew well how to speak English.

I saw three huge bergs born. Spray rose about two hundred feet. Lovely reflections showed of the pale-blue tones of the ice-wall and mountains in the calm water. Mirages are common, making the stranded bergs along the shore look like the sheer frontal wall of the glacier from which they were discharged.

I am watching the ice-wall, berg life and behavior, etc. Yesterday and to-day a solitary small flycatcher was feeding about camp. A sand-piper on the shore, loons, ducks, gulls, and crows, a few of each, and a bald eagle are all the birds I have noticed thus far. The glacier is thundering gloriously.

June 30. Clearing clouds and sunshine. In less than a minute I saw three large bergs born. First there is usually a preliminary thundering of comparatively small masses as the large mass begins to fall, then the grand crash and boom and reverberating roaring. Oftentimes three or four

heavy main throbbing thuds and booming explosions are heard as the
main mass falls in several pieces, and also secondary thuds and thun-
derings as the mass or masses plunge and rise again and again ere they
come to rest. Seldom, if ever, do the towers, battlements, and pinnacles into which the front of the glacier is broken fall forward head-long
from their bases like falling trees at the water-level or above or below
it. They mostly sink vertically or nearly so, as if undermined by the
melting action of the water of the inlet, occasionally maintaining their
upright positions after sinking far below the level of the water, and
rising again a hundred feet or more into the air with water streaming
like hair down their sides from their crowns, then launch forward and
fall flat with yet another thundering report, raising spray in magnificent, flamelike, radiating jets and sheets, occasionally to the very top
of the front wall. Illumined by the sun, the spray and angular crystal
masses are indescribably beautiful. Some of the discharges pour in fragments from clefts in the wall like waterfalls, white and mealy-looking,
even dusty with minute swirling ice-particles, followed by a rushing
succession of thunder-tones combining into a huge, blunt, solemn roar.
Most of these crumbling discharges are from the excessively shattered
central part of the ice-wall; the solid deep-blue masses from the ends
of the wall forming the large bergs rise from the bottom of the glacier.

Many lesser reports are heard at a distance of a mile or more from
the fall of pinnacles into crevasses or from the opening of new crevasses.
The berg discharges are very irregular, from three to twenty-two an
hour. On one rising tide, six hours, there were sixty bergs discharged,
large enough to thunder and be heard at distances of from three quarters
to one and a half miles; and on one succeeding falling tide, six hours,
sixty-nine were discharged.

July 1. We were awakened at four o'clock this morning by the whistle
of the steamer George W. Elder. I went out on the moraine and waved
my hand in salute and was answered by a toot from the whistle. Soon
a party came ashore and asked if I was Professor Muir. The leader,
Professor Harry Fielding Reid of Cleveland, Ohio, introduced himself
and his companion, Mr. Cushing, also of Cleveland, and six or eight

young students who had come well provided with instruments to study the glacier. They landed seven or eight tons of freight and pitched camp beside ours. I am delighted to have companions so congenial—we have now a village

As I set out to climb the second mountain, three thousand feet high, on the east side of the glacier, I met many tourists returning from a walk on the smooth east margin of the glacier, and had to answer many questions. I had a hard climb, but wonderful views were developed and I sketched the glacier from this high point and most of its upper fountains.

Many fine alpine plants grew here, an anemone on the summit, two species of cassiope in shaggy mats, three or four dwarf willows, large blue hairy lupines eighteen inches high, parnassia, phlox, solidago, dandelion, white-flowered bryanthus, daisy, pedicularis, epilobium, etc., with grasses, sedges, mosses, and lichens, forming a delightful deep spongy sod. Woodchucks stood erect and piped dolefully for an hour "Chee-chee!" with jaws absurdly stretched to emit so thin a note —rusty-looking, seedy fellows, also a smaller striped species which stood erect and cheeped and whistled like a Douglas squirrel. I saw three or four species of birds. A finch flew from her nest at my feet; and I almost stepped on a family of young ptarmigan ere they scattered, little bunches of downy brown silk, small but able to run well. They scattered along a snow-bank, over boulders, through willows, grass, and flowers, while the mother, very lame, tumbled and sprawled at my feet. I stood still until the little ones began to peep; the mother answered "Too-too-too" and showed admirable judgment and devo tion. She was in brown plumage with white on the wing primaries. She had fine grounds on which to lead and feed her young.

Not a cloud in the sky to-day; a faint film to the north vanished by noon, leaving all the sky full of soft, hazy light. The magnificent mountains around the widespread tributaries of the glacier; the great, gently undulating, prairie-like expanse of the main trunk, bluish on the east, pure white on the west and north; its trains of moraines in mag- nificent curving lines and many colors—black, gray, red, and brown; the stormy, cataract-like, crevassed sections; the hundred fountains;

the lofty, pure white Fairweather Range; the thunder of the plunging bergs; the fleet of bergs sailing tranquilly in the inlet—formed a glowing picture of nature's beauty and power.

July 2. I crossed the inlet with Mr. Reid and Mr. Adams to-day. The stratified drift on the west side all the way from top to base contains fossil wood. On the east side, as far as I have seen it, the wood occurs only in one stratum at a height of about a hundred and twenty feet in sand and clay. Some in a bank of the west side are rooted in clay soil. I noticed a large grove of stumps in the washed-out channel near the glacier-front but had no time to examine closely. Evidently a flood carrying great quantities of sand and gravel had overwhelmed and broken off these trees, leaving high stumps. The deposit, about a hundred feet or more above them, had been recently washed out by one of the draining streams of the glacier, exposing a part of the old forest floor certainly two or three centuries old.

I climbed along the right bank of the lowest of the tributaries and set a signal flag on a ridge fourteen hundred feet high. This tributary is about one and a fourth or one and a half miles wide and has four secondary tributaries. It reaches tide-water but gives off no bergs. Later I climbed the large Nunatak Island, seven thousand feet high, near the west margin of the glacier. It is composed of crumbling granite draggled with washed boulders, but has some enduring bosses which on sides and top are polished and scored rigidly, showing that it had been heavily over-swept by the glacier when it was thousands of feet deeper than now, like a submerged boulder in a river-channel. This island is very irregular in form, owing to the variations in the structure joints of the granite. It has several small lakelets and has been loaded with glacial drift, but by the melting of the ice about its flanks is shedding it off, together with some of its own crumbling surface. I descended a deep rock gully on the north side, the rawest, dirtiest, dustiest, most dangerous that I have seen hereabouts. There is also a large quantity of fossil wood scattered on this island, especially on the north side, that on the south side having been cleared off and carried away by the first tributary glacier, which, being lower and melting earlier, has allowed the soil of the moraine material to fall, together with its forest, and be carried off. That on the north side is now being carried off or buried. The last of the main ice foundation is melting and the moraine material re-formed over and over again, and the fallen tree-trunks, decayed or half decayed or in a fair state of preservation, are also unburied and buried again or carried off to the terminal or lateral moraine.

I found three small seedling Sitka spruces, feeble beginnings of a new forest. The circumference of the island is about seven miles. I arrived at camp about midnight, tired and cold. Sailing across the inlet in a cranky rotten boat through the midst of icebergs was dangerous, and I was glad to get ashore.

July 4. I climbed the east wall to the summit, about thirty-one hundred feet or so, by the northern most ravine next to the yellow ridge, finding about a mile of snow in the upper portion of the ravine and patches on the summit. A few of the patches probably lie all the year, the ground beneath them is so plantless. On the edge of some of the snow-banks I noticed cassiope. The thin, green, mosslike patches seen from camp are composed of a rich, shaggy growth of cassiope, white-flowered bryanthus, dwarf vaccinium with bright pink flowers, saxifrages, anemones, bluebells, gentians, small erigeron, pedicularis, dwarf willow and a few species of grasses. Of these, *Cassiope tetragona* is far the most influential and beautiful. Here it forms mats a foot thick and an acre or more in area, the sections being measured by the size and drainage of the soil-patches. I saw a few plants anchored in the less crumbling parts of the steep-faced bosses and steps—parnassia, potentilla, hedysarum, lutkea, etc. The lower, rough-looking patches half way up the mountain are mostly alder bushes ten or fifteen feet high. I had a fine view of the top of the mountain-mass which forms the boundary wall of the upper portion of the inlet on the west side, and of several glaciers, tributary to the first of the eastern tributaries of the main Muir Glacier. Five or six of these tributaries were seen, most of them now melted off from the trunk and independent. The highest peak to the eastward has an elevation of about five thousand feet or a little less. I also had glorious views of the Fairweather Range, La

Perouse, Crillon, Lituva, and Fairweather. Mt. Fairweather is the most beautiful of all the giants that stand guard about Glacier Bay. When the sun is shining on it from the east or south its magnificent glaciers and colors are brought out in most telling display. In the late afternoon its features become less distinct. The atmosphere seems pale and hazy, though around to the north and northeastward of Fairweather innumerable white peaks are displayed, the highest fountain-heads of the Muir Glacier crowded together in bewildering array, most exciting and inviting to the mountaineer. Altogether I have had a delightful day, a truly glorious celebration of the fourth.

July 6. I sailed three or four miles down the east coast of the inlet with the Reid party's cook, who is supposed to be an experienced camper and prospector, and landed at a stratified moraine-bank. It was here that I camped in 1880, a point at that time less than half a mile from the front of the glacier, now one and a half miles. I found my Indian's old camp made just ten years ago, and Professor Wright's of five years ago. Their alder-bough beds and fireplace were still marked and but little decayed. I found thirty-three species of plants in flower, not counting willows—a showy garden on the shore only a few feet above high tide, watered by a fine stream. Lutkea, hedysarum, parnassia, epilobium, bluebell, solidago, habenaria, strawberry with fruit half grown, arctostaphylos, mertensia, erigeron, willows, tall grasses and alder are the principal species. There are many butterflies in this garden. Gulls are breeding near here. I saw young in the water to-day.

On my way back to camp I discovered a group of monumental stumps in a washed-out valley of the moraine and went ashore to observe them. They are in the dry course of a flood-channel about eighty feet above mean tide and four or five hundred yards back from the shore, where they have been pounded and battered by boulders rolling against them and over them, making them look like gigantic shaving-brushes. The largest is about three feet in diameter and probably three hundred years old. I mean to return and examine them at leisure. A smaller stump, still firmly rooted, is standing astride of an old crumbling trunk, showing that at least two generations of trees flourished

here undisturbed by the advance or retreat of the glacier or by its draining stream-floods. They are Sitka spruces and the wood is mostly in a
good state of preservation. How these trees were broken off without
being uprooted is dark to me at present. Perhaps most of their companions were uprooted and carried away.

July 7. Another fine day; scarce a cloud in the sky. The icebergs in the
bay are miraged in the distance to look like the frontal wall of a great
glacier. I am writing letters in anticipation of the next steamer, the
Queen.

She arrived about 2:30 P.M. with two hundred and thirty tourists.
What a show they made with their ribbons and kodaks! All seemed
happy and enthusiastic, though it was curious to see how promptly all
of them ceased gazing when the dinner-bell rang, and how many turned
from the great thundering crystal world of ice to look curiously at the
Indians that came alongside to sell trinkets, and how our little camp
and kitchen arrangements excited so many to loiter and waste their
precious time prying into our poor hut.

July 8. A fine clear day. I went up the glacier to observe stakes and
found that a marked point near the middle of the current had flowed
about a hundred feet in eight days. On the medial moraine one mile
from the front there was no measureable displacement. I found a raven
devouring a tom-cod that was alive on a shallow at the mouth of the
creek. It had probably been wounded by a seal or eagle

July 10. I have been getting acquainted with the main features of the
glacier and its fountain mountains with reference to an exploration of
its main tributaries and the upper part of its prairie-like trunk, a trip I
have long had in mind. I have been building a sled and must now get
fully ready to start without reference to the weather. Yesterday evening
I saw a large blue berg just as it was detached sliding down from the
front. Two of Professor Reid's party rowed out to it as it sailed past
the camp, estimating it to be two hundred and forty feet in length and
one hundred feet high.

PIERRE BERTON

from *The Klondike Fever*

Pierre Berton was born in Whitehorse in 1920 and spent his teenage years as a laborer in the Klondike mining camps. His several books include *The Royal Family*, *Stampede for Gold*, *The Mysterious North*, which won the Governor-General's award for the best Canadian work of nonfiction in 1956, and *The Klondike Fever*. He also wrote *City of Gold*, a documentary on the Klondike gold rush which won an award from the National Film Board of Canada.

Of all the routes to the Klondike, the Skagway trail across the White Pass, more than any other, brought out the worst in men. None who survived ever forgot it, and most who remembered it did so with a sense of shame and remorse. It looked so easy: a jaunt through the rolling hills on horseback, not much more. And yet the men who traveled it were seized by a kind of delirium that drove them to the pit of brutality. Like drug addicts, they understood their dementia but could not control it. There was only one comfort—everyone was suffering from the same condition.

Frank Thomas of Plymouth, Indiana, expressed this feeling when he wrote this letter home from Skagway in the early fall of 1897:

"I am a few days older than when I left . . . and a great deal wiser. I have been working like a slave since I came here trying to get over the trail and am not over yet, and furthermore do not think I will be in time to get down the Yukon this winter. Since I came in we have lost our mule and one horse on this accursed trail. . . . This is the most discouraging work I ever did. . . . There are thousands of people here . . . all mad and crazy just like us. . . . I am undoubtedly a crazy fool for being here in this God-forsaken country but I have the consolation of seeing thousands of other men in all stages of life, rich and poor, wise and foolish, here in the same plight as I."

The trail on which Thomas found himself was a forty-five-mile switchback that plunged through bog and mire, over boulder and shale, skirted cliffsides, crossed and recrossed rivers, leapfrogged mountains, and followed canyon, valley, summit, and slope until it ended on the crescent beach of Lake Bennett, where the Yukon River has its beginning.

Unlike the Dyea trail that led directly to the base of the Chilkoot and then spanned the mountain barrier in a single leap, the Skagway trail straddled a series of obstacles. Its beginnings were deceptive—an attractive wagon road that led for several miles over flat timber- and swampland. Then began the series of precipitous hills, each hill separated by the almost continuous mire of the soggy riverbed, which had to be zigzagged by the narrow pathway.

First there was Devil's Hill, around whose slippery slate cliffs the path, scarcely two feet wide, wound like a corkscrew and where a single misstep by a badly loaded horse could mean death a sheer five hundred feet below.

Next there was Porcupine Hill, a roller-coaster ride where the wretched animals must pick their way between ten-foot boulders.

Then came Summit Hill, a thousand-foot climb, where liquid mud streamed down in rivulets, where sharp rocks tore at horses' feet and flanks, where slabs of granite barred the way and yawning mudholes swallowed the floundering animals, packs and all.

The summit marked the border between Canada and Alaska, but it was not the end. The slender trail skirted a network of tiny lakes and then hurdled Turtle Mountain, another thousand-foot obstacle, before descending into the Tutshi Valley. One more mountain pass blocked the way before Lake Bennett was finally achieved.

Of the five thousand men and women who attempted to cross the White Pass in the fall of '97, only the tiniest handful reached their goal in time to navigate the Yukon River before freeze-up. One man who succeeded compared the slow movement over the pass with that of an army in retreat, those in the forefront struggling on against hopeless odds, followed by a line of stragglers moving forward like a beaten rabble. On the coastal side of the divide an incessant gray drizzle shut out all sunlight, producing streams of gumbo that acted as a sort of mucilage for the hopeless tangle of men and animals, tents, feed, and supplies. As the trail was not wide enough to allow two animals to pass, time and again all movement ground to a stop. Fires sputtered and smoldered in the misty half-light while shivering men, haggard, dazed, and forlorn, hovered over them, waiting for the human chain to resume its slow movement across the dark hills.

During these tedious delays the wretched horses for miles back had to stand, often for hours, with crushing loads pressing down upon their backs because no one would chance unloading them in case movement might suddenly resume. An animal might remain loaded for twenty-four hours, his only respite being the tightening of the pack girths, and this was one reason why scarcely a single horse survived of the three thousand that were used to cross the White Pass in '97.

Here was the enduring shame of the Skagway trail. Many of these doomed beasts were ready for the glue factory when they were bought at Victoria or Seattle at outlandish prices, while others had never been broken or felt the weight of a pack. Few of the men who stampeded to the Klondike had ever handled animals before, hence it was not unusual for two partners to spend an entire day trying to load a single horse. By the time they reached the summit, horses that had fetched two hundred dollars in Skagway were not worth twenty cents, for the Klondikers felt impelled to get across the mountains at any cost—and the cost always included an animal's life.

A quarter of a mile from the Canadian border, each owner performed a grisly rite. He carefully unloaded his pack animal and then smoothed a blanket over its back to conceal the running sores that most horses suffered at the hands of amateurs. The Mounted Police would shoot a sore or injured horse on sight if he was brought across the line into Canada.

The macabre scenes on the trail that autumn and winter were seared into the memories of most of the men who witnessed them, so that fifty years later, when subsequent horrors had been blurred by the fog of time, these ghastly moments were as sharply etched as if they had occurred the week before. Samuel H. Graves, who was to play a leading role in the building of the railway over the White Pass, would never forget the day he passed a horse that had broken its leg a few minutes before at a point where the trail squeezed between two huge boulders. The horse's pack had been removed, and someone had knocked it on the head with an ax; then traffic was resumed directly across the still warm body. When Graves returned that evening there was not a vestige of the carcass left, save for the head on one side of the trail and the tail on the other. The beast had literally been ground into the earth by the human machine.

A veteran horseman, Major J. M. Walsh, one of the most famous officers of the original North West Mounted Police, now retired and on his way to the Klondike as Commissioner of the Yukon, crossed the trail that fall with a government party and was horrified at the spectacle. To Clifford Sifton, Canadian Minister of the Interior, he wrote that "such a scene of havoc and destruction . . . can scarcely be imagined. Thousands of pack-horses lie dead along the way, sometimes in bunches under the cliffs, with pack-saddles and packs where they have fallen from the rock above, sometimes in tangled masses filling the mudholes and furnishing the only footing for our poor pack animals on the march —often, I regret to say, exhausted but still alive, a fact we are unaware of until after the miserable wretches turn beneath the hoofs of our cavalcade. The eyeless sockets of the pack animals everywhere account for the myriads of ravens along the road. The inhumanity which this trail has been witness to, the heartbreak and suffering which so many have undergone, cannot be imagined. They certainly cannot be described."

T. Dufferin Pattullo, Walsh's secretary, who later became premier of the province of British Columbia, was one of several stampeders who report that the tortured animals were actually trying to commit suicide rather than negotiate the trail. To his dying day Pattullo insisted that he saw an ox trying to fling itself over a cliff. Tappan Adney, correspondent for *Harper's Illustrated Weekly*, reported a similar incident: a horse had walked over the edge of Porcupine Hill, and every man who witnessed the incident swore it was suicide.

In the crowd that fall was a sensitive young ex-sailor, his pack crammed with books —Darwin, Marx, Milton—and he, too, was to describe the ordeal of the horses on the White Pass.

"The horses died like mosquitoes in the first frost and from Skagway to Bennett they rotted in heaps," Jack London wrote. "They died at the rocks, they were poisoned at the summit, and they starved at the lakes; they fell off the trail, what there was of it, and they went through it; in the river they drowned under their loads or were smashed to pieces against the boulders; they snapped their legs in the crevices and broke their backs falling backwards with their packs; in the sloughs they sank from fright or smothered in the slime; and they were disembowelled in the bogs where the corduroy logs turned end up in the mud; men shot them, worked them to death and when they were gone, went back to the beach and bought more. Some did not bother to shoot them, stripping the saddles off and the shoes and leaving them where they fell. Their hearts turned to stone—those which did not break—and they became beasts, the men on the Dead Horse Trail."

Within a month the trail was almost impassable, and by September all movement had come to a standstill. Sylvester Scovel of the New York *World*, in a colorful gesture, offered several thousand dollars on behalf of his paper to dynamite the pass so that the stampede could resume. Scovel had come with his bride to Skagway, in a dashing costume complete with guitar—high leather boots, tight corduroys, white sombrero, and fancy buckskin shirt—but this final piece of flamboyance was too much for his paper, which refused to go along with the scheme and recalled him to New York. He had, in the meantime, spent some money widening a section of the trail and hiring a guard of twelve men at fifty dollars a day to barricade it against intruders. "Any man crossing the barrier dies!" the leader would shout, but with the press of three thousand behind it, the barrier did not last long.

By this time it was obvious to all that no one else was going to reach the Klondike until spring. Thousands were already in retreat and vainly trying to sell their outfits, which were to be seen strewn along the right-of-way for more than forty miles. The tidal flats of Skagway were black with a thousand horses, "For Sale" signs on their backs, blood streaming down their lacerated thighs. And everywhere a pall of despondency hung like a shroud over the multitude. Hal Hoffman of the Chicago *Tribune* happened upon one huge strapping gold-seeker in a red shirt, seated on a rock, a picture of despair; he could not get his goods across the first ridge, his money was gone, his adventure was at an end, and he was sobbing his heart out.

Men had been willing to pay any sum to reach Lake Bennett. Scores had given fifty cents apiece simply to use a log that one enterprising stampeder had flung over a stream. One packer, who landed in Skagway without a dollar, made three hundred thousand in transport fees before he blew out his brains. But, as these argonauts were to learn over and over again, money alone was not enough to take them to the Klondike.

Finally the trail was closed to all, and George Brackett, an ex-mayor of Minneapolis who had lost his fortune in the panic of '93, began to construct a wagon road along the mountainsides. When it was completed, the stampeders who followed in the winter were glad to pay tolls to use it, but each one who passed that way was haunted in some fashion by the ghosts of the pack animals that had died that fall. One winter evening a nineteen-year-old named Stanley Scearce, whose father raised thoroughbreds in the blue grass of Kentucky, was camped on the edge of Porcupine Hill. He had started an evening fire and set a kettle of beans to boil on it, and then, as the snow began to melt, he saw to his horror the outlines of a dead horse emerging beneath the glowing coals.

from
Jack London
Reports

Jack London was born in San Francisco in 1876 and, until his death in 1916, led a highly prolific literary career, publishing eighteen volumes of short stories, nineteen novels, seven books of nonfiction, and scores of articles, essays, and reviews. He is best known for *The Call of the Wild*, *The Sea Wolf*, *White Fang*, *Smoke Bellow*, *South Sea Tales*, and *The Iron Heel*.

Housekeeping in the Klondike—that's bad! And by men—worse. Reverse the proposition, if you will, yet you will fail to mitigate, even by the hair's breadth, the woe of it. It is bad, unutterably bad, for a man to keep house, and it is equally bad to keep house in the Klondike. That's the sum and substance of it. Of course men will be men, and especially is this true of the kind who wander off to the frozen rim of the world. The glitter of gold is in their eyes, they are borne along by uplifting ambition, and in their hearts is a great disdain for everything in the culinary department save "grub." "Just so long as it's grub," they say, coming off trail, gaunt and ravenous, "grub, and piping hot." Nor do they manifest the slightest regard for the genesis of the same; they prefer to begin at "revelations."

Yes, it would seem a pleasant task to cook for such men; but just let them lie around cabin to rest up for a week, and see with what celerity they grow high-stomached and make sarcastic comments on the way you fry the bacon or boil the coffee. And behold how each will spring his own strange and marvelous theory as to how sour-dough bread should be mixed and baked. Each has his own recipe (formulated, mark you, from personal experience only), and to him it is an idol of brass, like unto no other man's, and he'll fight for it—ay, down to the last wee pinch of soda—and if need be, die for it. If you should happen to catch him on trail, completely exhausted, you may blacken his character, his flag, and his ancestral tree with impunity; but breathe the slightest whisper against his sour-dough bread, and he will turn upon and rend you.

From this it may be gathered what an unstable thing sour dough is. Never was coquette so fickle. You cannot depend upon it. Still, it is the simplest thing in the world. Make a batter and place it near the stove (that it may not freeze) till it ferments or sours. Then mix the dough with it, and sweeten with soda to taste—of course replenishing the batter for next time. There it is. Was there ever anything simpler? But, oh, the tribulations of the cook! It is never twice the same. If the batter could only be placed away in an equable temperature, all well and good. If one's comrades did not interfere, much vexation of spirit might be avoided. But this cannot be; for Tom fires up the stove till the cabin is become like the hot-room of a Turkish bath; Dick forgets all about the fire till the place is a refrigerator; then along comes Harry and shoves the sour-dough bucket right against the stove to make way for the drying of his mittens. Now heat is a most potent factor in accelerating the fermentation of flour and water, and hence the unfortunate cook is constantly in disgrace with Tom, Dick, and Harry. Last week his bread was yellow from a plethora of soda; this week it is sour from a prudent lack of the same; and next week—ah, who can tell save the god of the fire-box?

Some cooks aver they have so cultivated their olfactory organs that they can tell to the fraction of a degree just how sour the batter is. Nevertheless they have never been known to bake two batches of bread which were at all alike. But this fact casts not the slightest shadow upon the infallibility of their theory. One and all, they take advantage of circumstances, and meanly crawl out by laying the blame upon the soda, which was dampened "the time the canoe overturned," or upon the flour, which they got in trade from "that half-breed fellow with the dogs."

The pride of the Klondike cook in his bread is something which passes understanding. The highest commendatory degree which can be passed upon a man in that country, and the one which distinguishes him from the tenderfoot, is that of being a "sour-dough boy." Never was a college graduate prouder of his "sheepskin" than the old-timer of this appellation. There is a certain distinction about it, from which the newcomer is invidiously excluded. A tenderfoot with his baking-powder is an inferior creature, a freshman; but a "sour-dough boy" is a man of stability, a post-graduate in that art of arts—bread making.

Next to bread a Klondike cook strives to achieve distinction by his doughnuts. This may appear frivolous at first glance, and at second, considering the materials with which he works, an impossible feat. But doughnuts are all-important to the man who goes on trail for a journey of any length. Bread freezes easily, and there is less grease and sugar, and hence less heat in it, than in doughnuts. The latter do not solidify except at extremely low temperatures, and they are very handy to carry in the pockets of a Mackinaw jacket and munch as one travels along.

They are made much after the manner of their brethren in warmer climes, with the exception that they are cooked in bacon grease—the more grease, the better they are. Sugar is the cook's chief stumbling-block; if it is very scarce, why, add more grease. The men never mind —on trail. In the cabin?—well, that's another matter; besides, bread is good enough for them then.

The cold, the silence, and the darkness somehow seem to be considered the chief woes of the Klondiker. But this is all wrong. There is one woe which overshadows all others—the lack of sugar. Every party which goes north signifies a manly intention to do without sugar, and after it gets there bemoans itself upon its lack of foresight. Man can endure hardship and horror with equanimity, but take from him his sugar, and he raises his lamentations to the stars. And the worst of it is that it all falls back upon the long-suffering cook. Naturally, coffee, and mush, and dried fruit, and rice, eaten without sugar, do not taste exactly as they should. A certain appeal to the palate is missing. Then the cook is blamed for his vile concoctions. Yet, if he be a man of wisdom, he may judiciously escape the major part of this injustice. When he places a pot of mush upon the table, let him see to it that it is accompanied by a pot of stewed dried apples or peaches. This propinquity will suggest the combination to the men, and the flatness of the one will be neutralized by the sharpness of the other. In the distress of a sugar famine, if he be a cook of parts, he will boil rice and fruit together in one pot; and if he cook a dish of rice and prunes properly, of a verity he will cheer up the most melancholy member of the party, and extract from him great gratitude.

Such a cook must indeed be a man of resources. Should his comrades cry out that vinegar be placed upon the beans, and there is no vinegar, he must know how to make it out of water, dried apples, and brown paper. He obtains the last from the bacon-wrappings, and it is usually saturated with grease. But that does not matter. He will early learn that in a land of low temperatures it is impossible for bacon grease to spoil anything. It is to the white man what blubber and seal oil are to the Eskimo. Soul-winning gravies may be made from it by the addition of water and browned flour over the fire. Some cooks base far-

reaching fame solely upon their gravy, and their names come to be on
the lips of men wherever they forgather at the feast. When the candles
give out, the cook fills a sardine-can with bacon grease, manufactures
a wick out of the carpenter's sail-twine, and behold! the slush-lamp
stands complete. It goes by another and less complimentary name in
the vernacular, and, next to sour-dough bread, is responsible for more
men's souls than any other single cause of degeneracy in the Klondike.

The ideal cook should also possess a Semitic incline to his soul. Ini-
tiative in his art is not the only requisite; he must keep an eye upon the
variety of his larder. He must "swap" grub with the gentile understanding; and woe unto him should the balance of trade be against him. His
comrades will thrust it into his teeth every time the bacon is done over
the turn, and they will even rouse him from his sleep to remind him
of it. For instance, previous to the men going out for a trip on trail, he
cooks several gallons of beans in the company of numerous chunks of
salt pork and much bacon grease. This mess he then molds into blocks
of convenient size and places on the roof, where it freezes into bricks
in a couple of hours. Thus the men, after a weary day's travel, have but
to chop off chunks with an axe and thaw out in the frying-pan. Now
the chances preponderate against more than one party in ten having
chili-peppers in their outfits. But the cook, supposing him to be fitted
for his position, will ferret out that one party, discover some particular
shortage in its grub-supply of which he has plenty, and swap the same
for chili-peppers. These in turn he will incorporate in the mess afore-
mentioned, and behold a dish which even the hungry arctic gods may
envy. Variety in the grub is as welcome to the men as nuggets. When,
after eating dried peaches for months, the cook trades a few cupfuls of
the same for apricots, the future at once takes on a more roseate hue.
Even a change in the brand of bacon will revivify blasted faith in the
country.

It is no sinecure, being cook in the Klondike. Often he must do his
work in a cabin measuring ten by twelve on the inside and occupied by
three other men besides himself. When it is considered that these men
eat, sleep, lounge, smoke, play cards, and entertain visitors there, and
also in that small space house the bulk of their possessions, the size of

the cook's orbit may be readily computed. In the morning he sits up in bed, reaches out and strikes the fire, then proceeds to dress. After that the centre of his orbit is the front of the stove, the diameter the length of his arms. Even then his comrades are continually encroaching upon his domain, and he is at constant warfare to prevent territorial grabs. If the men are working hard on the claim, the cook is also expected to find his own wood and water. The former he chops up and sleds into camp, the latter he brings home in a sack—unless he is unusually diligent, in which case he has a ton or so of water piled up before the door. Whenever he is not cooking, he is thawing ice, and between whiles running out and hoisting on the windlass for his comrades in the shaft. The care of the dogs also devolves upon him, and he carries his life and a long club in his hand every time he feeds them.

But there is one thing the cook does not have to do, nor any man in the Klondike—and that is, make another man's bed. In fact, the beds are never made except when the blankets become unfolded, or when the pine needles have all fallen off the boughs which form the mattress. When the cabin has a dirt floor and the men do their carpenter-work inside, the cook never sweeps it. It is much warmer to let the chips and shavings remain. Whenever he kindles a fire he uses a couple of handfuls of the floor. However, when the deposit becomes so deep that his head is knocking against the roof, he seizes a shovel and removes a foot or so of it.

Nor does he have any windows to wash; but if the carpenter is busy he must make his own windows. This is simple. He saws a hole out of the side of the cabin, inserts a home-made sash, and for panes falls back upon the treasured writing-tablet. A sheet of this paper, rubbed thoroughly with bacon grease, becomes transparent, sheds water when it thaws, and keeps the cold out and the heat in. In cold weather the ice will form upon the inside of it to the thickness of sometimes two or three inches. When the bulb of the mercurial thermometer has frozen solid, the cook turns to his window, and by the thickness of the icy coating infallibly gauges the outer cold within a couple of degrees.

A certain knowledge of astronomy is required of the Klondike cook, for another task of his is to keep track of the time. Before going to bed he wanders outside and studies the heavens. Having located the Pole Star by means of the Great Bear, he inserts two slender wands in the snow, a couple of yards apart and in line with the North Star. The next day, when the sun on the southern horizon casts the shadows of the wands to the northward and in line, he knows it to be twelve o'clock, noon, and sets his watch and those of his partners accordingly. As stray dogs are constantly knocking his wands out of line with the North Star, it becomes his habit to verify them regularly everynight, and thus another burden is laid upon him.

But, after all, while the woes of the man who keeps house and cooks food in the northland are innumerable, there is one redeeming feature in his lot which does not fall to the women housewives of other lands. When things come to a pass with his feminine prototype, she throws her apron over her head and has a good cry. Not so with him, being a man and a Klondiker. He merely cooks a little more atrociously, raises a storm of grumbling, and resigns. After that he takes up his free outdoor life again, and exerts himself mightily in making life miserable for the unlucky comrade who takes his place in the management of the household destinies.

The Forest of Eyes

Anthropologist Richard Nelson has
worked and traveled extensively
throughout Alaska. His books include
Hunters of the Northern Ice and *Make
Prayers to the Raven: A Koyukon View
of the Northern Forest.*

The sound of heavy surf awakens me well before dawn. I wait inside my sleeping bag, as the winter night gradually pales and the forest takes shape outside the tent door. When there is enough light, I eat a cold breakfast while Shungnak samples the morning scents around our camp. Last night's storm has eased to a gentle wind, and the rain has given way to passing showers, occasionally mixed with wet snow. Through the gaps between tree trunks, I can see walls of swell rising along the horizon, first gray, then darker, then black in their hollows, then suddenly white as they break with a force that reverberates through the timber and shore. I think of the skiff, safely anchored in a cove on the island's other side, of Nita and Ethan starting their day at home. There's no going back until these waters calm down. Most of the snow has washed away, so it looks like a good chance to explore a part of the island I've never seen before. Aside from the pristine coast and forest, I am especially curious about a nearby valley where the timber has been logged off, never having looked closely at any of the island's clearcut areas.

An hour later, Shungnak frolics down the shore ahead of me, stopping occasionally to sniff piles of kelp and other debris left by last night's tide. A rift opens between the high escarpments of cloud, and for a few minutes sunshine glistens on the black sand beach, the windrows of gray and amber drift logs. Beyond the shore of Roller Bay, the face of Kluksa Mountain is bright with new snow, and huge cornice purls down a thousand feet of fluted ridge beneath its crest. Radiating outward on the lower slopes are corrugated hills, patterned with forest and muskeg, descending toward points of black rock that drive beneath the fretting sea.

We come to a broad pond less than an inch deep, covered with rippled islets of sand floating on a mirror of our surroundings. Standing at its edge, I suddenly feel adrift in midair, gazing at the whole sweep of Kluksa Mountain that plunges into the earth and reaches toward the subterranean clouds. Then I look up, to see the same mountain soaring skyward and the clouds hovering high above. It makes a natural hallucination, suspended between images of a beauty too perfect to exist, afloat in a world beyond mind. I step across an abalone shell at the bottom of the pool and walk on through a daybreak dream.

The beach ends abruptly against a rockbound shore—beginning with a few cobbled coves separated by pillars and fists of stone, then rising to impassable cliffs with timbered mountain slopes above. We pick our way along the rocks just beyond reach of the waves, until a steep buttress forces us to climb up and follow the clifftop. Crowded tree trunks obscure the view, but we find a narrow ridge that extends seaward and follow it to a grassy overlook. Now the whole breadth of Roller Bay lays out beneath us, like arms opened to embrace the sea.

I trace the whole shore with binoculars, looking for dangerous submerged rocks, protected nooks where I could anchor the skiff, and hidden beaches that would make good camping places. Someday, I hope to explore this outer coast by boat, rather than coming across the island from its protected side. The coast is scalloped into a sequence of three promontories: Black Point the closest in, then Ocean Point, and finally Ragged Cape at the Bay's outermost edge. I watch towering waves sweep across the reefs a mile off Ragged Cape, five miles away from my cliff perch. They throw up clouds of spindrift and roil shoreward in bores of whitewater that must be enormous just to be visible from this distance. Much of the coastline is obscured by white spray and haze from waves detonating against the walls of rock.

A set of five or six large swells moves slowly into the bay, liquified ridges twenty feet high, lined up exactly parallel, extending across the mile between shores, building higher as the bight narrows and rises into shoals. I wonder how the billions of molecules inside these swells can be elevated to such a frenzy without a great whine rising from within or the water heating to a boil. Each wave gradually curves like an enormous wing, as its middle slides ahead in deeper water and its tips drag behind in the shallows, careening across rocks and raking the cliffs on either side. There is a terrifying inexorability and slowness in the way these swells sweep in from the open sea toward their impending collision with the land. It seems to take minutes from the time I first pick them out until they finally rise above the canyons of their own troughs and pour themselves against the coast.

The entire bay is alive with leaping water, scrawled with thick streamers of spume, and stained by patches of half-decayed organic debris washed off the shore or scoured up from the depths. At one place, the bottom slopes sharply enough so the biggest waves throw themselves against a perpendicular face of rock and hurl fountains of whitewater a hundred feet or more in the air. When the timing is right, backwash from one wave runs out to meet the next, so the two break against each other and splay upward in a spiralled geyser of colliding seas.

Farther offshore, three cormorants ride on the churning water and dive beneath the froth to hunt for fish. A bald eagle watches from its perch in a weathered snag on the clifftop. It makes no move for an hour, then suddenly launches, planes out over the bay, and sets its eye on a glint at the surface. A hundred yards from shore, its descent steepens like the down-curve of an arrow. The eagle bends its head to look straight below, releases its grasp on the air, drops abruptly, then swings out its opened talons and plunges bodily into the water. It lays there for a moment, its wings extended like pontoons. Then, with great effort and flailing, it strokes against the sea and rises, shaking streams from its feathers. A fish the size of a small cod swims helplessly in its grasp and stares uncomprehending at its lost element below.

The eagle labors back toward shore, circles at the timber's edge, drops down, then rises to the high bough it has chosen and grasps it with one foot, still holding its prey with the other. The slender treetop sways as the bird settles, shakes its head, ruffles the white feathers of its nape, and stares at the cold, shining fish.

I shrink away into the forest, mindful of the paradox that life sustains itself through the swift violence of that flensing beak, brought down beneath the closing shadow of wings.

Shungnak bounds ahead into the woods, released from her boredom, weaving her way through faint webs of scent, exploring a rich world of odors that scarcely exists for me. We work farther back along the hillside, through tall timber with a fair undergrowth of blueberry and menziesia bushes. The gales of fall and winter are channeled right along this exposed slope, yet the trees are not huddled or bent or gnarled. Apparently the straight-trunked forest protects itself by shunting storms over its heights. But while the whole community stands, each tree within it must eventually succumb. A massive trunk blocks our way, sprawled across the ground, its fractured wood still bright and smelling of sap, its boughs green and supple. Because it looks so healthy, I surmise it was suddenly twisted and brought down by a contrary gust, perhaps the only one to hit just this way in a hundred years, or five hundred. And I imagine the maelstrom that ripped through the forest when it fell, carrying two others with it and clouding the air with a mass of splintered debris.

Farther on, two fallen giants with an enormous mass of uptorn roots lean against a stone outcrop, half their length projecting like bowsprits over a cliff. They appear to have come down at least twenty or thirty years ago, perhaps even before I was born. Green algae coats the trunks, and the thick, branchless limbs are swaddled with patches of moss. Eventually these sodden hulks will snap and crash down the slope, then rot away to a lump in the forest floor. But they will not disappear until long after my every trace has vanished. Trees decay as slowly as they have lived and grown.

A sluggish stream runs along the base of the hill, closely bounded by impinging trees. We walk beside the bank looking for a place to cross. After a quarter-mile it opens to a long meadow bordered by alder patches and muskeg. I notice a few signs that spring plant life has already begun to stir. Alder, salmonberry, and red-stemmed blueberry have swollen buds with tiny fissures of embryonic leaves. In the yard at home, some of our domesticated plants are much more adventuresome. The little, drooping snowdrops came up in mid-January and are now in full bloom. A few crocuses have put up blossoms, though most of them only show grassy bladelets. Daffodil sprouts are finger-high; and fleshy red domes show at the base of last year's crumpled rhubarb leaves.

The wild flowers stay dormant and hidden well after our yard is bright with blooming domesticates. Yet our carefully tended plants show no sign of spreading into the thicket beyond. Garden flowers can afford their springtime gambles and flashy moves only as long as we're around to hold back the competition. But someday the house will decay, the walled gardens will crumble, grass and sedge will strangle the flowers' roots, while cow parsnip and salmonberry rise above them. The garden plants have cast their lot with us; and if we go, so will they.

As we wade across the gravelly stream, I notice the sky has darkened and gray haze has settled against the mountains. Shortly afterward, a mixture of drizzle, sleet, and snow begins to fall. But when we slip back beneath the canopy of trees there are no more needling flakes, no icy droplets, and the chilling breeze is gone. I feel enfolded by the soft, wet hands of the forest. As we move in from the edge, I realize this is one of the purest stands of ancient spruce and hemlocks I've found on the island. It has a dark, baritone richness, tinkled through with river sounds and chickadees. There are virtually no shrubs or small trees, just an open maze of huge gray pillars. And everything is covered with a deep blanket of moss that mounds up over decaying stumps and fallen trunks like a shroud pulled over the furnishings in a great hall.

These coastal forests must be among the wettest places on earth. My rubber boots glisten each time I lift them from the swollen sponge underfoot. Stepping over a mossy windfall, I press my knees against it and instantly feel the water soak through. When I call for Shungnak, the feathers of damp moss deaden my voice, as if I were in a soundproof room.

The sense of *life* in this temperate jungle is as pervasive and palpable as its wetness. Even the air seems organic—rich and pungent like the moss itself. I breathe life into my lungs, feel life against my skin, move through a thick, primordial ooze of life like an ancient amphibious fish paddling for the surface to gulp mouthfuls of air.

It seems that the rocks beneath this forest should lie under a thousand feet of soaked and decaying mulch. But the roots of a recently toppled spruce clutch small boulders torn up from only a foot or two below the moss. What has become of the trunks and boughs and branches that have fallen onto this earth for thousands of years? And the little showers of needles that have shaken down with every gust of wind for millennia? Digested by the forest itself, and dissolved into the tea-colored streams that run toward the island's shore. The thought makes me feel that I truly belong here—that I, too, hold membership in this community—because all of us share the same fate.

By looking carefully, I can pick out the shapes of many fallen trees and their root masses. They are nearly hidden by robes of moss that reduce them to hillocks and by the camouflage of trees that have grown up on top of them. Tendrils of living roots wind down through the lattice of older, decaying roots, straddle broken stumps, and wrap over prostrate trunks. Sometimes four or five large trees grow in a straight line, each supported by a thick, elevated, empty cagework of roots. These roots once enclosed a fallen mother log which has completely vanished. The whole impression is of a forest on contorted stilts, sheathed in moss, climbing over its own decay, breathing and wet and alive.

Only a few raindrops and oversized snowflakes sift through the crown of trees as the squall passes over. I feel grateful for the shelter and sense a deeper kind of comfort here. These are living things I move among, immeasurably older and larger and more deeply affixed to their place on earth than I am, and imbued with vast experience of a kind entirely beyond my comprehension. I feel like a miniscule upstart in their presence, a supplicant awaiting the quiet council of great trees.

I have often thought of the forest as a living cathedral, but this might diminish what it truly is. When I worked as an anthropologist among the Koyukon Athabaskan Indians of interior Alaska, I encountered a different sense of the world's spiritual dimensions. If I have understood Koyukon teachings, the forest is not merely an expression or representation of sacredness, nor a place to invoke the sacred; the forest is sacredness itself. Nature is not merely created by God; nature *is* God. Whoever moves within the forest can partake directly of sacredness, experience sacredness with his entire body, breathe sacredness and contain it within himself, drink the sacred water as a living communion, bury his feet in sacredness, touch the living branch and feel the sacredness, open his eyes and witness the burning beauty of sacredness. And when he cuts a tree from the forest, he participates in a sacred interchange that brings separate lives together.

The long boughs reach out above and encircle me like arms. I feel the assurance of being recognized, as if something powerful and protective is aware of my presence, looks in another direction but always keeps me in the corner of its eye. I am cautious and self-protective here, as anywhere, yet I believe that a covenant of mutual regard binds me together with the forest. We share in a common nurturing. Each of us serves as an amulet to protect the other from inordinate harm. I am never alone in this wild forest, this forest of elders, this forest of eyes.

After a long hike, taking the easy routes of deer trails, we move into a stand of shore pine that ends beside a half-overgrown logging road. This is the first sign of human activity since we left camp, and it indicates that we're approaching the clearcut valley. The road follows a narrow band of muskeg that has all the delicate loveliness of a Japanese garden, with reflecting ponds and twisted trees in banzai shapes. Farther on, it cuts through an alder thicket and runs up a steep, forested slope. A dense flock of birds sprays into the high trees, twittering like canaries, hundreds of them, agitated and nervous, moving so quickly they're difficult to hold for long in the binoculars.

The little birds are everywhere, hanging upside down from the twigs and working furiously on spruce cones. Each one plucks and twists at its cone, shaking loose the thin scales and letting them fall. The air is filled with a flutter of brown scales. I recognize the sparrow-sized pine siskins immediately, and then identify the larger birds with them as white-winged crossbills. I've never had a good look at a crossbill before, but the roadway atop this hillside gives an easy view into the treetops, where bright red males and olive females swarm through the boughs. With some patience, I can discern the tips of their beaks, that crisscross instead of fitting together like an ordinary bird's. This allows the crossbill to pry the scales apart and insert its tongue to extract seeds hidden deep within. I'm reminded that tropical animals aren't the only ones who have added a little adventure to their evolution. Suddenly the whole flock spills out from the trees and disappears, like bees following their queen.

A half mile farther on, a slot appears between the trees ahead. As we approach, it widens to a gateway out of the forest—a sudden, shorn edge where the trees and moss end, and where the dark, dour sky slumps down against a barren hillside strewn with slash and decay. Wet, oversized snowflakes blotch against the bare skin of my face and neck, and the breeze chills through me. I look ahead, then look back toward the trees, breathless and anxious, almost wishing I hadn't come. It's the same foreboding I sometimes feel in the depths of sleep, when a blissful dream slowly degenerates into a nightmare; I am carried helplessly along, dimly hoping that it's only a dream but unable to awaken and escape.

The road angles up into a wasteland of gray trunks and twisted wooden shards, pitched together in convulsed disarray, with knots of shoulder-high brush crowded along both sides. Fan-shaped accumulations of mud and ash splay across the roadway beneath rilled cutbanks. In one place, the lower side has eroded away and left ten feet of culvert hanging out in midair, spewing brown water over the naked bank and into a runnel thirty feet below.

A tall snag clawed with dead branches stands atop the hill. I decide to hike up toward it rather than walk farther along the road. At first, it's a relief to be in the brush where I can touch something above, and where my attention is focused on the next footstep rather than the surrounding view. But thirty yards into it, I realize that moving through a clearcut is unlike anything I've ever tried before. The ground is covered with a nearly impenetrable confusion of branches, roots, sticks, limbs, stumps, blocks, poles, and trunks, in every possible size, all gray and fibrous and rotting, thrown together in a chaotic mass and interwoven with a tangle of brittle bushes.

An astonishing amount of wood was left here to decay, including whole trees, many dozen of them in this one clearcut alone. Some flaw must have made them unusable even for pulp, but they were felled nonetheless, apparently so the others would be easier to drag out. Not a single living tree above sapling size stands in the thirty or forty acres around me.

I creep over the slippery trunks and crawl beneath them, slip and stumble across gridworks of slash, and worm through the close-growing salmonberry thickets. Even Shungnak struggles with her footing, but she gets around far better than I do, moving like a weasel through the maze of small holes and channels. I can tell where she is by the noise she makes in the brush, but only see her when she comes to my whistle. In some places I walk atop huge, bridging logs, but they're slick and perilous, with a risk of falling down onto a skewer of wood. I save myself from one misstep by grabbing the nearest branch, which turns out to be devil's club, festooned with spines that would do credit to any cactus. We also cross dozens of little washes that run over beds of coarse ash and gravel. There are no mossy banks, no spongy seeps, just water on bare earth. By the time we near the top I am strained, sweating, sore, frustrated, and exhausted. It has taken almost an hour to cover a few hundred yards of this crippled land.

I've heard no sound except my own unhappy voice since we entered the clearcut, but now a winter wren's song pours up from a nearby patch of young alders. I usually love to hear wrens, especially during the silence of winter. But in this topsy-turvy place the reedy, contorted phrases, rattling against the beaten hill, seem like angry words in some bewildering foreign tongue. I picture a small, brown-skinned man, shaking his fist at the sky from the edge of a bombed and cratered field.

A large stump raised six feet above the ground on buttressed roots offers a good lookout. The man who felled this tree cut two notches for footholds, which I use to clamber on top. It's about five feet in diameter and nearly flat, except for a straight ridge across the center, where the cutter left hinge wood to direct the tree's fall. The surface is soggy and checked, but still clearly ridged by concentric growth rings. On hands and knees, nose almost against the wood, using my knife blade as a pointer, I started to count. In a short while, I know that the tree died in its four hundred and twenty-third year.

I stand to see the whole forest of stumps. It looks like an enormous graveyard, covered with weathered markers made from the remains of its own dead. Along the slope nearby is a straight line of four stumps lifted on convoluted roots, like severed hands still clasping a nearly-vanished mother log. Many of the surrounding stumps are smaller than my platform, but others are as large or larger. A gathering of ancients once stood here. Now it reminds me of a prairie in the last century, strewn with the bleached bones of buffalo. Tall trees with bare trunks crowd along the clearcut's edge and seem to press forward like bewildered onlookers.

Two centuries ago, it would have taken the Native people who lived here several days to fell a tree like this one, and weeks or months to wedge it into planks. Earlier in this century, the handloggers could pull their huge crosscut saws through it in a couple of hours. But like the Indians before, they selected only the best trees and left the others. Now I gaze into a valley miles deep, laid bare to its high slopes, with only patches of living timber left between the clearcut swaths.

Where I stand now, a great tree once grew. The circles that mark the centuries of its life surround me, and I dream back through them. It is difficult to imagine the beginnings—perhaps a seed that fell from a flurry of crossbills like those I saw a while ago. More difficult still is the incomprehensible distance of time this tree crossed, as it grew from a limber switch on the dark forest floor to a tree perhaps 150 feet tall and weighing dozens of tons. Another way to measure the scope of its life is in terms of storms. Each year, scores of them swept down this valley—thousands of boiling gales and blizzards in the tree's lifetime—and it withstood them all.

The man who walked up beside it some twenty years ago would have seemed no more significant than a gentle puff of air on a summer afternoon.

Perhaps thin shafts of light glimmered down onto the forest floor that day and danced on the velvet moss. I wonder what that man might have thought as he looked into the tree's heights and prepared to bring it down. He placed the blade of his saw against the thick bark, pulled the cord that set it blaring, and filled the air with clouds of flying chips. Perhaps he thought only about the job at hand, or about his aching back, or how long it was until lunch, or how much he would earn in the time it took to fell this tree. I would like to believe he gave some thought to the tree itself, to its death and his responsibilities toward it.

The great, severed spruce cut an arc across the sky and thundered down through its neighbors, sending a quake deep into the earth and a roar up against the valley walls. And while the tree was limbed and bucked, dozens of other men worked along the clearcut's advancing front, as a steady stream of trucks hauled the logs away.

A Koyukon man named Joe Stevens once took me with him to cut birch for a dog sled and snowshoes. Each time we found a straight tree with clear bark, he made a vertical cut in the trunk and pulled out a strip of wood to check the straightness of its grain. When we finally came across a tree he wanted to cut, Joe said, "I don't care how smart a guy is, or how much he knows about birch. If he acts the wrong way—he treats his birch like it's nothing—after that he can walk right by a good birch and wouldn't see it." Later on, he showed me several large, old trees with narrow scars on their trunks, where someone had checked the grain many years ago. In the same stand, he pointed out a stump that had been felled with an ax, and explained that Chief Abraham used to get birch here before the river cut a new channel and left his fish camp on a dry slough.

Joe and I bucked the tree into logs and loaded them on a sled, then hauled them to the village and took them inside his house. It was important to peel off the bark in a warm place, he said, because the tree still had life and awareness in it. Stripping the bark outdoors would expose its nakedness to the winter cold and offend its spirit. The next day, he took the logs out and buried them under the snow, where they would be sheltered until he could split them into lumber. Later on, when Joe carved pieces of the birch to make snowshoe frames, I tried to help by putting the shavings in a fire. His urgent voice stopped me: "Old timers say we shouldn't burn snowshoe shavings. We put those back in the woods, away from any trails, where nobody will bother them. If we do that, we'll be able to find good birch again next time."

The clearcut valley rumbled like an industrial city through a decade of summers, as the island's living flesh was stripped away. Tugs pulled enormous rafts of logs from Deadfall Bay, through tide-slick channels toward the mill, where they were ground into pulp and slurried aboard ships bound for Japan. Within a few months, the tree that took four centuries to grow was transformed into newspapers, read by commuters on afternoon trains and then tossed away.

I think of the men who worked here, walking down this hill at the day's end, heading home to their families in the camp beside Deadfall Bay. I could judge them harshly indeed, and think myself closer to the image of Joe Stevens; but that would be a mistake. The loggers were people just like me, not henchman soldiers in a rebel army, their pockets filled with human souvenirs. They probably loved working in the woods and found their greatest pleasures in the outdoors. I once had a neighbor who was a logger all his life, worked in these very clearcuts, and lost most of his hearing to the chainsaw's roar. He was as fine a man as I could ever hope to meet. And he lived by the conscience of western culture—that the forest is here for the taking, in whatever way humanity sees fit.

The decaying stump is now a witness stand, where I pass judgment on myself. I hold few convictions so deeply as my belief that a profound transgression has taken place here, by devastating an entire forest rather than taking from it selectively and in moderation. Yet whatever judgment I might make against those who cut it down, I must also make against myself. I belong to the same nation, speak the same language, vote in the same elections, share many of the same values, avail myself of the same technology, and owe much of my existence to the same vast system of global exchange. There is no refuge in blaming only the loggers or their industry or the government that deeded this forest to them. The entire society—one in which I take active membership— holds responsibility for laying this valley bare.

The most I can do is strive toward a separate kind of conscience, listen to an older and more tested wisdom, participate minimally in a system that debases its own sustaining environment, work toward a different future, and wish for a pardon I fear I have not deserved.

A familiar voice speaks agreement. I squint up into the sleet as a black specter turns and soars above, head cocked to examine me. A crack of light shows through his open beak; his throat fluffs out with each croak and gurgle; downy feathers on his back lift in the wind; an ominous hiss arises from his indigo wings. Words and stories of the Koyukon elders flood into my mind. Grandfather Raven surveys what remains of His creation and I am the last human alive. I half expect him to spiral down, land on a broken branch beside me, and proclaim my fate. But he drifts away and disappears beyond the mountainside, still only keeping watch, patient, waiting.

I try to take encouragement from the ten-foot hemlock and spruce saplings scattered across the hillside. Interestingly, no tender young have taken root atop the flat stumps and mossless trunks. Some of the fast-growing alders are twenty feet tall, but in winter they add to the feeling of barrenness and death. Their thin, crooked branches scratch against the darkened cloud and rattle in the wind. The whole land-scape is like a cooling corpse, with new life struggling up between its fingers. If I live a long time, I might see this hillside covered with the beginnings of a new forest. Left alone for a century or two, the trees would form a closed canopy and the understory of smaller plants would flourish. Protected from the deep snows of open country, deer could again survive winter by retreating into the forest. The whole commu-nity of dispossessed animals would return—red squirrel, marten, great horned owl, hairy woodpecker, golden-crowned kinglet, pine siskin, blue grouse, and the seed-shedding crossbills. In streams cleared of sediment by moss-filtered runoff, swarms of salmon would spawn once more, hunted by brown bears that emerged from the cool woods.

There is comfort in knowing another giant tree could replace the one that stood here, even though it would take several centuries of unfettered growth. I wish I could sink down into the earth and wait, listen for the bird voices to awaken me, rise from beneath the moss, and find myself sheltered by resplendent boughs. And in this world be-yond dreams, such inordinate excesses toward nature will have become unthinkable.

Shungnak looks at me and whines, asking if we can leave, so I climb down and struggle along behind her. She leads us up over the hilltop, unwilling to retrace the tangled route that got us here. A short while later, we step from the last rakers of brush onto the glorious openness of gravel roadway. This might be the only time I ever feel so pleased to be on a logging road in the middle of a clearcut. Our other luck is a temporary reprieve from the mixed rain and snow. The clouds brighten above a spectacular view of the island's outermost shore. I pull the binoculars from inside my jacket and vow to ignore the foreground.

Across the breach of Roller Bay, Ocean Point and Ragged Cape stretch out beyond the slopes of Kluksa Mountain. For the past year, I've dreamed of riding into the bight between those forelands and anchoring the skiff behind a reef shown on navigation charts. Ragged Cape is six miles from where I stand, as plainly visible as the moon on a cloudless night and just as untouchable. I memorize every detail of the shore, reaching for whatever knowledge I can find. It's clear that the two promontories are fully exposed to the weight of storm winds, thrashing seas, and whatever else threatens a small boat on this coast.

The beach behind Ragged Cape is thirty miles from home, in stages of increasingly exposed water and diminishing access to help or shelter. Sometimes I wonder what lunatic cravings incite my longing to reach such places. More than anything else, their remoteness is what possesses me, the thought of arriving on a nearly inaccessible shore and experiencing the purity of its wildness. Right now the swells are so enormous, I can't imagine how a skiff could survive in any anchorage along that stretch of coast. My only chance to stand ashore at Ragged Cape is to wait until calm summer weather.

Looking along the island's outer flank also helps to take my mind off the devastation close at hand. From Ocean Point to Cape Deception, and from there to Tsandaku Point, the whole forest and shore remain as they were when the first square sail rose up from beneath the horizon. Sometimes I feel like a survivor from that age, a figure on a faded tintype, standing amid a long-vanished, pristine world. I read my scrawled island notebooks as if they've been discovered in someone's attic, recollections of a lost way of life. The envy and romanticism I feel seem oddly involuted, even bizarre. But it makes me live the miracle of this place all the more intensely.

Kluksa Mountain climbs away to its vanishing point amid the clouds. Spatters of cold sleet flick against my face. As I stare out across the ocean, a deep longing wells up inside, sadness for what is lost, mixed with gratitude for the wildness that remains, for being alive to experience it, and for the blessed gift of eyes.

The shadowed forest lofts over us, surrounds and shields us, smooths a way for us, and leads us gently back into itself. We hurry toward camp, amid the slow breathing-out of dusk. Hard exercise drives away

the chill and cleans out the residue from too much thinking. Shungnak paces beside me, ignoring the temptations of squirrel sounds and
beckoning scents.

An hour later we reach camp. It feels cold and clammy inside the
tent, but the little stove quickly changes that. I savor a cup of hot tea
and share a piece of last fall's smoked salmon with Shungnak, then
unwrap a slice of venison for tonight's dinner. While it cooks, I relax
on my sleeping bag, thinking of Nita and Ethan at work in our warm
kitchen, lights from the front window glowing out across the bay. Then
I listen to the steady throb of surf that resonates through the trees, and
the chatter of raindrops on the tent wall. My heart is torn between the
island and home. Born into a culture that keeps the worlds of humanity
and nature apart, I am always close to one love but longing for another.

The candle has burned down to a circular mound of hardened wax.
As I stare into the flame, my thoughts sift back through the day. First
to the mountainous surf, marching in from the Pacific to disgorge itself
against the shore. And to the high pleasures of exploring a part of the
island I've never seen before. Then the moss forest, nurturing itself
on the remains of its own dead and fallen. All the past generations of
trees are here, alive in the bodies of those now standing. And perhaps
alive in some communality of spirit that stretches back to the forest's
beginning and permeates all who come into it.

I think next of the clearcut and the gray, lichened stump, remnant
of a great tree whose body was taken away and lost to whatever future
generations might arise there. For thousands of years, the Indian people
also cut trees from this forest, but whatever they used remained here.
Generations of houses and canoes, ceremonial poles and paddles, spear
shafts and lost arrows rotted back into the place they came from, just
as Joe Stevens' sled and snowshoes and whittled shavings will do in my
own lifetime. A tree used in that way is little different from one thrown
down in a storm; its own land will have it back, spirit and body, still
rooted within its place on earth.

And what of rootedness in death among humans? I was raised to
believe that the souls of people who have lived well are given the reward of heaven, far removed from the place that nurtured them in

life, remote even from the earth itself. And those who commit evil are threatened with the punishment of hell—to spend eternity deep inside the body of the earth.

When I asked Koyukon people about death, they said a person's spirit is reluctant to leave the company of friends and family, so for a time it lingers near them. The spirits of virtuous people eventually wander along an easy trail to the afterlife, in a good place on the Koyukon homeland. Those who have lived badly follow a long trail of hardship and suffering, but they finally arrive among the others. The dead sustain themselves as hunters and mingle through the spirit world of nature, eternally rooted to their place on earth.

The candle's wick topples and drowns. Perfect blackness releases me into the free and boundless night, to roam in dreams through an everlasting, untrammeled forest; a forest that gives me breath and shelters me; a spirit forest; a forest that envelops me with shining, consecrated webs and binds me here forever.

Going Down in Valdeez

Harry Crews was born and raised in
Bacon County, Georgia. A contrib-
uting editor of *Southern* magazine,
he is the author of several books
including *The Gospel Singer, Naked in
Garden Hills, This Thing Don't Lead
to Heaven, Karate Is A Thing of the
Spirit, Car, The Hawk Is Dying, The
Gypsy's Curse, A Feast of Snakes, A
Childhood: The Biography of a Place,
Blood and Grits, Florida Frenzy,* and
All We Need of Hell.

I was standing there in front of the Pipeline Club in a fine, misting rain with my hand still on the door of the taxi that had brought me in from the airport to Valdez, Alaska (pronounced *Valdeez*, so that the last syllable rhymes with *disease*, by the folks who lived thereabouts, folks who do not take the pronunciation of their town lightly and who are subject to become very pissed very quick if you do not come down hard on the *eez*, drawing it out in a long sibilant *z*); I was standing there looking at a legless man where he sat on the sidewalk on his little wheeled dolly, a beatific look of ecstasy on his thin, pale face as he looked not back at me but up into the cold, slanting mist, and the lady cabdriver was saying for the fourth time since I got into her cab: "These goddamn *new* people think they own this goddamn town, but I'll tell you one goddamn thing: They don't own it yet."

I was stunned with exhaustion. The flight from Atlanta to Chicago to Seattle to Ketchikan to Juneau to Yakutat to Cordova had left me confused and disoriented. Then my ordinary morning terrors had been compounded by the flight from Cordova in a Piper Aztec, bouncing and dropping and tilting through winds that anywhere else in the world would have been called a hurricane.

The ecstasy on the legless man's face had changed to a gentle, bemused satisfaction. I turned to see if the taxi driver was looking at the legless man. I thought she might tell me about him, tell me maybe that he was a religious mystic famous in Valdez for seeing through to the secret heart of things. But she was still staring curiously up at me, and through her clenched teeth, she said: "You just goddamn remember that."

"Look, lady," I said, but she was already squealing in a U turn, roaring off toward the airport.

When I started across the sidewalk, the legless man put his padded fists down and gave himself a shove, shooting his little dolly past me. I stopped, blinked. There on the cement where the legless man had been sitting were two symmetrical, perfectly formed human turds. I turned just in time to see the man and the dolly being lifted by two young boys into a camper on the back of a Ford pickup. I knew I'd been given a sign. Because I believe most devoutly in such things, I knew I had been given a sign to reckon with.

Inside the Pipeline Club I asked the bartender for double vodka and tonic with no ice and then found myself a corner where I could lean my head back against a wall and collect myself.

When I got off the Alaska Airlines plane in Cordova, the flight up to that point had only been exhausting. An hour later, when I got into the Piper Aztec, it went from exhausting to terrifying. We were in heavy rain and wind under a lowering sky. It couldn't have been much more than noon, but it seemed like dusk dark. I was the only passenger, and I rode up front by the pilot. He looked to be in his early twenties, wearing Levi's and a work shirt. His damp hair was hanging in a wet curling bang over his eyes. He was impossibly young to be taking me up in an airplane.

"What airline is this?" I shouted over the noise of the engine. The Aztec was unmarked except for the numbers on the fuselage, and I thought wildly as we approached the runway that I was on the wrong plane and, such being the case, I could get off.

"Chitina," he shouted back. "We do ferrying work for Alaskan over to Valdeez."

He moved the throttle to full rich, and the plane shook and groaned, its little wings flapping like a crippled bird's. "Listen," he screamed, "the ride'll be a little choppy today. But I think it'll be all right."

He thought it would be all right. Yes, indeed. Once aloft, I opened my eyes and watched him expertly light a Lucky Strike while the horizon tilted everywhere about us. I asked him where he'd learned to fly, thinking perhaps the Army or the Air Force.

"Aw, it's just something I picked up back in Texas. Always been interested in it and I just picked it up."

His name was Jerry Austin. From Austin, Texas. There was a story that the town had been named for some of his people somewhere back there. He didn't know if it was true. Thought it might be a lie. But you never can tell.

"Only been up here in Alasker three months. Hope to git a job with a jet out of Anchorage. Don't know if I can, though. Ruther not fly this rig up here in the winter."

We had been in the air for about twenty minutes when we turned away from the coast, following a wide body of water up between two mountains that rose 4000 or 5000 feet above us on either side.

"Valdeez Bay," he shouted. We had come out of the rain now, and the day had brightened under patches of blue sky showing through the clouds. "Right up yonder beyond that rise is Valdeez. This is where the tankers'll come in to pick up the oil off the pipeline." He looked down at the shimmering surface of the bay. "Seems a shame to ruin that water. Won't be fit to wash your feet in when they git through with it." He pointed off to the left as he banked the plane. "There she is."

From the air Valdez looked like a mobile-home court. It was a city on wheels. House trailers were jammed into every available space.

"What's that over there?" I asked.

"That's four hundred miles of steel pipe. Thirty-foot sections. Four-feet diameter." He looked at me and smiled. "Made in Japan. It's stacked over there right where Valdeez used to be."

"Used to be?"

"A few years back Valdeez was wiped out by a earthquake and tidal wave. When they built it up again, they moved it up here."

We were coming in fast now toward the airport. All manner of heavy machinery—packers and stackers and dirt buggies and backhoes and scrapers—raced about over the barren landscape. For no apparent reason, two helicopters hovered a half mile away on the side of a mountain. Raw lumber was everywhere, stacks of it, and the naked sides of buildings in various stages of construction shone in the sun but only briefly because as we made our approach, the sky closed again as if by magic and a misting rain began to fall.

"Jesus," I said, "is that a dirt runway?"

"Yeah," Jerry said, putting his cigarette out with one hand and bringing us in with the other. "But when they finish over there"—he pointed to the madly racing machinery—"when they git through over there, you'll be able to bring a 727 in here."

The lady cabdriver laughed when I told her to take me to a motel. "No rooms in this town. None. I can check if you want me to, but there won't be any." She got on her radio, and sure enough, there were no rooms.

"Take me to a bar then," I said.

After I'd had enough vodka to steady me down, I asked the bartender to sell me a bottle.

"Not but one place you can buy a bottle of vodka in Valdeez. Just a block over there. Pinzon Liquor Store. Truck Egan's place."

"Egan?" I said, the name trying to remind me of something. Then I knew where I'd heard it. "Say, he's not. . . ."

"That's right," he said. "Governor of Alaska's brother. Truck's the smart one in the family. Shit, Bill Egan's on the phone two, three times a day, asking Truck what to do."

I walked through the rain across Egan Drive to the Pinzon Liquor Store on Tatitlek Avenue. Truck Egan was a very small man with wet eyes, a sad, gentle face, and a badly twisted hunchback. His long, slender white fingers trembled as he put the vodka in a bag.

There were no other customers in the store, but he didn't want to talk. Or rather, his sister, Alice, an imposing lady with bluing hair, didn't want to talk, and that seemed to discourage Truck. It was apparent Alice was displeased over the prospect of anybody writing anything about Valdez.

I got back into the rain and walked toward a neon sign I'd seen from the taxi coming in from the airport advertising the Club Valdez. Egan Drive is the main street going through town. It is wide and paved with sidewalks and curbstones. But once you turn off that and head up toward the place where the house trailers are stacked in cheek to jowl, up toward the little marina where the fishing boats swing at anchor, the streets dissolve into mud and potholes and rock. Packs of dogs scavenge in overflowing dumpsters and garbage cans, snarling and fighting among themselves. Scraps of lumber and twisted sheets of corrugated tin litter the edges of swampy streets. Construction is going on everywhere in and among the house trailers. Even the Alaska National Bank of the

North is in a house trailer, but they're building right next door, going at it with hammer and Skilsaw, and even as I write this, they might be out of their house trailer and into something new and fine.

The Club Valdez was one enormous room, a bar across the front, two pool tables in the back, and, in the space between, maybe ten or twelve round wooden tables. The smoke was heavy. The jukebox was playing Charlie Pride. A lone couple two-stepped across the bare wooden floor as a line of men at the bar watched them.

I got a vodka and went to the head. The sweet smell of grass clung to the damp calcimined walls, and clouds of smoke hung in the air, mixing nicely with the odor of vomit and piss. "My, my, my," I said to myself while I watered off, "it's everywhere, even here in Valdeez."

As if on cue, a boy popped out of the stall. "You wanta buy some?"

I looked at him and thought, *Now, ain't you a dumbass?* but I said, "What you selling?"

He had on a beaded headband and a fringe leather jacket over greasy Levi's stuffed into mud-spattered cowboy boots.

"What you lookin to buy?" The words turned to grits in his mouth, and it occurred to me that most of the talk I'd heard since I'd been in town, including the taxi driver's, had been Grit talk.

"What you selling a lid for?" I asked.

"A weighed ounce," he said, "is worth ninety dollars."

"Not to me it isn't," I said.

"All right then," he said, "sixty dollars."

"You're hurt," I said. "Something's burned in your fuse box."

He shrugged. "People expect to be robbed up here. Anythin is worth anythin you can git for it. But sixty's all right. Sixty wouldn't cheat me."

"I bet it wouldn't," I said. As I was going out the door, he went back into the stall.

I went to the bar and watched the couple two-step. The girl was very skinny and she had a baby with her. She had thoughtfully tied it to a chair with a leather belt. She and the man went back to the table between numbers to chug some beer and pet the baby. She gave it a sip from time to time, and the baby sat strapped to the chair, gurgling and mewling contentedly, now and then nodding off. Which reminded me I was looking for a place to put my head down.

"Writin a letter home, are you?"

I looked up from the notes I was scribbling. The man was on the stool next to me. He seemed to be about as drunk as I was. I would have guessed his age at thirty, but he had a marvelously weathered and ruined face. On his hard hat was a faded McGovern sticker.

"Yeah," I said. "I'm just writing the old lady it ain't nowhere to stay in this town."

"You just git in?"

"Yeah."

"You ain't got on yet?"

"Not yet, but I'm supposed to git on."

"You got some cash money in your pocket?"

"I wouldn't come off up here without some cash money."

"Go out yonder to the airport then and tell Dave Kennedy I sent you. My name's Bugger Wells. Kennedy's building a camp out there the other side of the airport. It'll cost you, but you can stay. Ask anybody out there for Dave Kennedy. You won't have no trouble."

The cabdriver took me to a tiny two-story building that had an outside stairway leading to the top. The second floor was a single room with a half partition. The whole thing couldn't have been more than twenty feet square. Maps and overlays and blueprints and papers of every sort were stuffed into shelves along the walls. Two Teletype machines rattled next to the semipartition. A polar-bear skin covered the top of a dun-colored couch. The bear's mouth was open, and its stunned marble eyes stared past me through the window where the helicopters still hovered in the distance and the yellow, growling machinery still raced about over the airport. Dave Kennedy stood at his desk, the top of which was a foot deep in papers, most of which seemed incredibly dusty. He was on the phone, cradling it between his shoulder and right ear. His left ear was pinned against his head and grown shut.

A lady in corduroy trousers sat in the corner at a typewriter. She stopped typing and looked at me. I told her what the guy at the Club Valdez had told me.

"Valdeez," she said. "You say *Valdeez*!"

"He was right," said Dave Kennedy, who had just put the phone down. "You can stay at the camp. Thirty-three dollars a day. You looking for work?"

I decided to tell him what I was doing in Valdez.

"No way," he said. "Take you a year to write this and you still wouldn't have it right. You'd have it wrong. The only way to measure what's happening here? You know? You want me to tell you? I'll tell you. A six-inch ruler made out of rubber that stretches to seventeen feet. That's how. Nothing like this ever been done. And you can't worry because a ruler's got twelve inches to the foot. In Valdeez, there may be twelve feet to the inch. OK?"

The explanation seemed to satisfy him immensely. It tended to confuse me, but I thought better of asking him to explain it. I'd noticed a National Car Rental sign downstairs and asked if I could get a car. Rent you a plane if you want one, he said. I said, no, a car would do nicely. While the girl was writing out the ticket for the car, Dave Kennedy took me over to the window and pointed. "See where they're building down there?" It looked to me as if they were building *everywhere* down there, and I told him so.

"No, no," he said impatiently, "there by the trailer. Right there with the silver top. Go in there and ask for Hap. Hap, the cook. He'll fix it. Give him the money."

I found Hap in a house trailer that had been converted into a kitchen and dining room with enough seats to feed 54 people. Directly next to it, a whole covey of carpenters was building a permanent dining hall that would eventually feed 600.

Hap was feeding some of the early night crew when I got there and he asked me to wait. I sat at a table, looking at a cup of coffee he had given me and thinking how nice it was going to be to put my head down, when a foreman came in. Like most of the men there, the foreman's skin was ruined from the wind and the sun and the snow. He had what looked like might be skin cancer across the bridge of his nose. He was pissed when he came in. He kicked a couple of chairs, hustled his balls, and sat down. He started talking loudly, a little out of breath, to nobody in particular.

"I'll tell you one damn thing: if you pick up something in this town, don't set it back down. Because if you do set back down even for a minute, it'll be another price when you pick it up." He got off his chairs, hustled his balls again, sat back down, crossed his legs, uncrossed them, and sat kicking one heavy boot against the other. "Went into town there to buy a damn alarm clock. Wanted to make sure the crew was up and ready. Went in the store there. Didn't have but one kind of clock. Looked like a piece of shit, but I thought it'd get us up: Young kid behind the counter. Asked him how much it was. Said he didn't know, but the boss was next door and he'd run ask. While he was gone, I picked up one of the goddamn things. Had a sticker on it said six dollars and fifty cent. Kid come back and said the boss said nine dollars and fifty cent. I told the kid the one in my hand said six-fifty. He said he just knowed what the boss said. Fuck it, I didn't want to stand around there all day talking to a shirttail kid, so I bought it. Brought it down here to camp and the goddamn thing quit in the middle of the night. Crew was half a fucking hour late. Took the goddamn thing down there a while ago. Man runs the place said he was sorry, but it was as is. *Sold as is.* No refund, no nothing. But the sonofabitch *did* say he was sorry. I told him to stick it up his ass, and I hope the alarm went off. I'd already checked all over town and there weren't no more clocks. Not another goddamn one in town. I guess he knowed it too because when I told him I'd have to buy another of the goddamn sorry things, he looked me dead in the eye and said just as slick as you'd want: 'That'll be twelve dollars and fifty cent.' "

Hap came out of the kitchen and took my money, $165 for five nights, and gave me over to a bull cook named Paul, a dark boy of about twenty-two with very white teeth and short, curly hair. On the way over to where I would be bunking he explained to me that a bull cook was the all-round good guy in camp who made the beds, carried the trash, swept the floors, and did whatever else was necessary to keep the bunkhouse crew happy.

The bunkhouse in this case turned out to be a house trailer. The entire camp was made out of house trailers joined together by a walkway and covered over with a little roof. Each trailer had a deep sink, a bathroom, and slept five men. The floors were covered with gold-speck carpeting, and the walls were all paneled with imitation wood. It was exactly the sort of thing that would have passed for elegance in Waycross, Georgia. Paul told me there was a washing machine and dryer in the back that I could use for nothing. If I needed anything, I should let him know. When he left, I walked outside and sat on an empty gas can. It was gray and still raining, but the sun was brilliant and brittle as glass high on the sides of the Chugach Mountains where they rose 5000 feet and better on all sides of town. I was finally at the end of the line, Valdez, Alaska.

Alaska is an awesome place where exaggeration and outrage are the norm. It is a place where Eskimos live and work in cold so extreme it often reaches 80 degrees *below* zero. Three percent of the state is made up of active glaciers and ice fields—20,000 square miles—more than is found in the rest of the inhabited world combined. It is a land of unimaginable wealth that we ripped off from the Russians on October 18, 1867, for about two cents an acre. The shortest distance separating North America from Asia is between Little Diomede and Big Diomede islands. On Little Diomede a picture of Abraham Lincoln hangs on the schoolhouse wall. In the schoolhouse on Big Diomede is a picture of Karl Marx. Everything about Alaska stuns the imagination—including the proposed trans-Alaska pipeline. To understand what is happening to the town of Valdez, to the people there, it is necessary to have some notion of the dimensions, the magnitude of the pipeline itself.

In the northernmost part of the state, between the formidable mountains of the Brooks Range and the Arctic Ocean, lies the North Slope. And it is there at Prudhoe Bay that the trans-Alaska pipeline will rise. It passes the Sagavanirktok River, the Atigun Valley and crosses the mountains of the wild Brooks Range itself through the 4500-foot Dietrich Pass; and from there it goes south to the Yukon River and on south, passing only 15 miles to the east of Fairbanks. Once past Fairbanks, it goes into the Alaska Mountain Range, where it will reach an elevation of 3500 feet as it crosses the Isabel Pass before descending into the Copper River Basin. The line then climbs the Chugach Mountains and descends through Keystone Canyon into Valdez, the nearest year-round ice-free port capable of accommodating tankers of the size that will be needed to haul the oil to West Coast refineries. The distance covered is exactly 798 miles.

The line itself will be buried when the terrain it crosses is solid rock or well-drained gravel. When it is not buried, it will be raised on special pipe supports. It will go over rivers and under rivers—more often than not under them—and when it does go under rivers, it will be encased in concrete four inches thick.

The pipe out of which the line will be constructed comes in sections about 40 or 60 feet long, 4 feet in diameter, with thicknesses ranging from .462 inches to .652 inches. In Berkeley, California, where the pipe was tested, a section of it was subjected to a maximum force of 2.52 million pounds and a lateral deflection force of 459,000 pounds before it wrinkled. There is, as I write this, a total of 418.54 miles of this pipe stacked and waiting in Valdez. It was made in Japan and the first shipment arrived in Valdez September 13, 1969, the last shipment October 21, 1971. The other pipe-storage yards are at Fairbanks and Prudhoe Bay.

By the best estimates, there are an incredible 9.6 billion barrels of oil on the North Slope, and that is said to be as much as the combined reserves of Louisiana, Oklahoma, Kansas, and half of Texas. When the pipeline is completed, the oil will go into it hot (at times as hot as 140 degrees Fahrenheit) and remain warm through the line because of the heat of the twelve pumping stations along the route and the heat generated by the friction between the oil and the pipe itself. Initially, the line will move 1.2 million barrels a day—that's 50.4 million gallons —but ultimately it is designed to move 2 million barrels a day. Under normal pumping conditions, there will be, at any given moment, approximately 11,000 barrels, or 462,000 gallons, in any single mile of line. When the line first begins pumping, the oil will move about 2 miles per hour inside the line; but when it reaches capacity, the oil will travel at something just over 7 miles per hour.

The entire line will be under computer control, with a monitoring station in Valdez. At the first sign of a loss of pressure, which would mean there had been a rupture or a leak somewhere along the way, the entire line could be shut down within twenty minutes. Shutting down a system that includes almost 800 miles of line and that much moving oil would create tremendous backup pressures, so designers have contrived to build into the lines a series of valves and overflow tanks to accommodate that pressure. All tank facilities will have dikes built around them for protection against earthquakes. The Valdez terminal, which will be across the bay from the actual city of Valdez, will be constructed on solid bedrock far above the highest recorded seismic sea wave.

All of this planning and designing and construction is being carried out by the Alyeska Pipeline Service Company. Alyeska was formed in August of 1970, by Amerada Hess Corporation, ARCO Pipe Line Company, SOHIO Pipeline Company, Exxon Pipeline Company, Mobil Alaska Pipeline Company, Phillips Petroleum Company, BP Pipeline Company, Inc., and Union Alaska Pipeline Company and is owned outright by these eight companies today. Certainly, it would appear that the designers have done everything they could do to prevent despoiling a beautiful irreplaceable wilderness by visiting ruination upon a balanced, though delicately so, animal and plant life.

But there is some question as to whether what they have done is enough. There is the matter of those caribou, for instance. Everybody has heard about the pipeline and the caribou—that magnificent herd of animals balanced off nicely on the scales of progress against this magnificent herd of people, you and I. There are better than 205 million of us; there are only 450,000 of them. Each of us—every man, woman, and child—uses an average of three gallons of oil a day. Numbers count for something, by God. So what does Alyeska intend to do about the fact that 450,000 caribou are up on the North Slope every summer to calve and then migrate through the Brooks Range, where they are sure to encounter the pipeline? Where sections of pipe are aboveground and would interrupt the natural migratory patterns of the caribou, Alyeska will build underpasses for the animals to walk through. That's right, *underpasses*. Will the caribou walk through the underpasses? They'd damned well better if they want to get to where they've been going for hundreds of years.

What of the spawning of fish when they are laying all that pipe under all those rivers? Simple. They are going to time the operation so they won't be putting the pipe down when the fish are spawning. But will the fish spawn after their natural beds have been upset by inevitable noise, vibration, and the ubiquitous debris of construction? Many of us hope so, but many of us doubt it.

Alyeska also plans to time its construction to minimize the disturbance to Dall sheep, a rare species, grazing and lambing in the Atigun Canyon. But they will be disturbed, however minimally, and nobody can predict with certainty what the outcome will be. The peregrine falcon is an endangered species, and yet there will be many places along the pipeline where the peregrine falcon nests. It is stupid and absurd to say the pipeline work will not disturb and upset the peregrine. *Anything disturbs and upsets the peregrine, so delicate is its nervous system* and so finely attuned is it to the natural rhythms and cycles of the earth.

Many people who love the idea of the pipeline will point out to you that Alyeska doesn't want or need much land to carry out its project—a ridiculously small percentage of the state as a matter of fact. The right-of-way will extend only 25 feet on each side of the 4-foot pipeline, and if you add all the additional working space required for the job, it will only come to about 7680 acres, or 12 square miles. The state of Alaska contains 586,412 square miles. That figures out to be .002 percent of the total area of the state. But it is not, of course, *what* they want, it's *where* they want it. The quarrel comes from the fact that the 12 square miles form a thin knife-edge line and therefore a barrier of some sort, if nothing but an access road, across the entire interior of Alaska from the Arctic Ocean at Prudhoe Bay to the Bay of Valdez.

The final nut buster is that there are men who have every reason to know about such things who think we did not need to go onto the North Slope to start with. One of these men is Barry Commoner, director of the Center for the Biology of Natural Systems at Washington University in St. Louis. In a *Playboy* "Interview" of July 1974, he said: "It's been estimated that the oil on Alaska's North Slope may provide the U.S. with a two-or-three-year supply. So we've extended the country's oil resources from, say, 20 years to 23 years. For that, we may permanently wreck the ecosystem in Alaska. Is it worth it? I don't think so."

But all this has been hashed over. And for every expert you can find who thinks the pipeline is a horror, the oil companies can find five who think it is an unmitigated blessing. In the meantime, the actual welding of the line has not started; but those miles and miles of pipe are lying there in Valdez, waiting. Barges are on the way from Washington State, loaded with supplies. Men and equipment arrive every day. The town is gearing up as best it can for the onslaught. Dave Kennedy is completing a camp to house 600 men. Another camp is going up to house 1700 men. And across the bay at the site of the proposed terminal, Fluor Alaska, Inc., is about to start construction of a camp where 3500 men will stay. Valdez will change from a village of about 1000 people to a boomtown of 17,000 in the next few years. There is a tension, even a violence, in the air of Valdez, poised on the brink of becoming something it has never been before. What that something is, nobody knows. But you can hear it in the growling machinery, the whine of ripsaws, the constant beat of hammers. You can smell it in the smoky bars. You can see it in the faces of the people.

I was standing out on the dock in the rain, freezing, while they headed and gutted fish. That morning Dave Kennedy had asked me down at the camp if I knew why the men had to drink so much in Valdez. No, I told him. He said you had to stay as wet on the inside as you were on the outside, so you wouldn't warp. I had done the best with it I could, but I was beginning to warp bad. The boy standing beside me, whose name was Chris Matthews, stood not as I did with my back to the rain but rather with his face into it, looking out toward the flat gray water of Valdez Bay. He didn't seem to notice the rain or the wind even though my teeth were chattering so I could hardly talk. The rain was fine as mist and driven by a thin, cold wind. Chris was sixteen years old with corn-colored hair cropped close and a mouth full of broken teeth. He had just brought the fish in off the boat where it was anchored out in the flats off Cordova. A seaplane had taken him and the fish off the boat. He was a quiet, almost shy boy, but when he spoke, his voice carried the flat authority of a man who had been around the block.

"It's a seaplane that'll take you off the boat and bring you in for fifteen dollars. Cain't bring my boat in. Got a Indian fishing out there with me. Good man. But a drunk. I bring him in, I cain't git'm back out again."

He was popping the heads off the salmon, expertly ripping their bellies, lifting out long pink roe, and dropping it into a zinc bucket at the end of the bench. Directly he quit with the fish and wiped his hands on the end of his shirt. He walked over to the edge of the dock and spat in the water. Straight across the bay from where we were standing was the site of the terminal where tankers would take the oil off the pipeline. Even from there we could see the yellow scrapers and dirt buggies and Cats, small as ants, digging away at the mountain, preparing for Fluor Alaska to build a camp for 3500 men.

"We'll all end up working for Fluor," he said and spat again. "The money's too good."

We went back over to the bench where Chris' daddy, Bob Matthews, and Bob's partner, Johnny Craine, were finishing up with the fish. Johnny's wife, Lynn, was packing them into long fish boxes.

"We'll freeze'm and sell'm locally in the winter," Chris said. "Ain't no fish here then much. Sell'm wholesale for forty, forty-five cent. These reds will bring that; the king'll go for a little more maybe."

"Let's go across the street for a drink," somebody said.

Wet, smelling slightly of fish, we went up the ramp with the fish boxes to the pickup truck. We walked across the muddy, unpaved street to the Club Valdez. It was late afternoon, and the bar was beginning to fill up. Four couples were two-stepping to Merle Haggard. The boy ordered a Coke and I got a vodka. The others asked for Olys, by which they meant Olympia beer. I never heard anybody order any other kind of beer but Oly while I was in Valdez. I know there were other kinds of beer there because I had been into several Budweisers myself. But everybody else drank Olympia because goddamn it was Alaskan beer. They didn't care what people Outside drank; they drank Olympia. (*Outside* is the word they use for anyplace that is not in Alaska. Sometimes they'll refer to the Lower Forty-eight, but mostly it's Outside.) Native Alaskans, as well as people who are not native Alaskans but who have been through one or more Alaskan winters, have a tremendous contempt for people Outside. And like people everywhere, they do not gladly suffer fools to instruct them on the error of their ways. It is common to see bumper stickers saying: "SIERRA CLUB GO HOME" and "WE DON'T GIVE A DAMN HOW YOU DO IT OUTSIDE."

Earlier, out on the end of the dock, Chris had been standing there kicking one rubber boot against the other when he looked up and said: "Family of pukers."

I looked where he was pointing and saw a man and a woman and a child coming down to the dock from a fifty-foot yacht with raised fishing chairs and curtains on the windows of an enclosed cabin. The man was double-knitted and color-coordinated and wearing a braided cap at a jaunty angle. The woman was pants-suited in something phosphorescent pink.

"Pukers?" I said.

"This is one of the best fishing waters in the world—commercial, sport, anything. People like them there come from Outside with they damn boats and git one of us to guide'm. Only thing is, they spend all day puking. Pukers ought not to have boats."

I eventually learned that *puker* had become one of the kinder generic words for anybody from Outside.

Johnny got up to dance with his blond and handsome lady, Lynn. They sailed smoothly about the wooden floor, Johnny's cheek pressed against hers, she humming the words to the song softly, the two of them two-stepping as only people can who have been together thirty years and better. Lynn had followed Johnny to Valdez, but Bob's wife was Outside. She didn't like it in Alaska. Johnny and Bob had been partners for twenty-one years, worked dirt jobs all over Alaska, had been up on the North Slope together back in the early days. They were Cat drivers and together owned some heavy equipment they leased out. They were just about to bid on the sewage contract the town of Valdez was going to put out in a few days.

A friend of theirs came in and Bob waved him over. He was lean, not big but set up thick in the shoulder and narrow in the hip. His hands were wedge-shaped and laced with heavy veins. His eyes were dark; his hair thick and straight and black. He was a little drunk. The lady with him was slender, with flat cheeks and deep eyes and a beautifully formed mouth. Bob introduced us. His name was Jay and hers was Chris. They were both native Alaskans. He was Irish and Indian. She was Eskimo.

She hugged my neck like a good buddy and said: "You met your first full-blood Eskimo in the Club Valdeez." Then to her husband: "Show'm what you got for Father's Day, honey."

Jay wasn't feeling good. He looked at me, "Gone come up here and write it all down in a week or two, are you?" I told him I didn't think I'd get it *all*, no. I was feeling about like a snake by then myself. "You know where I just come from?" he said.

"Show'm what you got for Father's Day, honey," his wife said.

"I'll tell you where I just come from, a meeting with the pipeline people; Impact Meeting, they call it. Had a goddamn Texan there, ten-gallon hat, cowboy boots, sunglasses, and he was telling us what to expect from these Alaskan winters." His voice was thin and bitter. "Telling us how to dress and what to do—you know, the dos and don'ts of Alaska. I sat there wondering how the hell I got through forty-some-odd years up here without a goddamn Texan to tell me what to do."

His wife didn't like the way things were going. "Somebody ask him what he got for Father's Day. A gold watch is what I gave him."

Jay shook his head and drained his Oly. "Goddamn Texans took over this state and never fired a shot."

His wife said: "You know what Father's Day meant? It meant I could go back for seconds." She laughed nervously. She had tremendous teeth.

"You know the difference between cowboy boots and farmer's boots?" asked Jay. "Farmer's boots got the bullshit on the *outside*."

His wife came over and took his arm. "I want to dance," she said. He didn't seem to want to, but he got up, anyway, and they two-stepped away to Hank Williams, Jr.

A lady, rather heavy and smelling of talcum, had joined us at the table and had begun a long story in a sour, quarrelsome voice about what was happening to food prices.

"We're not all on the pipeline money, you know." she said. "A eight-ounce can of vegetable juice, the kind I like and all, jumped from seventy-nine cent to a dollar and three cent in one week."

I'd walked around town that day myself, seeing what the stores were like. There was not a single bar of hand soap in any store in all of Valdez. Neither was there any milk. None. A Coke, a small one, cost fifty cents. Generally anything that is brought in by truck is very expensive, if you can get it at all. Anything that is flown in is, given the scheme of things, fairly reasonable. Meat, for instance, comes by plane, and round steak in the grocery store was $2.25 a pound.

Jay and his lady came back to the table, and he was in a better mood. He showed us the gold watch she had given him for Father's Day. He said he was going to be a grandfather any day now. Except for his beat-up face, he looked thirty. He was forty-two.

His wife started telling me how her mother used to make ice cream. When she got to the place where her mother was adding seal oil, she suddenly stopped and said, "Do you boogie?" I told her I'd boogie her back off. "Goddamn, let's do it," she said. And we did, but it was science-fiction boogie, because we had to do it to "Tie a Yellow Ribbon Round the Old Oak Tree."

We came back to the table, and Jay put his hand on my arm. "You serious about writing about this?" I told him I was. "Then I want to tell you," he said. "I'm native Alaskan. I never went Outside until I was grown. Still haven't been Outside but two or three times in my whole life." He waved his arm to include the room. "There's not but seventy thousand of us. Think about that. This country and there's not but seventy thousand natives. We're Eskimos, Aleuts, Indians, and people like me, a cross, but born here and raised here. And this pipeline's gone kill us, kill the country." He was speaking with great intensity, his face flushed, his hand where it held my arm gripped hard enough to hurt. "Ruin it all forever."

I thought he meant the pipeline itself, running across the interior of the country. I thought he was talking about ecology.

"Shit, no," he said. "I was Outside a couple of years ago in a bar and a couple guys started in on me about how the line was gone ruin Alaska and they had a river right there in their own state that'd kill a horse if he was to drink out of it. They're so full of shit in the Lower Forty-eight. Let'm look to their own backyard before they start telling us what's ruining our country. What's gone kill us is the scumbags that'll follow the line, follow the men and the money. The Alaskan people are delicate—the seventy thousand—so . . . so . . . innocent. You know innocent?" I told him I knew innocent. "It's not the workers. Hell, the men are all right. Look at'm up there." We turned to look at the long line of men at the bar, solemnly staring at three couples two-stepping over the smooth wooden floor. "Scumbags always follow construction, but there'll be scumbags here like they've never been scumbags before. This job is so big, the money's so. . . . Look, a laborer on this line'll make seven, eight hundred dollars a week. A guy driving a dirt buggy can make twelve hundred a week. The companies put these men in camps, feed'm, give'm a place to sleep. All that money's free and clear. Only a few of'm got their wives up here. So what'll the men do? They'll give their money to scumbags. And I don't give shit about that. You think I give a shit? But this job's going to draw every high roller, promoter, hype artist, con man, pimp, and dopester. . . . It's gone suck'm up here from Outside. And once they're here, it'll be all over. They'll go through this country, every city, every town, every village, like maggots through meat."

He stopped and chugged an Oly. The whole table had grown silent, listening. It was a little embarrassing, because he was so obviously sincere, so impassioned about something he could do nothing about.

The boy, who had sat all this time drinking a Coke, said in his flat, laconic voice: "That's why I'm staying on the boat. Me and that drunk Indian. They'll have to come take me off that boat."

Everybody laughed, and the boy's daddy, Bob, slapped the table with the palm of his hand and said: "Hey, let's go have a fish fry!"

I said I'd go by Truck's and pick up some beer and meet them at the trailer. After they had gone, I had another vodka and thought about the mess that was Valdez, Alaska, and how pleased I was that it was their mess and not mine, or, if in some larger sense it was mine, that I wouldn't have to deal with it. I'm a coward that way.

I'd gone by a couple days before to see the mayor, but he was out delivering the mail, had a mail route. The mayoralty turned out to be one of those dollar-a-year-jobs. So I dropped by to see the city manager, Mr. Lehfeldt, a neatly dressed man with slicked-down black hair and nervous eyes. He in effect told me he was scared to death. "There's not enough sewers and there's not enough water and I had a meeting with Alyeska last week. . . ." He stopped and drew a deep breath before his tight, petulant voice ran on. "And they're talking about coming in here to start building housing for a thousand supervisory personnel. That's more than all the permanent housing in the rest of Valdeez put together!" When I got through talking to Mr. Lehfeldt, the mayor was still out delivering mail.

So I stopped by to see Police Chief Dave Ohler, a big man with enormous hands, whose gentle, whispery voice almost put me to sleep even though I only spoke with him for a minute or two. He seemed to see no cause for alarm in the fact that there were only three men on the police force. "Course, we've got a state-trooper office here with two men permanently assigned to it, so that gives us five officers, and we've only got at this moment about two thousand people in town." What about when it jumped to 5000 or 6000 or 10,000? Well, he wasn't sure. But so far things seemed to be going along OK. "I guess we can expect some trouble, but so far everything in town seems to be pretty clean." Drugs? Whores? Not that he knew of.

I went over to the Pinzon Liquor Store for some beer and vodka. Alice wasn't there, but Truck was still as reticent as ever. We exchanged pleasantries about the weather, and I went back out into the rain. Just as I was getting into the car, a guy called to me from across the street. There were two of them, both young, both bearded, sitting in a Volkswagen bus.

"Step over here a second," the one behind the wheel leaned toward the window. "You want a tattoo?" he said.

First I thought I'd heard him wrong; then I thought he was crazy. "No," I said. "No, I don't want a tattoo."

"Listen," he said. "I'm from L.A. I worked for Lyle Tuttle. You know Lyle Tuttle?"

"No," I said.

"Tattooist to the stars," he said. "He's the one tattooed Janis Joplin."

"How you know you don't want one? You ain't seen my work. Pete, show him my work." The boy nearest me got out of the Volkswagen. I took about three steps back when he stepped down to the street. I was pretty freaked by then. "This here's Pete. He's a walking advertisement for my work." Pete shucked out of his shirt, held his arms out, flexed, and slowly turned. He ws intricately and beautifully illustrated. From neck to navel he was a complicated network of interlocking eagles and jaguars and anchors and hearts and legends written in a kind of Germanic script. I couldn't take my eyes off him. Among other things, he must have been an iron freak. Muscles, as he turned, rippled and slid, ridged and quivered, making the smooth, multicolored skin come alive, pulsing in an undulant motion.

"Jesus Lord," I finally said.

"See," the guy in the truck said. "You don't know what you want. I got lots of designs you can choose from, or I'll work from something you design. We're camped right out. . . ."

"I've got to go see some people," I said. "They're waiting."

The illustrated iron freak was still turning, and I could not bring myself to say I didn't want one of his tattoos. They were too beautifully and skillfully done to tell him that.

"OK, that's OK. Come by our place anytime."

He told me where they were camped, out beyond the Pipeline Storage Yard on the road to Anchorage. You turned left on the first dirt road beyond the yard.

I was just turning to go when he said: "One last thing. You wanta buy a watch?" He whipped open the door to the bus and there in a shallow suitcase must have been 150 watches of all kinds—wrist, pocket, and pendant.

"When I got more time to look at them," I said. "When I come for my tattoo, maybe."

"Good enough," he said and closed the case.

Bob Matthews was already cooking the fish when I got there. He was doing it outside even though it was raining. They walk through the rain in Valdez the way the rest of the world walks through sunshine. They don't seem to notice it. I went inside and drank with Johnny

Craine while Lynn made coleslaw and cooked cornbread. A guy came in and said hello and asked if he could take a shower. Lynn told him sure and said there were towels by the sink.

"That's something you get used to up here quick," she said. "Somebody says hi; then they ask you if they can have a shower. Nobody's got any water up here much, you know."

Bob came in with the fish, and we ate and drank and told sea stories. No alcohol is allowed in the pipeline camps up on the North Slope by the oil companies because the men are working in such cold weather that a drunk could easily wander out into the snow and freeze to death. So Lynn baked a cake for Johnny one Christmas, hollowed it out, put a quart of whiskey inside, and sent it to him. (I think I understand the story, but I'm not sure.) Up on the North Slope no engine is ever turned off during the winter months. Tractors, Cats, trucks, run day and night for the good reason that if anything ever shuts down, you can't start it again. Rubber tires shatter like glass. Bob told a story about getting outstanding on some bootleg stuff and decking an Eskimo only to wake up later that night to find the Eskimo outside on a Caterpillar bulldozing down the camp.

And so it went late into the night, through outrageous quantities of fish, cornbread, slaw, and beer and vodka, until we were full, talked out, laughed out, and sensationally drunk. At which time I thought I was going back to the camp, and I'll never know how it happened (maybe I just wanted to see the illustrated man again) but I ended up out on the road to Anchorage, left on the first dirt road past the Pipeline Storage Yard. None of it's too clear, but I do remember sitting in a trailer with these two guys explaining that my right leg was game, a really bad knee, broken, torn, bad cartilage, unrepairable, and saying that I thought I needed hinges on that knee, four tattooed hinges, one on the front and back and one on each side. I think I was joking. It's all very hazy. Anyway, that's the last thing I remember.

I woke up the next morning in the rented National car with a pounding head and a dry mouth. I thought at first an ant or maybe even a bee had stung my right arm, was stinging it. I looked down to knock

it off and damned if I didn't have a tattoo. A hinge on my right elbow.
I was still parked in front of the trailer where the tattoo artist and his
walking advertisement lived, and I went bellowing out of the car, my
head hurting ninety miles an hour, into the trailer. The two guys were
asleep on a ratty bed.

"You sonofabitches," I was shouting, "you tattooed me!"

Their eyes were open now. One of them yawned and said, "That's
right."

I started yelling and screaming that you just didn't tattoo somebody
when he was out on his ass, that I never would have agreed to being
tattooed, that only assholes got tattooed and I was not an asshole. And
then I really started foaming at the mouth when he told me it had cost
me $65. Out with the old wallet. A quick look. Sure enough, I was
lighter by $65.

"You bastards, what if I get hepatitis?"

The iron freak got off the bed, his eagles and jaguars flashing, walked
right up and leaned into my face and said softly: "If you get hepatitis,
you'll turn yellow as shit."

As I was driving back to town, I said to myself: You have been rolled
and permanently discolored in Valdeez, Alaska.

The whore was twenty-two and her name was Micki (spelled with two
i's that way). Her husband's name was Buddy. They were from Los
Angeles.

"So, you know, I'm reading the paper one morning and the wire service has picked up a story about a girl who got permission to go up on
the North Slope and sell subscriptions to *Argosy* magazine. Two months
later some security people stopped her. She had five subscriptions to
Argosy magazine and nineteen thousand dollars in her pocket.

"So, you know, we were swinging down in Los Angeles, right? I
mean, you know, Micki was turning four or five guys a party anyway.
So I said why not go up there and make some money? Micki said sure,
why not? In three years we'll retire to France forever."

"The Riviera," said Micki.

We were in a mobile home, a double wide. Micki had come out of her little room and was sitting in a housecoat. Buddy was tricked out in the best tradition of pimpdom. He was all ruffles and lace and stacked heels and wraparound goggle-style amber sunglasses and a gold earring and on and on. He'd been going through this long number about how cool he was (I think he'd read Iceberg Slim's autobiography) when Micki leaned forward in her chair and said, looking at my discolored, swollen, scabby hinged elbow: "How long've you had that?"

"About three days," I said.

"Is the guy here in Valdeez?"

"Who?"

"The man who gives tattoos."

"Yes."

"Buddy," she said, "I want a tattoo."

"Bullshit," he said.

They were immediately in an awful argument. He'd flown her out to Seattle not long ago for a little R & R, and she'd seen the movie *Papillon*. She wanted a tattoo of a butterfly on her ass. He shouted that she wouldn't be able to fuck for a week with a tattoo on her ass. Just look at that goddamn hinge on his goddamn elbow! She screamed she wouldn't turn another trick if he didn't get her a tattoo. It was very embarrassing. I hate to witness family disputes. But he relented finally and stomped out of the room. He wasn't gone but a minute before he was back, zipping himself into a pair of muddy Levi's and buttoning a mackinaw that was torn and raveling at both sleeves.

He shrugged. "I have to get out of my good stuff and put on this shit when I go out of the trailer."

He wanted me to go with him, but I told him the tattoo artist and I had had words. He didn't like me and I didn't like him; further, I thought they were doing a bad thing getting the butterfly, at least from the man out by the Pipeline Storage Yard. But Micki was adamant, and Buddy left with the directions I gave him. While he was gone, we talked about her situation there in Valdez.

"They mostly want head. Hell, I don't mind giving head. I'm in the business. It comes with the package."

"Well," I said, because she had paused and I didn't know quite how to react to that, "it's so cold and wet here in Valdeez."

She didn't understand what I meant by that any better than I did. She regarded me blankly for a moment. "I think they think I might have the clap or something. Shit, we got a doctor who looks after me. See, most of'm have their old ladies Outside in Seattle or up in Anchorage and they fly out to see'm every couple of weeks and I don't think they want to risk carrying home the clap."

She'd broken out a little cellophane bag and dumped a small hill of white powder onto the table in front of her. While she talked, she chopped it fine and then laid it out in little rows with the edge of a razor blade.

"Like I say, it don't matter to me, but you'd be surprised how many insist I swallow. In a long day that can work out to a lot of come."

With considerably more show than I thought necessary she took out a $100 bill—going to some pains to make sure I knew it was a hundred — rolled it up, put one end in her right nostril, her thumb against her left, and leaned forward over the table and snorted a row of coke. Then she gave her left nostril the same shot.

She smiled a laid-back smile. "I figured out one day I took nine yards of cock. Later on I won't have to work so hard. Once all the men are here and the camps are full, Buddy plans to expand to take some of the load off me. Maybe then, too, Buddy can wear his clothes on the street. It kills him to have to get out of his fine things to go out, but Valdeez is still so small and our cover's not good enough to let him flaunt himself. He wants to flaunt himself."

The telephone rang, and she answered it. "Yeah, if you come right over."

The guy must have been calling from the corner because he was there in about four minutes. He was a fisherman. He reeked of salmon. She took him into her little room. In less than five minutes they were out again. She sat down and snorted another row of coke.

"This has got to be one of the greatest places in the world to work. These guys are so horny I can bump into them and they come. Of course, everything has its drawbacks and disadvantages. That poor creep probably hasn't had a bath in a month." She gave me her dreamy little smile again. "I washed about six inches of him. It'll be the last bath he has until he sees me again."

The telephone rang. She picked it up, listened, then put her hand over the mouthpiece. "How soon do you think Buddy ought to be back?"

"He ought to be back now," I said.

"No," she said into the phone. "No, not even later. Call tomorrow."

I commented that business seemed to be good, trying to make it as objective and professional as I could, just the sort of thing you might say to a used-car dealer who had lately opened a lot and was trying to establish himself.

"Oh, this is slow," she said. "The middle of the week is never any good much. But weekends? You ought to see weekends. It's a madhouse around here. They all seem to be hornier on weekends."

I asked if it was a Friday, a Saturday, or a Sunday when she took the nine yards, because I'd done some quick, easy arithmetic in my head and—using a modest six inches as a standard—found six guys to the yard, times nine, and got the, at least to my mind, phenomenal number of fifty-four.

"It was a Sunday," she said. "Sundays are always good here."

Buddy came in with the illustrated iron freak and the tattoo artist. They were both carrying stuff: alcohol, gauze, swabs, a little metal case that held the electric needle.

They were very friendly to me, as though nothing had happened out there at their place three days ago.

"How's you 'too?" said the iron freak. "You ready for another one?"

"No," I said.

"They're addicting," said the artist. "Everybody comes back for another one, and then another, and pretty soon you'll look like Lyle Tuttle."

"I've never seen Lyle Tuttle," I said.

"Tattooist to the stars," he said.

"You told me," I said.

"Well, he's got more pictures than Pete here. Right, Pete? Lyle Tuttle's got no space left."

"Great," I said. "That's just great."

Buddy went immediately and changed into his street-corner flash. Micki was looking over some designs the artist had brought over. He had plugged in what looked like a baby-bottle warmer to get some steam to sterilize his equipment. While he made all these motions of cleanliness—hospital conditions, he called them—I couldn't help noticing that his fingernails were extravagantly dirty. Micki finally found the butterfly she wanted. It was a big thing, nearly as big as my hand, with blue, green, and yellow in its wings.

Buddy came out and looked at the design she had chosen. "Good Christ," he said. "You'll be out of commission for a week."

She said: "You know as well as I do I do most of my work on my knees." He started to protest again, but she stopped him by saying, "Shut up, Buddy, or I'll send you back to Los Angeles."

While she was lying face down on the couch, pulling her robe up around her shoulders and sharing the last few rows of coke with Pete and the artist, Buddy leaned in close to me and said behind his hand: "Regular pimps get treated with respect. Hell, they're gods to their girls. Right? Am I right?"

I told him I'd heard that what he said was true.

"Don't ever hustle for your wife," he said. "You get no respect."

I told him I'd remember that. We turned to watch the artist at work. He was swabbing down Micki's cheek. She had a fine ass. The little machine with the tattooing needle in the end of it made a sound like a small eggbeater. The artist held it lightly in his hand and, I was pleased to notice, made quick, sure strokes with it. After each stroke, he swabbed the stroke with an alcohol-soaked piece of cotton. Micki lay with her face turned to the side and her eyes closed. She never once flinched.

Buddy, the first time the artist missed with the cotton swab and the blood coursed down off her snow-white ass, grabbed his mouth with his hands and said: "Oh, oh, blood, my God, the blood!" and ran to the rear of the double wide.

Finally, the tattoo was done. And a handsome tattoo it was after the colors were traced and blended into the wings and all the blood was wiped away. There was slight redness around the edges of the butterfly, but other than the redness it might have been painted on with bright watercolors instead of embedded in her flesh with an electric needle. In a few days, of course, it would swell. It would scab. It would turn ugly, and if Micki couldn't keep her fingers off it, there would be infection —not much, but still infection—a little pus, a little blurring of the line with scar tissue. But as everybody knows, if you want a tattoo (and why in God's world would anybody want one?), you have to run the risk of infection, of pus and scar tissue.

It was no doubt gratuitous, even sentimental, but looking at the butterfly on the young whore's ass, I thought of the long snaking pipeline falling from Prudhoe Bay across the interior of Alaska to the Bay of Valdez. I thought: If Alaska is not our young whore, what is she? She is rich, but who can live with her? She is full of all that will pleasure us, but she is hard and cold to the bone. And if we scar her, leave her with pestilence and corrupted with infection, irrefutably marked with our own private design, who can blame us? Didn't we buy her for a trifling sum to start with?

Watching the freshly wiped butterfly that had so lately been bloody, knowing that before it would be beautiful again it must first be scabby and unlovely, I came to a kind of bilious outrage and depression. It was a green and sour thickness I could taste on my tongue. It was a taste and feeling that would stay with me for weeks after I left Valdez.

I stood up, made my apologies for leaving early, and, without waiting for Micki to answer, went through the door into the fine, misting rain. I walked back toward the car in the dark thinking about the town out there, the people I'd met: Dave Kennedy building, Hap cooking, Chris on the flat with the drunken Indian fishing, Johnny Craine's wife cooking and giving showers to those who had none. I thought about it all and watching the bloody butterfly going on Micki's snowy cheek; finally, all I could think of or remember with any pleasure was that over in the Club Valdez they were still two-stepping. Charlie Pride was singing and Hank Williams, Jr., was next and at the bar, a long line of quiet, almost solemn men watched the dancers two-stepping, gliding over the smooth wooden floor, their faces touching, the lips of the women parted, softly humming the words of the song.

OLAUS MURIE

With Dogs Around Denali

For thirty-one years, from 1914 to
1945, Olaus Murie earned a living as
a field biologist in northern Canada
and Alaska, working first for the
Carnegie Museum and then for the
United States Fish and Wildlife Service. Author of *Journeys to the Far
North*, he spent much of his active
life working for the preservation of
the wilderness, serving as both president and director of the Wilderness
Society. Before his death in 1963,
Mr. Murie was presented with the
John Muir Award by the Sierra Club,
for his achievements on behalf of
conservation.

You can see a dogteam is approaching, but the day is so cold that the team is enveloped in a cloud of vapor, and the dogs seem blurred. When they come closer, you see that the dogs are frosted with rime and the driver's parka and cap are white. Your own dogs, too, are rimed with frost.

These are some of the memories of frontier Alaska in the dog mushing days, before the automobile and airplane. There was struggle, of course—hard, wintry days of deep cold, minus forty, fifty, sixty, or more degrees.

Why do we look back to those days as something precious? Perhaps there was something there we do not yet understand. On those long dog trails, leading through miles of scrubby spruce forest, across lowland flats, over rolling hills, every traveler I met was a friend. We would maneuver our respective dogteams past each other in the narrow trail, plant a foot on the brake, and talk.

"How's the trail?"

"Pretty fair. Got into an overflow back there on the Toklat; but nothing bad. You'll have no trouble. Good-looking lead dog you've got there."

"Yeah, he's all right in trail. A little footsore today. You come from Kantishna?"

"Came from McGrath, really, but I've been quite awhile. You headed for Kantishna?"

"I'm going to the Iditarod. How's the dog feed? Can I get some at the Turk's?"

Nothing weighty, those conversations. We were complete strangers, but in a sparsely settled land each person has more value. You're glad to see each other. When you release your brake and your dogs perk up and yank the sled loose, you wave a mittened hand to your departing acquaintance with the warm feeling of a few shared moments. Even the dogs have taken on new life after a brief sniff of canine fellow travelers.

And you remember such meetings. Perhaps when the grass is green and the arctic flora in full bloom, you see a fellow somewhere on the Yukon. "Say, I met you on the Koyukuk, remember? How'd you make out on that trip?"

Is it a hard life? Yes. In a roadhouse of an evening, when the stars are out in myriads and the logs are cracking with the cold, old-timers may cuss this "so-and-so" country. They are tired of falling into overflows up to their necks at forty below. "Why in hell didn't I stay in California? I didn't have to do this!"

Another may chime in: "Yeah, I lost a dog up there on the pass today. Froze to death right there in harness. Should know better than to use a bird dog on a trip like this."

But they didn't leave. The next fall their hands were again itching for the handlebars. They wanted once again to hear the hullabaloo when the dogs were being hooked up in the morning. Perhaps the arctic winter had gotten into their blood. Low on the southern horizon in a sky of old rose, the sun tints the snow a faint pink. There's not much warmth in the winter sun, and it shines for just a few hours, but it's part of the wonder of the Arctic.

I was starting on a long trip and spent the first night at the roadhouse near the recently completed government railroad, on which the dogs and I had come to the south side of Broad Pass in the Alaska Range. I learned that the mailman was due any time, with his seventeen-dog team, and the old-timers were all waiting for him to go first to break the trail. I was new to Alaska and thought it was unfair to wait for someone else to go first and break trail. I decided to start out alone in the morning.

When I went out to hook up my team, I found that I had only four dogs left! One had been killed in a dog fight during the night. There I was, a stranger just learning the Alaska type of dog mushing, starting out for Rainy Pass in the Alaska Range and points far beyond—with only four dogs.

On this February morning in 1922 my objective was to reach the Rainy Pass country, a wintering ground of the caribou.

I met several travelers along the way, among them a United States marshal and a prisoner he was taking from McGrath out to the railroad (dogteam was the only means of travel). We stopped to pass the time of day, and I learned what the situation was. The prisoner didn't say much, but there was no sign of handcuffs or other legal paraphernalia. Up here, there seemed to be little distinction made between the lawman and the prisoner—they were just fellow travelers.

I had been warned to pass up the Mountain Climber Roadhouse if I possibly could, because even by frontier standards its accommodations were very poor. Besides, I was allowed only $5.50 per day for expenses, and roadhouses charged two dollars per meal and two dollars for a bed. So I camped out whenever I could.

Accordingly, instead of going on to this roadhouse, I made an early camp. I tramped down the snow, put up my seven-by-nine tent, and set up my small Yukon stove. I chained the dogs to trees, out of reach of each other. They jumped and howled in anticipation as the salmon were being pulled out of the sled load. I tossed a dried salmon to each and with what wholesome gusto they tore at that fish, eating every morsel. Then, realizing there was no more coming, each curled up in his snowy nest, nose in tail, and slept.

I cooked my simple meal of bacon, rice, dried fruit, and "Jersey Creams," a tasty, softer "hardtack" widely used in Alaska. I didn't care for tea or coffee myself, but coffee was the universal drink in Alaska, as tea had been in Hudson Bay. After dinner I spread out my warm sleeping bag of woven rabbit skins from Hudson Bay, laid a little kindling for morning, blew out the candle, and soon I was snug for the night, like the dogs curled up out there in the snow.

In the morning it was storming, and I knew we faced heavy going, but fortunately I had learned about gee poles. I cut and trimmed off a small spruce tree, fastening it with rope and thongs under the right front end of the sled so that it slanted out at my hand height. Thus I could straddle the towline behind the dogs, become one of them, and guide the sled. Then the mailman, with his big seventeen-dog team, caught up with me, and he took the lead. From that point on my four dogs trotted along gleefully, and we all made good time. In midafternoon we came to Mountain Climber, my companion's regular stop. We were met by the owner and put our dogs in the low kennels he had —I had lost all ambition to go on alone.

"I'm going after some wood. Go in and make yourself at home," the proprietor told us, and with an axe over his shoulder he strode off down a slope into the snowy woods.

We went inside and I looked around curiously. I was thirsty so I walked over to a pail with a dipper beside it. There was a little water in the pail, but it looked quite dingy. How many days ago had he fetched it? There were successive rims of ice in the pail down to the water, showing the level at which ice had frozen each night. But I was thirsty and used to such things, so I took a drink.

Then I happened to look out the window and saw the owner returning. The axe head was stuck in a chunk of wood, and he was carrying it with the axe handle over his shoulder. It seemed to me a very strange way of gathering wood.

We finally sat down to supper, and I wondered how it would be. But the mailman had been here often and was very pleasant and understanding. By suggestions and humorous remarks, he had our host bringing us a variety of food, including some cookies. So the next morning when we pushed on, I was not sorry we had stopped at Mountain Climber Roadhouse.

As we went along together on the trail that day, I was surprised to see a heavy gasoline engine on the mailman's sled. The charge for such freight was a dollar a pound. I wondered who wanted an engine that badly.

That same day I had another experience with his load. I was collecting specimens for the Biological Survey collection in Washington whenever I had opportunity. We saw a flock of ptarmigan on the snow in among the trees, and we stopped the two sleds. To get one of the birds, I pulled the shotgun out of the top of my load. The skin would be a specimen, the meat would be my dinner.

Now whenever there was any sudden commotion, the dogs would get excited and go off on the run. No matter from what direction the diversion might come, they would keep to the trail and speed straight ahead. (They reacted the same way to the smell of game. When there was caribou scent in the air, we would make wonderful time as long as the scent lasted.) At the sound of my gun, my dogs started forward

pell-mell, right up along side the mail sled, and my gee pole pierced
one of the mail sacks, bringing my sled to a sudden stop. Think of my
dismay! The mailman was a friendly and understanding soul, noted my
discomfiture, and did his best to put me at ease. But I have often wondered in what condition some of those letters reached their destination.

In a few days the mailman went on, and I stopped along the way to
investigate the winter wildlife. In addition to studying the caribou, I
was to report on the birds and mammals living in the areas I traveled.
I was also commissioned as federal fur warden, and my district was
interior and northern Alaska. I had little time or taste for the latter
duty, but appropriations were small and we were short of personnel.

As I traveled over the lowland and up the outer slopes of the mountains, I enjoyed recording what I saw. I was pleased to see the chickadee
among the lower branches of a spruce, always busy and much alive,
adding a cheery note to any winter woods. This bird often came to the
spruces near the trail, as if he too were glad to see someone. There was
also the magpie, always aloof and wary, traits to be expected in a bird
so persecuted by man. His dark body with striking stripes and patches
of white gave a vivacious accent to the winter landscape. Then there
were the tracks in the snow—tracks of squirrels, tiny shrews, and snowshoe hares. I knew there were wolverines, for now and then I saw the
tracks of this elusive animal, too. At night I sometimes heard the great
horned owl. All of this made me aware that underneath the apparent
lifelessness in this wintry northland the landscape was still alive.

But I kept looking up to the higher mountains, the Rainy Pass country I was heading for. What would I find up there? When I arrived at
the point where I was to leave the dog trail and go off into the desolate
high caribou and mountain sheep country, I spent the night at an old-
timer's cabin. For two days and nights I had suffered with a toothache,
and I spoke of my trouble to my host, a pioneer Alaskan. Of course he
had a remedy—a drastic one—if I wanted to take a chance on it.

"I'll tell you what I done once, and it helped. I put iodine on it. I
got a bottle of iodine here."

I was horrified at the idea of putting pure iodine in my mouth, but I
was desperate.

My friend brought out his little bottle of iodine and a ptarmigan feather to dip with. I took the feather and thoroughly smeared the gums on both sides of the aching tooth with iodine. Immediately the pain of the remedy was much greater than the toothache it was to cure, and I resolved not to swallow any of this poison, but that night I slept. Next morning all pain was gone. I had no more trouble until I reached Fairbanks and a dentist in the spring.

I always felt that the best part of my journeys came after I left well-traveled dog trails. I had crossed the lowlands south of the mountains and gone through the Rainy Pass. Now there rose before me the high mountain country just north of the summit of the Alaska Range. From my maps and the verbal directions of roadhouse keepers, I knew about where I wanted to go. So off we went, the four dogs and I, to explore high mountains new to us.

As the days went by, I wondered what the dogs got out of it. I had a supply of dried salmon on the sled, and they eagerly looked forward to their meal each evening. They loved to be in harness; as a matter of fact, as they were being hooked up in the morning, they were so happy that it was hard to handle them. The minute we were ready, off they would go in a great burst of speed.

We encountered many obstacles as we went along, but the dogs seemed to take everything as a matter of course. When we came to the Rhone River, our route lay straight across it. It had been blown free of snow and there was glare ice. We were at the mercy of the elements. The dogs' feet had no traction, the sled swerved, and a few times we went round in a circle. Fortunately, the wind was at our backs, and somehow we drifted and slid across the ice river and continued on our journey.

As I lived with those four dogs and we shared the little vicissitudes of the trail, I was impressed with the thought that we human creatures share with dogs certain characteristics of behavior. There is a primeval truculence which appears at times—a real joy in the fight. I have seen my lead dog, Snook, sail into a mass of fighting dogs with what appeared to be a smile on his face. There was also the joy in simply being active that was so obvious on this trip. The dogs were eager to be up and doing, to go somewhere, to pull the sled. I had a similar feeling, wanting to clamber over the mountains, to discover, to achieve. I suppose we can say that both man and dog have the joyous impulse to *do*.

One day, from an old, deserted cabin where I had camped, I went up on a high mountain to look around. There I came upon a band of mountain sheep. Mindful of the needs of the museum on the other side of the continent, I obtained two of them for specimens. It was late in the day, and I was unable to finish and carry both back to camp. One sheep would have to be left overnight. But I had seen wolverine tracks and knew what to expect—the wolverine has been cursed as a trap robber, and our literature is full of lurid tales about the sins of this animal. Much of this has arisen because of our tendency to hate any animal that interferes with *us* in any way. I decided to make a bargain with the wolverine. I wanted the skin and skull for a specimen; the wolverine would want some meat to eat. So I partially skinned the animal, pulled the skin over the head, laying bare much of the carcass of pure meat. Then I filled my packsack with the other specimen and went down to camp.

Next morning I went back up the mountain for my specimen sheep. As I approached, two magpies flew off; those canny birds had found this source of food. Coming closer, I saw that the wolverine had been there, had his feed of meat, and gone his way. He had accepted the bargain; he had his meal, the museum would have its specimen, and the dogs and I still had a supply of camp food.

These were unforgettable days high above timberline, on slopes where I found the caribou spending the winter. This was one of the many places where these hardy arctic travelers found they could paw down through the snow and find the tasty "reindeer moss," or lichens, below. Both forms of life, these particular lichens and the caribou, have found the Arctic a suitable place in which to live. This little alpine wintering place, high in the mountains of Rainy Pass, is one spot in the vast circumpolar Arctic that has nourished the caribou for many centuries.

I spent some time in this area, collected a caribou specimen, and weighed the animal with a steelyard that I carried in my pack. In nearby rugged uplands were bands of mountain sheep living serenely through the winter as they had done for many centuries.

It was hard for me to pull away from this peaceful arctic-alpine paradise. But I had a mission to perform—to learn about the distribution of caribou in Alaska and Yukon—and I could not linger. So the four dogs and I started off for other parts. We went to visit domestic reindeer herds to the west, and eventually, about the middle of March, we were back on the mail trail, headed for Lake Minchumina and the Kantishna country.

At the last roadhouse I had hoped to get dog feed for the long trail-less trip to the Kantishna, but the proprietor explained that he was obligated to serve only those who stopped at his place for the period of their stay, and could not undertake to outfit a longer expedition. But he did tell me all he could about the route. Someone had been through and had headed in that direction about a week before. "He musta left a sled track. I hope you can find that sled track most of the time. It will help you."

So I started off the next morning, short of dog feed and with only a vague notion of where I was going. But over on my right, far away, rose lofty Mount McKinley, called by the Indians *Denali* ("The Highest One"), and Mount Foraker beside it. These would guide me. By going eastward, I hoped to reach the Kantishna River by the end of March.

I had good fortune. I came upon an occasional Indian camp and moved along steadily. Yet the going was difficult, and the dogs had lost all their enthusiasm. Theirs was hard, steady, never-ending work. Finally Jack, my old standby in the team, became so tired that I had to take him out of his harness and let him run loose. Then I had only three dogs and myself to wrestle with the sled. Most Alaskan travelers had five to seven dogs, at the least. Moreover, I was reduced to sharing my own food supply with the dogs, and we were all living on very meager rations. I could find no rabbits but I shot an occasional ptarmigan (using the big rifle since I was short of shotgun shells) so that the dogs could have at least a little meat.

One day I met an Indian coming along the faint trail, and we had a good visit. Most important, he gave me a moose heart, and I lived on this for several days. He also gave me good directions, mentioning a lake as a landmark. As I started off, he warned me, "Watch out dat lake. Big fish stop dere!" I thanked him for his warning, but as I went on, I wondered about the belief in a mythical spirit fish that lived in a frozen lake. It seems inherent in the human mind to reach into the spirit world and create myths.

Those days sound tough and desperate in the telling, and I wonder whether it is misleading to relate such experiences on paper. Yes, we were all hungry, but the dogs took it philosophically (they can work for a couple of days without any food, I have found), and somehow I don't remember that I felt badly either. Kantishna and supplies lay ahead somewhere. And I remember the inspiration I got from seeing those great mountains off on the horizon.

Occasionally in the evening we would see the aurora. The dogs took no notice, but for me the lights never lost their excitement.

Part of this time we had wind and cloudiness, but I recall one night when it was still and clear, and close to forty degrees below zero. I knew it would not storm on such a night. I fed the dogs some ptarmigan meat and ate a little of the moose heart myself. I didn't bother to put up the tent but simply spread out my sleeping bag, took off my boots, and crawled in, parka and all. For some reason this clear, cold night remains vividly in my memory. As I lay there, cozy and warm in the sleeping bag, the four dogs curled up close around the edges of my bed, life seemed good. We had a special comradeship, camping and traveling together.

One day we came to an Indian camp. The trail they had made lay among their tents—and their dogs. Ordinarily, strange dogs will fight, but my four were hungry. They paid no attention to the bedlam of those chained dogs, but pushed eagerly forward, their noses alive for any scent of food. I got the team through to the edge of the village, and after a brief visit with the Indians, we went on.

I was entering a more inhabited region now. Soon I came to another well-worn trail, at right angles to my course. Which way? I decided to go to the right, but just then heard dogs howling off to the left. My dogs pulled in that direction, so I changed my mind and turned left. Soon we came to another Indian village, where we learned that we were now headed for Tanana. With new information about the trail, we turned around and took the direction of my first, instinctive choice. We could not make it to any settlement that night and again camped out. There was just a little bite to eat all around—the last of the moose heart.

On March 22 we reached a little place called Roosevelt on the map, with a few old miners' cabins. I noted in my official diary: "Clear again today. I went on and early in the morning reached Roosevelt, where I was invited to stop by Mr. Einar Hansen."

Here was plenty to eat. The dogs tore at the whole quarter of meat Mr. Hansen provided. To replenish his supplies, he and I took our rifles down to a frozen stream and shot moose. He was in meat again, and we were all well fed.

Now I was back on a traveled dog trail, back in easy living. With comfortable travel, I reached the railroad at Nenana on March 30, after crossing the flats for forty miles.

On that last night in the Kantishna country there was another great display of the aurora—a colorful farewell to a long trip in the wilderness surrounding Denali.

Ice

Poet and essayist John Haines home-
steaded in Alaska for seventeen years.
His books of poetry include *Winter
News*, *The Stone Harp*, *Twenty Poems*,
Leaves and Ashes, *Cicada*, *In a Dusty
Light*, and *News from the Glacier*. His
collections of essays include *Living
Off the Country*, *Other Days*, and
Stories We Listened To. He has twice
received a Guggenheim Foundation
Fellowship for poetry, a National
Endowment for the Arts Fellowship,
and the Governor's Award in the Arts
for his life contributions to the arts in
Alaska.

For some time now in the woods, away from the sun, in ravines and hollows where the ground is normally wet, the soil has darkened and is hard and cold to the touch. The deep, shaded mosses have stiffened, and there are tiny crystals of ice in their hairy spaces.

Water has sunken in the pools of the footpaths; in the high ridge trails the small potholes are ringed with transparent ice, or they are filled with whitened splinters shattered by the foot of some passing animal. Ice thickened with leaves surrounds a circle of open water in the flowing pool of the creek below the house.

The waters are freezing. From the reedy shallows outward to the centers of the roadside ponds: black ice, clear and hard, with bubbles that are white; opaque patches of shell ice that shatter easily when stepped on. The last ducks that kept to the open centers of the ponds are gone. Clumps of stiff, dry grass stand upright there, held fast, casting their shadows on the evening ice.

Now that the steady frost has come, I have been thinking about the river. It is time to take a walk over the sandbars and islands, while there is still so little snow. It is late October, and the smaller channels of this broad and braided river have long since stopped flowing, and their remaining pools are frozen. Far out in mid-river, beyond the big, wooded island, a single large channel is now the only open water. The sound of that water comes distant, but strong and pervasive, over the dry land dusted with snow: a deep and swallowed sound, as if the river had ice in its throat.

One afternoon I take the steep path downhill to the riverbed. I make my way across to the big island over sandbar and dusty ice, past bleached piles of driftwood and through waist-high willows and alders, to the gravelly, ice-coated shore of the open channel. I walk a short distance out on the shore ice and stand there, looking at the water. A little wind comes down the wide river, over the frozen bars, smelling of winter.

Free of its summer load of silt, the water is clear in the shallows, incredibly blue and deep in the middle of the channel. Ice is riding in the water, big rafts of it crowding each other, falling through the rapids above me and catching on the bottom stones. Here where the current

slackens and deepens, the water is heavy and slow with ice, with more
and more ice.

Call it mush ice, or pan ice. It forms at night during the colder days
in the slack water of eddies and shallows: a cold slush that gathers
weight and form. Drifting and turning in the backwaters, it is pulled
piecemeal into the main current and taken down.

Now on the heavy water great pans of ice are coming, breaking
and reforming, drifting with the slowed current: shaggy donuts of ice,
ragged squares and oblongs, turning and pushing against each other,
islands of ice among lakes of dark blue water. Crowded shoreward by
the current, they rush the shore ice with a steady "shsss" as they catch
and go by. And with each sheering contact a little of that freezing slush
clings to the outer edge of the shore ice. The ice is building outward,
ridged and whitened, thickening with each night of frost, with each
wave of shallow water that washes it.

As I look intently into the shallows, I see that boulder ice, a soft,
shapeless and gluey mass, is forming on some large, rounded stones not
far below the surface; the river is freezing from the bottom also. Now
and then a piece of that water-soaked ice dislodges and comes to the
surface, bobbing in the moving current, turning over and over. It is
dirty ice, grey and heavy with sand, small stones, and debris.

Where it gathers speed in the rapids above, the sound of all this ice
and water is loud, rough, and vaguely menacing. As the cold gradually
deepens and the sunlight departs in the days to come, the floating ice
will become harder and thicker, and the sound of its movement in
the water will change to a harsher grinding and crushing. Now in the
slowed current before me, it is mostly that steady and seething "shsss"
that I hear, and underneath it a softer clinking as of many small glasses
breaking against each other.

Standing here, watching the ice come down, I recall past years on
the river. Each fall when the salmon season was over and the nets
were dried and mended and put away for the winter, it was time to
move our big poling boat upriver to safe storage. And how with a steel-
tipped pole and a pair of lines I worked that heavy wooden boat against
the current. Standing braced at the stern, I slowly poled through the

shallows, finding purchase for the pole in the shifting gravel of the river bottom. At intervals when the current was too swift or the water too deep, I walked and lined the boat along the shore against the oncoming water, breaking the thin shore ice underfoot with my rubber boots.

One year an early freeze caught us before we had time to move the boat. Overnight in the sudden cold there was ice in the channel. I spent the better part of a day attempting to maneuver the boat against a current that was heavy with slush. Ice clung to the pole and the oars, and the boat grew sluggish with the drift that was freezing against it. I was unable finally to make sufficient headway. At last we reached a point of land with a bank out of reach of the winter ice. We beached the boat, its bottom and sides now heavy with ice, and with much labor we drew it out of the water and onto the sandbar. We raised it on a pair of dry poles and left it there for the winter. That was the earliest freeze-up I can remember; it was well below zero by the second week of October.

I think of the early days in this country when the rivers were the primary means of summer travel. And of the people—natives and whites —working their heavy wooden boats upriver to the trapping ground: poling, wading the ice-choked water with a growing urgency, as the days shortened, to reach their winter stations before freeze-up. And of the big shallow-draft steamboats finally stopped by the shoaling water. Their wood fires dampened, they were warped into shore below Fairbanks and secured for the winter against the crush of the ice.

Like rainfall in a land of dryness, life on a northern river is ruled by the ice, its presence and its absence. And to struggle day by day upriver into the current and the ice is to feel oneself part of something so old that its origin is lost in the sundown of many winters. A feeling intensified, made rich by the smell of ice and cold fish slime; by the steely color of the winter sky, the whiteness of early snow on the sandbars; by the occasional crimson flash of a salmon in the ice-blue water, and by the strong blackness of a solitary raven flying with a remote, hollow call from one wooded island to another.

I see no salmon now as I stand here by this ice-filled channel, searching its green, bouldery shallows and bluer depths for a tell-tale flash of crimson. It may be that there is not a good run this fall, that I am too early or too late, or that the fish have taken another way upriver. The sound of the water and the ice before me is one sound, familiar over the years. But there are other sounds of the ice, among them the strange and eerie moaning that comes from under the new ice of a pond when it is walked on, as if some sad spirit in the depth of the pond were trying to speak. In midwinter, a large sheet of ice will split with a rippling crack when the temperature suddenly changes or the ice bed shifts underneath, the ripple traveling fast with a winnowing sound at the end. And there are those small, ticking sounds of the ice in the evening when the cold slides toward its deepest zero, as if a thousand hidden insects were chirping bitterly in chorus under the ice and snow. And, finally, the thundering crack and plunge of the shelf ice breaking off in the spring as the rising water wears away its support, a sound that can be heard for miles, like the detonation of a heavy building.

The ice sings, groans, howls, and whistles like a living thing. Years ago when I was stopped by the side of a gravel road in the Alaska Range I heard the oldest lament of the ice. It was early in October, and as I stood there alone and listening—with the slow freeze coming down over the empty land and its many lakes—I heard on the nearly windless air, as if from the earth itself, a muted and forsaken moaning from the lakes and ponds. It was a sound out of prehistory, of something deeply wounded and abandoned, slowly giving up its life to the cold. There were fleeting ghost-fires on the tundra, white-maned shadows from the bands of caribou fleeing before something I could not see. Then, distant shots, gunfire, the sound of a truck rattling by on the frozen road.

Here before me the river is still awake, still speaking in its half-choked mutter and murmur, still surging, pushing its ice-filled way across the open stand and gravel. But one day—it may be soon, or it may be very late, when the solstice sun clears the south horizon—the sound of all this surging and grinding, this shredding and crushing, will stop. The great silence will have come, that other sound of the ice, which is almost nothing at all. This channel will have finally filled, the last open water will close, and the river will go under the ice. Snow will drift and cover the ice I stand on.

If I were to walk out here in midwinter, the only sound I would be likely to hear would be the wind, pushing snow across the ice. Only now and then, while walking over the frozen shallows, would I hear under my feet the sound of trickling water finding its way somehow through the ice. And later still, when ice has thickened to a depth of many feet on the deepest channel, I might hear far down in some snow-filled crevice the deep murmur and surge of the river running beneath me.

For the ice and the river under it are never still for long. Again and again throughout this long winter, water will find its way into the open, welling up from a seam in the ice, and spreading over the existing surface of ice and snow to freeze again in a perilous sheet. The wind will bring its dry snow to polish the new ice and turn it into a great slick and glare. Delicate flowers of frost will bloom upon it: small, glittering blossoms standing curled and fragile on the gritty ice, to be scattered by the first passage of air. And over the renewed expanse of ice there will be silence again, the silence of ice unchanged since the first winter of Earth.

But all this is still to come, as it has come before. Winter is making its way across the land over slope and plain, bog and high meadow, across lake and pond, outlet and feeder. It has progressed slowly this fall in an even, majestic tread, with a little more frost each night, a little less warmth each day. Meanwhile, the open water of the river flows at my feet, steady and heavy with ice, the deep sound of it filling the landscape around me.

I turn and walk back to the home shore whose tall yellow bluffs still bare of snow I can see nearly half a mile to the north. I find my way as I came, over dusty sandbars and by old channels, through shrubby stands of willows. The cold, late afternoon sun breaks through its cloud cover and streaks the grey sand mixed with snow.

As it has fallen steadily in the past weeks, the river has left behind many shallow pools, and these are now roofed with ice. When I am close to the main shore I come upon one of them, not far from the wooded bank. The light snow that fell a few days ago has blown away;

the ice is polished and is thick enough to stand on. I can see to the bottom without difficulty, as through heavy, dark glass.

I bend over, looking at the debris caught there in the clear, black depth of the ice: I see a few small sticks and many leaves. There are alder leaves, roughly-toothed and still half green, the more delicate birch leaves and aspen leaves, the big, smooth poplar leaves, and narrow leaves from the willows. They are massed or scattered, as they fell quietly or as the wind blew them into the freezing water. Some of them are still fresh in color, glowing yellow and orange; others are mottled with grey and brown. A few older leaves lie sunken and black on the silty bottom. Here and there a pebble of quartz is gleaming. But nothing moves there. It is a still, cold world, something like night, with its own fixed planets and stars.

JOHN MCPHEE

Riding the Boom Extension

John McPhee was born in 1931 and
attended Princeton University and
Cambridge University. A staff writer
for *The New Yorker*, he is the author
of *A Sense of Where You Are*, *The
Headmaster*, *The Pine Barrens*, *A
Roomful of Hovings*, *Oranges*, *Levels
of the Game*, *The Deltoid Pumpkin
Seed*, *Pieces of the Frame*, *The Survival
of the Bark Canoe*, *Basin and Range*,
In Suspect Terrain, *Table of Contents*,
and *Coming into the Country*.

At the end of the day in slowly falling light a pickup truck with a
camper rig came into Circle City, Alaska. It had a Texas license plate,
and it drove to the edge of the Yukon River. Piled high on the roof were
mining gear, camping gear, paddles, a boat, and a suction dredge big
enough to suck the gold off almost anyone's capitol dome. To operate
a suction dredge, swimmers move it from place to place on floats as
it vacuums uncounted riches from the beds of streams. For the moment, though, no one was about to swim anywhere. In the gray of
the evening, the Fahrenheit temperature was thirty-one degrees, smoke
was blue above the cabins of the town, and the occupants of the pickup
—having driven four thousand miles, the last hundred and twenty on
an unpaved track through forest and over mountains—were now paus-
ing long to stare at a firmly frozen river. May 4, 1980, 9 p.m., and the
Yukon at Circle was white. The river had not yet so much as begun to
turn gray, as it does when it nears breaking up.

There was a sign to read. "CIRCLE CITY, ESTABLISHED 1893. . . . MOST
NORTHERN POINT ON CONNECTED AMERICAN HIGHWAY SYSTEM. . . . THE
END OF THE ROAD." The new Dempster Highway, in Yukon Territory,
runs a great deal farther north than this one, but the Dempster is in
Canada and is therefore not American. The haul road that accompanies the Alyeska pipeline goes to and over the Brooks Range and quits
at the edge of the Arctic Ocean, and if the haul road is ever opened to
the public it will destroy Circle City's sign, but meanwhile the community maintains a certain focus on this moribund credential. Circle
City was given its name in the mistaken belief that it was on the Arctic Circle, which is somewhere nearby. The town was established not
as a gate to the Arctic, however, but as a result of the incontestable
fact that it would stand beside the Yukon River. This was the trading port that supplied the Birch Creek mining district, which lies immediately to the south, and where miners around the turn of the century working streams like Mammoth Creek and Mastodon Creek—in a
country of mica schists and quartz intrusions, of sharp-peaked ridges,
dendritic drainages, steep-walled valleys, and long flat spurs—washed
out in their cleanups about a million ounces of gold. Circle was for
a time the foremost settlement on the Yukon, and proclaimed itself

"the largest log-cabin city in the world." It was served by woodburning stern-wheel steamers. They ran until the Second World War. In 1896, there were ten thousand miners out on the creeks of the district, with their small cabins, their caches. The resident population of Circle was twelve hundred, its all-time high. Works of Shakespeare were produced in the opera house. The town had a several-thousand-volume library, a clinic, a school, churches, music and dance halls, and so many whorehouses they may have outnumbered the saloons. A large percentage of these buildings have since fallen into the river. Circle is considerably smaller now and consists, in the main, of two rows of cabins, parallel to the Yukon and backed by a gravel airstrip. The center of commerce and industry includes the Yukon Trading Post ("SOUVENIRS, TIRE REPAIRS"), the Yukon Liquor Cache, and the Midnite Sun Cafe—names above three doors in one building. The cabins are inhabited by a few whites and for the most part by a group of Athapaskans who call themselves Danzhit Hanlaii, indicating that they live where the Yukon River comes out through mountains and begins its traverse of the vast savannas known as the Yukon Flats. Circle, Alaska 99733.

In a thousand miles of the upper Yukon, the largest vessel ever seen on the river in present times is the Brainstorm, a barge with a three-story white deckhouse, an orange hull; and on that chill May night a few weeks ago even the Brainstorm was disengaged from the river, and was far up on the bank, where it had been all winter, canting to one side in Circle City. To the suckers in their pickup from Texas, the appearance of the Brainstorm may have been one more suggestion that they had come a little early with their dredge. The pickup turned around, eventually, and moved slowly back into the forest.

If the arrival was untimely, the rig was nonetheless the first of a great many like it that would come to the End of the Road in a summer of excited questing for gold. The price of one troy ounce had gone up so much over the winter that a new boom had come to a region whose economy has had no other history than booms. In Fairbanks, a hundred and sixty miles away, dealers in the goods of placer mining were selling their premises bare. Bulldozer parts were going like chicken livers—and whole bulldozers, too, many of them left over from the construction of

the pipeline. Placer miners have recently discerned the hidden talents of
AstroTurf. They use AstroTurf in sluice boxes—in much the way that
the Greeks washed auriferous gravels over the unshorn hides of sheep.
Gradually, the hides became extraordinarily heavy with arrested flecks
of gold. They were burned to get the metal. What for Greeks was Gold
Fleece for us is AstroTurf. To be sure, the AstroTurf of Alaska is not the
puny Easter-basket grass that skins the knees of Philadelphia Eagles.
It is tough, tundric AstroTurf, with individualistic three-quarter-inch
skookum green blades. In a cleanup, this advantageous material will
yield its gold almost as readily as it has caught it. AstroTurf costs about
four hundred dollars a roll. Sold out.

People from all over the Lower Forty-eight are fanning into the
country north of Fairbanks. As they represent many states, they also
represent many levels of competence. The new price of gold has penetrated deep into the human soul and has brought out the placer miner in
the Tucson developer, the Denver lawyer, the carpenter of Knoxville,
the sawyer of Ely, the merchant of Cleveland, the barber of Tenafly.
Suction dredging is a small-time effort made by people without established claims, who move up and down streams snipping gold. The real
earthmovers are the Cat miners, with their steel sluice boxes and their
immense Caterpillar D8s and D9s. Some people named Green from
Minnesota have shipped the family bulldozer to interior Alaska for five
thousand five hundred dollars. There are a lot of new people in the
country who know how to move gravel but will not necessarily know
what to do with it when it moves. Whatever the level of their skills
may be, the collective rush of suction dredgers and Cat miners is so
numerous that, like their counterparts of the eighteen-nineties, most
of them will inevitably go home with pockets innocent of gold. Gold is
where you find it, though, and not all of it lies in the beds of creeks.
Richard Hutchinson, who has been in the country for sixteen years,
knows where the gold is now. He has struck it right here in Circle City.

Three years ago, Hutchinson went down to Fairbanks and returned
with a telephone exchange in the back of his pickup. It had been in the
Tanana Valley Clinic and was of a size that could deal with only about

eighty individual lines, which had become too few for the expanding needs of the Tanana Valley Clinic but would be more than adequate for Circle City. Hutchinson prefers not to mention what he paid for it. He will say that he got it for "a song," but when asked he will not sing it. "The thing is called a PABX. It was on its way to the dump. Luckily, I came along—the big boob at the right time. I got it for next to nothing." Hutchinson is a dust-kicking type, modest about himself and his accomplishments. He is big, yes, six feet one, and trim in form, with blue irises and blond hair, cut short in homage to the Marine Corps. But he is away from the mark when he calls himself a boob, as almost everyone in Circle will attest.

"He gave us lights."

"He gave us telephones."

"He did it all by himself."

Eight hours over the mountains he drove home with his PABX. A tall rectilinear box full of multicolored wires and wafery plates, it might have been a computer bought in an antique store in Pennsylvania. Hutchinson had no idea what its components were, what their purposes might be, or how to advance his new property into a state of operation. Remembering the extent of his knowledge of telephone technology at that time, he says, "I knew how to dial a number." There was a manual, but with its sequence charts and connecting schemes, its predetermined night answers and toll-diversion adapters, its spark-quench units and contact failures, the manual might as well have been for human sex. He had friends, though, who knew the system—telephone technicians and engineers, in Fairbanks, in Clear. They would give him his training, on the job. He emptied his tool shed and put the PABX in there. He strung wires. He sold subscriptions. In July, 1977, he opened his local service.

Carl Dasch was having none of it.

"Would you like a telephone, Carl?"

"No."

"A phone is a real convenience, Carl."

"When I say no, I don't mean yes."

Dasch, from Minnesota, has been in Alaska forty years and lives on a pension from the First World War. He trapped for many seasons, and he used to take passengers on the river in his boat. He wears high black shoes and, as often as not, a black-and-red checkered heavy wool shirt. He has a full dark beard. He is solidly built, and looks much younger than his years. His cabin is small and is close to the river. "Why would I need a telephone? I can stand on the porch and yell at everyone here."

The village otherwise clamored for Hutchinson's phones. He soon had twenty subscribers. Albert Carroll, the on-again-off-again Indian chief, speaks for the whole tribe when he says, "I don't get out and holler the way we used to. I call from here to here. We stand in the window and look at each other and talk on the phone. I don't have to walk over next door and ask Anne Ginnis if she has a beer. I call her and tell her to bring it."

The wire cost Hutchinson a couple of thousand dollars. He already had the poles. In 1973, he bought a fifty-five–kilowatt generator and a seventy-five–kilowatt generator to bring light and power to the town. He went to Fairbanks and bought used telephone poles, which he set in holes he dug in frozen gravel, with an ice chisel, by hand. He strung his power line. "When I put it in, I couldn't wire a light fixture. It was comical." He sent away for "The Lineman's and Cableman's Handbook" and "The American Electrician's Handbook." Before he was off page 1 he had almost everyone in town signed up for electricity. The only holdout was Carl Dasch. Soon there was a record-player in nearly every home. There would have been television everywhere, too, but television has yet to reach Circle City.

Hutchinson in his books learned how to install meters. His son, who is called Little Hutch, was five years old when the generators began to operate. He is now twelve and is the reader of the meters. A number of people in Circle have two Mr. Coffee coffeemakers, one for coffee and one for tea, which they brew in the manner of coffee. They have big freezers, in which king salmon are stacked like cordwood. Albert Carroll has at least three freezers for his moose, ducks, fish, and geese. For four years, Carl Dasch observed all this without a kind word, but then one day he mentioned to Hutchinson that he wouldn't mind a little current after all. Hutchinson dropped whatever he was doing and went home for his wire, and Dasch was on line that day. Dasch has a small freezer, and a single forty-watt bulb that hangs from his cabin ceiling. With the capitulation of Carl Dasch, Hutchinson's electric monopoly became as complete as it ever could be, with a hundred per cent of the town subscribing.

At some point early in the history of the company, the thought occurred to a number of customers that plugging in an electric heater would be, as one of them put it, "easier than going out and getting a log of wood." In various subtle ways, they brought heaters into Circle. They did not want Hutchinson to know. They did not understand the significance of the numbers on his meters. Now there are not so many heaters in town. There are wringer-style electric washers but no dryers and no electric stoves, except at the school. The government and the pipeline are paying for the school. Hutchinson charges thirty-two cents a kilowatt hour for the first hundred kilowatt hours used each month, twenty-two cents through the second hundred, and seventeen cents after that—rates that are regulated by the Alaska Public Utilities Commission and are roughly double the rates in New Jersey. There are no complaints, and, according to one subscriber, complaints are unlikely from the present generation—"People remember what it was like to use kerosene lamps." In Hutchinson's electric-lighted home, an old Alaskan kerosene lamp is on display like a trophy: an instant antique, garlanded with plastic daisies.

For about a year and a half, the telephone customers of Circle Utilities, as Hutchinson has named his diversified company, had no one to call but themselves. That, however, was joy enough, and for five dollars a month they were on the telephone twenty-four hours a day, tattling, fighting, entertaining their neighbors. "It's almost like having TV," Hutchinson observed. "They're always on the phone, calling each other. Suddenly they can't live without it. A phone goes out and you ought to hear them squawk." From the beginning, he has been busy with his manual, practicing the art of repair. When conversations turn bellicose, people will rip phones off the wall. They shatter them on the floor. Albert Carroll, one winter night, opened the door of his wood stove and added his phone to the fire. Hutchinson makes cheerful rounds in his pickup, restoring service. The cost to him of a new telephone instrument is only twenty-eight dollars. He says, "Phones are cheap if you own the phone company."

At the end of 1978, RCA-Alascom and the Alaska Public Utilities Commission, the communications power of Arctic America, completed a long series of discussions about Hutchinson, with the result that Circle City subscribers were let out of their closed circuit and into the telephone systems of the world. There is a white dish antenna outside the Circle City school, facing upward into the southeast toward a satellite in geosynchronous orbit more than twenty-two thousand miles high. When someone telephones a relative in Fort Yukon, which is the next town downriver (sixty miles), the call travels first to the dish antenna, and then up to the satellite, and then down to the Alascom earth station at Talkeetna (beyond the summits of the Alaska Range), and then back up to the satellite, and then down to Fort Yukon. The relative's voice reverses the caroms. The conversation travels ninety thousand miles in each direction, but the rate charge is reckoned by the flight of the crow: Circle City to Fort Yukon, forty-five cents for three minutes.

Alascom allows Hutchinson to keep about eighty per cent of the tolls. When someone at Alascom first acquainted Hutchinson with this nineteen-carate percentage, he could not believe what he was hearing.

"That's not right," he said.

"What? You want more?" said Alascom.

"No. That's too much," said Hutchinson.

And Alascom said, "Don't ever say it's too much."

Circle City people are running up phone bills above a hundred dollars a month, calling their kin in Fort Yukon. They call Metlakatla. They call Old Crow. They call Anchorage, Fairbanks, and Chalkyitsik. They call New York, Deadhorse, and San Jose. Albert Carroll's toll calls exceed fifteen hundred dollars a year. "When I'm drinking, I call my brothers in Fort Yukon and my sister in Florida," he says. "Before the telephone, I wrote letters. It took me two years to write a letter. Don't ever take the phone out of Circle City. It's our best resource." When it is suggested to the sometime chief that the dish antenna is drawing out of his pocket thousands of dollars that might otherwise be spent on something sollder than words, he says, "Money is nothing. Easy come, easy go. I make good money trapping. I'm one-third partner in the Brainstorm."

Carroll is the captain of the Brainstorm. He goes to Black River, Coal Creek, Dawson, hauling diesel fuel and D8 Cats. He does not resemble Lord Nelson. He is short and sinewy, slight like a nail. With his dark felt eyebrows and black beard, his dark glasses and black visored cap, he is nearly illegible, but there is nothing enigmatic in his rapid flow of words. For the moment, he is not the chief. "Margaret Henry is the chief. But I'll straighten that out when I get good and ready," says Carroll. His wife, Alice Joseph, is the Health Aide in Circle, and school cook. "Her great-grandfather was Joe No. 6," he says, with evident pride. "I am Albert No. 1, you see—Albert Carroll Senior the First." The pelts of half a dozen ermine decorate their cabin wall. Hutchinson and Carroll used to trap together. Sometimes Hutchinson comes into Carroll's cabin, sees only one light on, and asks, "How am I going to make any money?" "He turns on every light there is, inside and out," Albert says. "If a bulb is missing, he'll go and get one."

Alice earns about fifteen thousand dollars a year. A doctor in Fairbanks calls her frequently to discuss the health of Circle. Last year, Albert trapped thirty lynx. A lynx skin was worth thirty-five dollars not long ago and was worth five hundred last year. Meanwhile, the State of Alaska has been making so much money from its one-eighth share of pipeline oil that the legislature is in a feeding frenzy. Pending court approval, Alaskans are to receive fifty dollars in 1980 for every year they have lived in Alaska since statehood. Alice and Albert Carroll will together get twenty-one hundred dollars. Next year, they will get twenty-two hundred, twenty-three hundred the year after that. The oil will last about twenty-five years. Easy come, easy go. The state will soon have a surplus in its treasury of nearly four billion dollars. It will cover many calls to Fort Yukon.

Circle is now a part of the Fairbanks and Vicinity Telephone Directory, wherein many businesses stand prepared to serve few people. There are five hundred yellow pages, a hundred white ones. The "vicinity" is about three hundred thousand square miles. It includes communities as far as six hundred miles from Fairbanks. One telephone book. One-tenth of the United States. Only eighteen towns are in the directory, because few villages have a Dick Hutchinson and telephones are little known in the bush. Circle, with its seventeen listings, is not the smallest community in the book. The Summit Telephone Company, of Cleary Summit, Alaska, lists seven subscribers. The Mukluk Telephone Company, an intercity conglomerate, has twenty-three listings in Teller (sixty miles north of Nome), thirty-two in Wales (on the Bering Strait), and fifty-six in Shishmaref (eighty miles up the coast from Wales). Up the Koyukuk, there are forty-one listed telephones in Bettles (Bettles Light & Power). Of course, there is no saying how many unlisted telephone numbers there might be in a given village. In Circle, there is one. Also, there are eight credit-card subscribers—trappers whose cabins are thirty, forty miles up the Yukon. They come into town and use other people's phones.

There is a shortwave transmitter in the Yukon Trading Post. People used to come into the store and call Fairbanks, where they would be patched into the national telephone system. The charge was seven dollars and fifty cents to Fairbanks plus the toll from there. Hutchinson's rate charge for three minutes to Fairbanks is a dollar and ten cents. Two dollars and thirty-five cents to Anchorage. Of course, three minutes mean nothing to an Alaskan. They take three minutes just to say hello. When they talk, they talk. An encountered human being is like a good long read.

When the trappers come in from the country and appear over the riverbank, Hutchinson can be counted on to intercept them with their phone bills. Monthly statements are not mailed out in Circle. They are hand-delivered by Hutchinson in his Chevrolet pickup, a vehicle he starts with a hammer. In it is a gimballed cage in which a glass tumbler swings always level. Levi Ginnis, a hundred and ten dollars. Ruth Crow, a hundred and forty dollars. Albert Carroll, two hundred dollars. Helge

Boquist's toll calls come to eight dollars and twenty-three cents. Helge is a Swede and he is married to an Athapaskan. Long since retired, he once worked Mastodon Creek. It is said that his Athapaskan relatives take advantage of his good nature, making free use of his telephone for long-distance calls. At eight dollars and twenty-three cents, he would seem to have the problem under control.

The Reverend Fred Vogel has a modest bill, too. Vogel is more or less a one-man denomination. He holds services in his cabin. The return address he sends out with his mail is "Chapel Hill, Circle, Alaska." He has been in and out of Circle City for nearly thirty years. "He's all bent out of shape because the Episcopals give wine to kids during Communion," Hutchinson says. Once, when Vogel was off doing missionary work, he tried to close the Yukon Liquor Cache by mail from Liberia.

Calvary's Northern Lights Mission, of North Pole, Alaska, near Fairbanks, has a small outpost here in Circle—a young couple, who also have a low-toll phone bill. At its home base, the mission operates a fifty-thousand-watt radio station called KJNP—King Jesus North Pole. A great deal of bush communication is accomplished by a program called "Trapline Chatter" on KJNP—people announcing their travel plans and their babies, people asking favors or offering fragments of regional news, people begging and granting forgiveness. "Trapline Chatter" knits the lives of citizens of the bush, but its audience has declined in Circle City. As a result, Circle City people are much less current with what is going on around the bush. What they know now is what has been said on their own telephones. And there are no party lines.

From time to time, a bill will become seriously overdue, the subscriber indefensibly delinquent. Hutchinson has yet to disconnect a phone. "I strap their lines," he says, which means that he takes a pair of pliers to the PABX and turns off their access to the satellite.

Gordon MacDonald's aggregate phone bill approaches five hundred dollars a month. He has two or three lines. Young and entrepreneurial, MacDonald and his wife, Lynne, own the Trading Post, the Liquor Cache, the Cafe, and a helicopter-and-fixed-wing flying service, which takes geologists into the country in a three-place Hiller for a hundred and fifty dollars an hour, or twice that in a five-place Hughes. Mac-

Donald carries supplies to trappers in winter and to miners in summer. Hutchinson works for him as a part-time fixed-wing pilot. Certain trappers resist MacDonald, who has been in the country four years. They say that if he brings his geologists around their home streams they will open fire. "Just try that once" is MacDonald's response, "and a fifty-five-gallon drum filled with water will land on the roof of your cabin."

On billing days, Hutchinson does not call on Carl Dasch. Now and again, Hutchinson has renewed his attempts to sell Dasch a phone, but the prospect seems unlikely. "He knows it's no use," says Dasch. "I have no one to call." Living alone in his cabin, with his two rifles above his bed, Dasch has achieved a durable independence that he obviously enjoys. In the nineteen-seventies, Dasch's brother appeared one day in Circle. The two men had not seen each other in forty years. They had a pleasant conversation for fifteen or twenty minutes, and then Carl's brother went back down the road. The brother is dead now.

"This is a good country to get lost in if you want to get lost," says Carl.

"Yes, it is," Helge Boquist agrees. "One guy was lost here three months."

"That's a different kind of lost," says Carl Dasch.

Dasch went to Fairbanks last summer, and he has visited Anchorage. "Yes, I was in Anchorage just after the Second World War."

He has found much to interest him here in the country. He used to watch ornithologists from the Lower Forty-eight shooting peregrine falcons off the bluffs of the Yukon. "They were allowed to do this. It was a scientific deal. They wanted to see what the falcons had been eating. All they had to do was look at the bones in the nest to see what the falcons had been eating."

As advancing age increases his risks, would he not be assured by having a telephone at hand?

"I'm a hard guy to convince. When I say no, I don't mean yes."

"What happens if you get sick, Carl?"

"If I get sick enough, I'll die, like everybody else."

Dasch's obstinance notwithstanding, Circle Utilities is in such robust condition that Hutchinson has become deeply interested in the growth of the town. This past school year, he was pleased to note five new first graders. He referred to them as "future customers." Hutchinson is the town welcome wagon. "Circle has plenty of capacity for expansion," he says. "I think it could probably stand a hundred and fifty people and still be comfortable." The new census has amazed and gratified him. "The count was eighty. That really surprised me. I thought there were sixty-five." To prepare himself for the demands of the future, he has bought a Pitman Polecat, the classic truck of the telephone lineman, with a plastic bucket that can lift him forty-one feet into the air and a big auger that can drill holes deep in the ground. While Hutchinson is up in the bucket, Little Hutch is operating the truck below, his hands flying to the levers of the pole-grabber, the outriggers, the load line, the boom extension. It is Hutchinson's hope that one day Little Hutch will inherit the place in the bucket.

Hutchinson's father was a Boston fireman, and Hutchinson grew up in South Weymouth, Massachusetts, where he read a little less than he hunted and fished. He learned offset printing in the Marine Corps, and had been working for a job printer in Los Angeles when he first got into his pickup and drove to Alaska. Unlike most people who experiment with Alaska, he spent no time in Anchorage or Fairbanks but directly sought the country of the upper Yukon. The year was 1964, and he was twenty-three. He lived in the woods some miles from Circle. His adventure ended one day when, just after killing a wolf, he tripped and accidentally shot himself in the leg. After time in the hospital in Fairbanks, he went Outside to recover. It is a measure of his affection for Alaska that he returned as soon as he could, with intent to stay forever. He trapped from a cabin on Birch Creek and, as the expression goes, made his groceries. He worked as "a flunky for a biologist," live-trapping lynx, shooting them with tranquillizers, putting radio collars around their necks, and then tracking their movements. He worked in the Yukon Trading Post, and in Fairbanks printing *Jessen's Weekly*, among other things, while assembling the capital to establish his utility.

His flight instruction was under the supervision of the late Don Jonz, who was at the controls when the plane carrying Congressmen Hale Boggs and Nick Begich disappeared over the Gulf of Alaska. Hutchinson has had a commercial flying license since 1972. He also worked as a generator operator on the construction of the Alyeska pipeline, making well over five thousand dollars a month, at Franklin Bluffs and Prudhoe Bay, doing "seven twelves"—twelve hours a day, seven days a week. Hutchinson's wife, Earla, thinks a more accurate translation of "seven twelves" would be "seven days a week, twelve minutes a day," but Earla has the so-called work ethic deep in her fabric. From Standish, Michigan, she came to Circle to teach in a Bible school that was run by the Episcopal Church. The Hutchinsons have two children: Earl Francis (Little Hutch) and Krista, who is ten. For ten years, the family lived in a small cabin that had one bedroom. They now live in a handsome new house that stands eight feet in the air on steel poles like a giant cache. Last year, an ice jam on the Yukon at Circle backed up water until it went over the bank and flooded much of the town. The PABX telephone exchange stood boot-deep in water. So Hutchinson, later constructing his new home, backed the Pitman Polecat up to the site and planted his metallic stilts—ten feet into frozen ground. The house is all second floor—forty-two feet long, three bedrooms, galvanized roof. Temperatures in Circle reach seventy below zero. There's a foot of insulation in the elevated floor. Even the outhouse is raised off the ground on what appear to be short stilts. A chorus of sled dogs is chained in the yard.

Inside, Hutchinson sits back with a contented grin, a Calvert's-and-water. He listens to the static on his radio. "Music to my ears," he says. The static indicates that at least one long-distance telephone call is in progress in Circle City. It is an almost purring static. It stops when the parties hang up. The static caused by a local call is different. Local-call static is staccato, crackly, arrhythmic, and not particularly pleasing to Hutchinson's ears.

He wears a black-and-gold Ski-Doo cap, an elbow-patched canvas shirt, blue jeans, and L. L. Bean's shoepacs, which he calls "breakup boots." In his living room and kitchen, he is surrounded by mementos of life on the Yukon River: the locally obsolescent kerosene lantern, a wolverine pelt, a model of a log cabin (very much like the cabin the Hutchinsons lived in for so many years). There is a model dogsled and a model Yukon River fish wheel. A red fifty-five-gallon drum full of water stands beside the kitchen sink. It is the house water supply, and he fills it from a neighbor's well. There is a tall refrigerator-freezer, a microwave oven, an electric coffeemaker, an electric can opener, a toaster, a washing machine, an electric typewriter, an electric adding machine, and a Sears electric organ. Along a bookshelf are "Livingstone of the Arctic," "Cultures of the North Pacific Coast," "How to Select and Install Antennas," "McGuffey's 5th Eclectic Reader." Dick and Earla are partners in Circle Utilities, which earned for them about sixty-five thousand dollars last year. Earla now teaches in the public school. With her salary and his income from flying and trapping, their grand total has broken the six-digit barrier and gone into the proximate beyond. Hutchinson tugs apologetically at the visor of his Ski-Doo cap. He says, "Of course, that won't sound like much to people in the Lower Forty-eight."

Helge Boquist remembers that when he came here fifty years ago a telephone line ran from Circle a hundred and sixty-five miles among miners out on the creeks. Galvanized wire went through the forest from tripod to tripod of spruce. It was an all-party line "with one long, three shorts, that sort of thing, a box on a wall with a crank," and everybody heard everybody else, from Circle to Ferry Roadhouse to Central to Miller House, and on Birch and Independence, Deadwood and Ketchum, Mammoth and Mastodon Creeks.

"Helge knows where gold still is," says Carl Dasch. "He should get a skookum young partner and go out there."

"Today, they get five hundred dollars for a teaspoonful of gold" is Boquist's contemplative response. "And the old telephone wires that went out to the creeks are clotheslines now, here in Circle."

Brooks
Range

William O. Douglas was born in 1898
in Maine, Minnesota, and graduated
from Whitman College and the
Columbia University School of Law.
From 1931 to 1939 he was a professor
of law at Yale University and from
1939 to 1975 was a member of the U. S.
Supreme Court. He was the author of
*Of Men and Mountains, Strange Lands
and Friendly, Beyond the Himalayas,
North from Malaya, We the Judges,
The Right of the People, Mr. Lincoln
and the Negroes* and *My Wilderness:
The Pacific West.* He died in 1980.

The Arctic has strange stillness that no other wilderness knows. It has loneliness too—a feeling of isolation and remoteness born of vast spaces, the rolling tundra, and the barren domes of limestone mountains. This is a loneliness that is joyous and exhilarating. All the noises of civilization have been left behind; now the music of the wilderness can be heard. The Arctic shows beauty in this bareness and in the shadows cast by clouds over empty land. The beauty is in part the glory of seeing moose, caribou, and wolves living in a natural habitat, untouched by civilization. It is the thrill of seeing birds come thousands of miles to nest and raise their young. The beauty is also in slopes painted cerise by a low-bush rhododendron, in strange mosses and lichens that grow everywhere, and (to one who gets on his hands and knees) in the glories of delicate saxifrage, arctic poppies, and fairy forget-me-nots. The Arctic has a call that is compelling. The distant mountains make one want to go on and on over the next ridge and over the one beyond. The call is that of a wilderness known only to a few. It is a call to adventure. This is not a place to possess like the plateaus of Wyoming or the valleys of Arizona; it is one to behold with wonderment. It is a domain for any restless soul who yearns to discover the startling beauties of creation in the place of quiet and solitude where life exists without molestation by man.

I was sitting under a white spruce on the upper reaches of the Sheenjek River in the Brooks Range of Alaska. Our camp was at 68 degrees 36'N., 143 degrees 45'W. Glaciers estimated to be 1400 feet thick once moved over this country. Only a few remnants of them are left and they are at the very head of the Sheenjek. But their work is evident on every hand. The mountain ridges are rounded and polished; the valley is U-shaped; morainal deposits cover the valley floor; potholes dot the area.

We were camped on one pothole filled with dark blue water and over 200 acres in size. It lies at an elevation of about 2000 feet. It is the last one up the Sheenjek Valley large enough for a seaplane to negotiate. And therefore Olaus J. Murie, biologist and conservationist, and his wife Mardy, who were heading a scientific expedition into these mountains, appropriately called it Last Lake.

I sat for an hour or more under my spruce tree. The first friend to approach was an arctic ground squirrel. He was a quiet body, not chattering or scolding like our western species. He had a quiet call, "sik sik"; and that is his Eskimo name. He was curious about my presence but not unduly alarmed. After inspecting me he went to work with a great burst of energy collecting roots and plants for his den under the hummock where I sat. This arctic ground squirrel is a true hibernator, and his winters are long. In June, when the Muries first arrived, the valley of the Sheenjek was still brown. Summer came in a great rush, July being the month when the bloom of the flowers was at the peak. By mid-August Summer was gone and Fall had set in. Even the first part of August showed fresh snow on the mountains. The arctic ground squirrel had his job cut out for him if he was to finish all his household tasks before freezing weather set in.

This busy animal that ran to and fro at my feet is important in the ecology of the Brooks Range. The grizzly bear digs into hummocks looking for him. The red fox, the lynx, and the wolverine are heavily dependent on him. The golden eagles, whose nest I saw on a cliff some miles east of camp, also hunt the arctic ground squirrel. Gyrfalcons and hawks join the chase. The arctic ground squirrel is essential in the food chain of the Sheenjek.

The next friend to appear was the willow ptarmigan. This bird, which mates in May and nests by the first of June, was quite silent in July and August. The white body feathers had been molted and the birds now wore the brown plumage of summer. This color blends perfectly with the willow, dwarf birch, and spruce boughs where the nests are cleverly hidden. The eggs have the same brown-splotched appearance; and the downies are so perfectly camouflaged they are almost impossible to see. The bird that approached me this morning was a male. He kept at a respectable distance, feeding on bearberries. Once he was startled and fled. It was a short, swift flight with a low trajectory; and though I saw where he landed I could not, for the life of me, see him.

The ptarmigan, like the ground squirrel, is important in the Sheenjek's food chain. Man, of course, finds this bird a delicious dish. The red fox hunts its eggs and its young. So do the ground squirrels. The golden eagle, marsh hawks, short-eared owls, and goshawks pursue the ptarmigan. So do the wolf and the wolverine. Every predator seems to rely on this bird for a part of its diet. And its feathers are important too. They are used by many birds, particularly the tree sparrows and white-crowned sparrows, to line their nests.

Last Lake, which was below me, suddenly seemed to come alive with birds. Cliff swallows hurried by; Brewer's blackbirds set up a chatter; some gray-cheeked thrushes were calling. An old squaw duck came gliding in. A pin-tailed duck with a young brood cruised a marshy point looking for food. Two Pacific loons—whose calls we were to hear infrequently—came out of some reeds, heading quickly for the middle of the lake. A number of lesser yellowlegs and numerous sandpipers— common shore birds in this region—combed the shores of Last Lake, looking for food. But the most frenzied activity was by the short-billed gulls. Two of them had a nest somewhere in the marsh by the lake. We were to see one large young one before we left. This day it was not in view. One of the gulls sat on the high stub of an ancient spruce, guarding the lake. I decided to walk over and inspect the site. I had no sooner started along the shore of the lake then several lesser yellowlegs flew from spruce to spruce, sounding the alarm with their ear-splitting cry—"whew, whew, whew, whew." But the short-billed gull needed no notice of my coming. I was still fifty yards from its perch when it dived on me. I kept going, and it dived again and again. I held my hands over my face as I splashed through the marshy stand of sedges and willows. Once more the gull dived, this time hitting my hat. I ignominiously retreated, taking as my excuse the antics of a female mallard, who feverishly scattered her young ones into the marshes and scuttled toward the middle of the lake showing a "broken wing."

I resumed my seat under the white spruce and noted that I was not the only intruder whom the short-billed gull resented. Out of the deep stillness of the Sheenjek came the clear, metallic croak of the raven—a friendly sound in the Arctic, where most voices are muted. I looked up to see two circling. The short-billed gull left like a fighter plane after bombers, chasing the ravens and diving on them from above.

The gull resumed its vigil. The loons, which had been cruising Last Lake, got close to the shore where the nest of the gulls was located. Down came the gull over their heads, screaming and scolding. Again and again during our stay at Last Lake the short-billed gull stayed on guard, driving off any of our party that ventured close and chasing golden eagles and goshawks with a vengeance I had never seen.

I love fishing in the Arctic. There were many tributaries of the Sheenjek below camp—streams that drained Last Lake and the marshy ponds that lay below it. Some of these were deep sluices showing black bottoms from the sphagnum moss that flourishes in this valley. These fresh-water streams ended in a rather extensive piece of overflow ice that occupied perhaps ten acres or more. This overflow ice is formed by the pressure of water against the ice that forms in the stream bed. When the pressure is great, the water breaks through the ice and flows over it. It in turn is frozen. The process is repeated until many layers are formed, creating a body of ice six feet or more deep and many acres in size that lasts all summer.

Above the overflow ice were large holes in the deep, still water where I fished with flies. An old friend, the robin, hopped furtively in a stand of spruce. It was no longer the gay, spirited bird I had known farther south. But when I turned my back it burst forth with its old, familiar song. An Alaska jay flew up and scouted me, filled with curiosity. But in this arctic domain they are not the "camp robbers" I had expected them to be. They, too, seemed shy and furtive.

I was whipping my line preparatory to the first cast upstream when a muskrat came up from some pocket on the side of the stream and, seeing me, dived with a splash. These animals that are very much in evidence when the ice goes out and the mating season is on are inconspicuous as July advances. Their secretiveness must be rewarded, for they are sought after by all the birds of prey; and the wolf and the fox find them a delicacy.

I whipped the first piece of open water above the overflow ice without reward. My first cast in the next pool produced a slight swirl that would have gone unnoticed had not my eyes been glued on the spot.

I set the hook and brought to net a fourteen-inch grayling. It did not show the fight our rainbow trout give. There was no standing on its tail, no shaking of its head. It went down like a pike and tried to stay there. I was to be rewarded over and again with grayling, striking a wet fly. Bob Krear, a member of the Murie party, knew these fish well and was adept at catching them. He explained that one of their mainstays was the beetle larvae. These waters hatch great quantities of caddis flies; and the pools I saw were rich with nymphs that I was not able to catalogue.

These grayling, which run up to three pounds or more, are not prepossessing. Their small heads and broad-beamed bodies make them seem a bit awkward compared with our streamlined rainbow. But whatever they lack in grace they make up in food. Their flesh is white and their thick steaks cook up into a sweeter and more delicious dish than any trout I have sampled. Bob Krear and I cleaned the grayling by Last Lake, throwing the offal into the shallow water. The short-billed gulls that had attacked me so relentlessly quickly appeared to enjoy the feast. They brought with them their lone offspring, who still was awkward and clumsy; and it was gray, not white like its parents. But it had its parents' aggressive instincts. A pin-tailed duck flew in to examine the shore line and was immediately attacked by the youngster.

It is said there are other fish in the Sheenjek—a word meaning "dog salmon" in the Kutchin Indian language. But I saw no salmon, nor did I see any lake trout, pickerel, or whitefish that have been reputed there. My only rewards were the grayling, and they were enough to satisfy any fisherman.

We discovered on one of our exploratory hikes some pools that lie on one of the low knolls that dot this area. The pools, which drain to the river only when the rains come, are deep in the shade of white spruce, which generally forms an open forest but here had grown into a thick stand. Willow—a browse that caribou and moose enjoy in winter—was mixed with the spruce; and there were some stands of dwarf birch. Some of the spruce was hung with beardlike lichens, giving them almost a patriarchal appearance. Others were decorated with crustose lichens that grew like scales on the limbs—some red, some yellow, some gray. The ground around the pools was spongy and soft and covered with a thick mat of mosses. The mountain avens was in bloom, adding streaks of creamy white to the dark green. A dark blue saxifrage was mostly hidden. A tall lousewort—bright blue—showed its tiny heads. A small black berry, known as the crowberry, made a carpet. The arctic poppies were brilliant. Bush cinquefoil added a touch of gaiety. White, yellow, and gray lichens gave life and zest to the leaf litter; and the lovely, delicate, tiny bluebell flower was almost hidden from view. But what caught my eye was a moss I had never seen before, one which George Schaller, also in the Murie party, assured me was scarce. George gave me its technical name, *Splachnum luteum*. It has stems almost eight inches high, topped by small yellow umbrellas or hats. This moss has become so specialized that it can survive only on the dung of moose, an article in abundance around these pools.

It was difficult to express my feelings as I stood beside these dark quiet pools, shaded by spruce. They were so beautiful, so exquisite, that they were unreal. They seemed withdrawn from the earth, though a glorious part of it. The day had been cloudy; now the sun came out, brightening the dark waters. The black of their bottoms showed various tints of green. The delicate colors along the shore added life and zest. Here were pools never touched by man—unspoiled, uncontaminated except perhaps by the awful fall-out from the atomic bombs that is slowly poisoning the whole earth. Here was life in perfect ecological balance. A moose had stopped here to drink. Some water beetles skimmed the surface. Nothing else had seemed to invade this sanctuary. It was indeed a temple in the glades. Never, I believe, had God worked more wondrously than in the creation of this beautiful, delicate alcove in the remoteness of the Sheenjek Valley.

These white-spruce forests are interesting to explore. They never grow above 3000 feet and their northernmost limit is just short of 69 degrees N. In moist places they sometimes form thick stands. But they usually appear as long fingers, stretching northward up to Sheenjek Valley. They are a small tree with branches that cover the trunk. The branches are short, giving the tree a slim appearance, and the tip is peaked. Their average height is fifteen or twenty feet; and a foot or so from the ground they are usually not more than seven inches in diameter. There are some, however, that are nearly eighteen inches through. The Murie expedition found that it takes over thirty years for a white spruce in the Brooks Range to reach five feet and 100 years to reach twenty feet. The oldest white spruce they found was nearly 300 years old.

These white spruce are slowly reclaiming the Arctic. Their scarcity is due, it is thought, not to unfavorable environment but to the fact that they could take hold only after the ice sheets had receded. Since then the migration of the white spruce northward has never ceased.

But except for the soil hummucks where the white spruce grows, most of this Sheenjek Valley country is tundra. In lowland meadows are small islands a foot or so high. The land they enclose is called a polygon, a wet area where mosses, sedges, rushes, and prostrate willow grow. A horsetail—perennial aquatic—flourishes there, as does the wild cranberry. This swampy land surrounds Last Lake. One sloshes through it as he does in any marsh. The more typical tundra is a few feet higher. It is marked by tussocks formed from a variety of vegetation. Most conspicuous is a cotton grass, sometimes known as hare's-tail. In June this cotton grass is in bloom, showing hundreds of acres with a bluish-gray cast. Mosses and lichens grow thick on these tussocks. A bog rosemary with lovely pink blossoms adorns them. Bog bilberries (smaller than blueberries and not good for eating) flourish there. Bearberries with white flowers make a mat. A dwarf and prostrate rhododendron decorates many tussocks. A dwarf trailing willow possesses much of this high ground in the bogs. A vigorous species of the grass of parnassus grows here, mixed with a purple lousewort, violet butterwort, violet-purple milk vetch, a low, greenish bunchflower, a white false asphodel.

The tussocks are from a few inches to a foot or two broad. They are like tall mushrooms with grassy heads. They are not steady underfoot, sinking and sometimes swaying. Mardy Murie said that one who walked them had to be limp like a rag doll. A hike through the tussock meadows is more strenuous than climbing. One is continuously on edge to keep his balance, for a misstep sends him down into deep slush. The result is that a hiker tends to put on speed, barely touching one tussock and practically jumping to the next. A day of walking a tussock meadow is exhausting. Horses would flounder hopelessly. In the summer this is country only for men with packs. I had seen this tundra on an earlier trip stretching from the north side of the Brooks Range to the Arctic Ocean. That tundra, though differing in botanical detail from the tundra of the Sheenjek, has the same general appearance. It is in the main a dwarf-shrub heath marked by tussocks, and it runs for miles and miles. There is a dreary monotony in its northern expanse. But here on the Sheenjek it is a colorful community broken by knolls where willow, alder, and birch form thickets, by the long fingers of spruce reaching north, and by the backdrop of rounded mountains covered with a soft nap of lichen and moss heath.

One day we hiked far up the Sheenjek, resting frequently on the dry hummocks where the white spruce grow. Usually the Sheenjek is crystal-clear; but the day of our hike was after a storm. So the river was muddy from drainage. Above Last Lake the Sheenjek breaks up into many small streams. The riffles were shallow; the gravel beds highly polished. Small sand bars had built up from favorable currents, and the islands between the fingers of the river were thick with willow. These stands of willow along the river are a favorite habitat of moose. There were many fresh tracks, but we saw none of the animals. Wolves travel this river bed in their hunt for game. The wolf signs—especially the scat—were fresh and numerous this day. Olaus found one track where a front paw measured 6 inches by 5.1 inches. I was to see wolves later, but we saw none on this hike. Red fox also follow the river bed, and while we found their tracks we did not see them. But I heard one barking far off to the west in some willow. We looked at every mud bar for signs of the grizzly bear, but found none. One of our great rewards this day was the low, lush blueberries that grow in splendor on the east bank. Hundreds of acres were in full fruit. The berries were ripe, and they were the sweetest we have known. We picked several pints and ate many for lunch. Then we lay on our backs in these stands of blueberries and took a nap to the soft music of the purling Sheenjek.

The day was bright. The storm that brought us rain left six inches or so of snow on the mountains. These 8000-foot ridges glistened with their white mantles and seemed cool and inviting. No tree broke the soft flow of their lines, and cloud shadows changed their moods and our fantasies.

A turbulent tributary that comes into the Sheenjek about three miles north has white spruce growing thick along it. A few stray cottonwoods are to be found, and poplars flourish there. Beaver frequent the Sheenjek Valley, and some of them had been fresh at work cutting these poplars. These woods were thickly carpeted with moss—rich in color, springy underfoot. Some of it reminded me of the star moss that grows high in the Cascades and Wallowas. One type was a bright green. When we came to higher ground, we found a bright-yellow moss that made a deep carpet on the wilderness floor. And choicest of all was a gray lichen (endemic in Alaska) that Mercedes, my wife, and Mardy collected for its decorative effect on women's hats.

Not far up this tributary we found two large spruce poles standing upright in the ground, spanned by a third one. This was a cache for food made by prospectors, who designed it years ago to keep their supplies safe from animals.

This was ancient land of the Athabaskan Indians, composed of eight tribes making up the Kutchin nation. Their domain extended over the Brooks Range to the Arctic Ocean. Occasionally they fought the Eskimos. But they were essentially hunters and fishermen who settled on the Yukon and the larger rivers that feed it. Probably only a few frequented the Sheenjek, at least in its upper reaches. Things changed when the gold rush started. Prospectors came into the Sheenjek Valley. Before then, in 1847, the Hudson's Bay Company established a post at Fort Yukon and the fur trade began. The Indians accommodated the fur traders; even Eskimos crossed the Brooks Range and came down the Sheenjek, bringing furs to the trading post. Some of the Eskimos stayed, establishing villages. But since the 1920s little hunting or trapping has been done here. A few Indians still make excursions into the Brooks

Range from the Yukon flats, looking mainly for wolves, on which there has been a $50 bounty; but not many of them make the effort. They are mostly congregated at Fort Yukon, 150 miles to the south and in Arctic Village, nearly 50 miles to the southwest of our camp. Some white men have come into the Sheenjek, but they have been few and far between. The Sheenjek since the 1920s has known only its primeval quiet and stillness. Life has gone on undisturbed by men. No food chains have been broken by the introduction of civilization. There is no more thrilling place to observe life in complete ecological balance than in this valley on the south slopes of the Brooks Range.

The spread of the tree line far into the Brooks Range has some relation to the temperature range. This relationship has been put by some students into a formula which suggests that if the mean temperature for the coldest month of the year is -14 degrees F, the mean for the warmest month must be 50 degrees F. If the mean for the coldest month is -40 degrees F, the mean for the warmest month must reach 55.4 degrees F. The requirements of this formula can be satisfied on the southern slopes of the Brooks Range.

The summers on the Sheenjek are mostly sunny and warm, the July daytime average being about 61 degrees F. At night the temperature drops to 40 degrees F and sometimes lower. While the summer days are in the main bright, clouds often drift in by midday. And July and August are the months of the year when there is the heaviest precipitation. We knew several all rain days, the storms coming mostly from the south and southeast. But the precipitation on these south slopes of the Brooks Range is so slight that but for the arctic conditions this would be semidesert. The total precipitation over the period of a quarter century averages slightly under seven inches a year, which is only a bit more than half of that of Wyoming's high plateau. The yearly snowfall is less than four feet on the average. But the winters are long and cold, the average January temperature being -21 degrees F. Summers are short in the Arctic. Early June flowerings produce seeds by July first. Early in August most arctic plants have completed the cycle and entered the seed phase. Even while the seeds are maturing, new leaf and flower buds develop near the surface of the soil, ready for next season's growth. Most of the seeds of these arctic plants are light and specially adapted for transportation by wind. A high percentage of plants depend, indeed, on the high velocity of arctic winds for their spread and migration. This early flowering that comes with such a rush is aided by the fact that the microclimate at which the plants live is warmer than ordinary temperature readings would reveal. For the temperature just under the soil surface may be as much as 40 degrees F higher than the air temperature. So there may be enough warmth for photosynthesis to take place in the earth, though the air temperature indicates freezing.

But under the soil is permafrost, which conditions much of the life of the Arctic. It lies about fourteen inches beneath the surface in the Sheenjek Valley. This permafrost acts as an impervious layer which prevents normal drainage. Rainfall that would be absorbed by the earth under normal conditions, producing no runoff, has startling effects in the Sheenjek. A half inch of rain or less will raise the level of Last Lake a foot or more, since the water runs off permafrost as it would off concrete. One morning after an all-night rain we found a new creek running by our camp.

These arctic soils are quite acid, due to poor drainage and poor aeration; and they are deficient in nitrogen, because organic decay by bacterial action is very slow.

The thin soil and short growing period emphasize how perishable the arctic wilderness is. Overgrazing would cause great tragedy here. Lichens, on which caribou depend so heavily, would take a century to restore. This arctic wilderness is truly fragile. Never can it survive the full impact of civilization.

The Eskimos have graphic names for these summer months:

> May—month-of-fawning
> June—egg-month
> July—mosquito-month
> August—berry-month

July ran true to the Eskimo experience.

I had heard horrible stories of the mosquitoes of Alaska and went prepared with head nets. But I never used them. There are mosquitoes —many of them. Even after a frost—one of which we experienced—

new crops of mosquitoes are born. They swarm up out of the marshland and tundra. They are not too bothersome when the wind blows. Once it dies down they rise from the ground on every step; and they are always present where the stands of spruce or poplar are thick. But the use of modern mosquito "dope" keeps them off the skin and hands. They still envelop the head and shoulders like a cloud, following one everywhere. But one gets accustomed to this—except when he eats. Then he must be in a tent to avoid getting a mouthful of mosquitoes. A tent with a floor and zipper flap can be made mosquitoproof with the help of a spray. At night the greater worry for one raised in a temperate zone is not the mosquito but the light. In July the sun sets over the Sheenjek Valley about midnight and rises an hour or two later. This means it sinks below the limestone peaks to the west, travels only a short arc, and rises. We are accustomed to darkness for deep sleep and the unraveling of cares. The newcomer misses night in the Arctic. But there are special rewards. Cloud effects, sunsets, the long afterglow, and the sunrise produce a riot of colors that even Arizona does not know.

There are lemmings and voles in this arctic region. These rodents —along with snowshoe hares and arctic ground squirrels—support an aristocracy of clever predators that include the fox, the lynx, and the arctic weasel. They are most active in the summer, collecting and storing roots and grass for their winter needs. Olaus and George were busy trapping them by day and preparing the specimens by night. I followed them as they ran their trap lines, learning much about these animals that a casual visitor to the northland would never know. These tiny mouselike animals live at various elevations in the Brooks Range. Some of them possess networks of runways extending from tussock to tussock in the wet land around Last Lake. There are ponds, higher in the mountains, where they are also found. Some types of voles are found several thousand feet above the Sheenjek with their runways built through carpets of moss and through bare rocky outcrops. They seem never to be found on high, dry slopes. Their preference is for damp edges of lakes and swamps. And when the waters rise and their runways are flooded, they merely retreat temporarily to higher, drier ground.

The lemmings and voles travel cycles of life with periods when the population reaches crash proportions and times when it is at low ebb. The low point for lemmings had been reached this summer, for they were not much in evidence. Lowell Sumner and John Christian have shown that once these animals build to a high population level and then come into a period of food scarcity, they are subject to tremendous emotional stress. This stress leads to an exhaustion of the adreno-pituitary system. The effect on voles and lemmings is similar to the effect of stress on man. These rodents develop inflammation or ulceration of the digestive tract and a permanent metabolic derangement that directly or indirectly causes death. In lemmings this tension becomes so great that it leads to mass migration. This migration is not an orderly, methodical one, like settlers looking for new homes. It is a panicky outburst which amounts to mass suicide. The lemmings go on and on, stopped not even by rivers, lakes, or the ocean where they are destroyed.

There are Dall sheep in the Brooks Range; but they come down into the Sheenjek only in winter. George Schaller scouted the high slopes and found them in alpine meadows protected both above and below by talus slopes.

There are grizzly bear in these mountains, and their tracks and scat were evident on every trip. I also saw many places where they had dug for roots or for squirrels, and some where they had bedded down. But I never came across one, nor did I even see one from a distance. One charged to within thirty feet of George Schaller; another got even closer to Bob Krear on the charge that came to a sudden, grinding stop when Bob thought the end was near. These grizzlies—inherently shy—have very poor eyesight. Even at a hundred feet a man probably looks much like a caribou. The grizzly may have to come much closer to pick up the scent. When he does, he usually will run unless cornered or hurt. The scent of man is the signal of danger. The grizzly gets this message intuitively, for the sight or even the odor of a man is an experience that would come to a grizzly in the Sheenjek only once in a lifetime.

There are many caribou in the Sheenjek, the total number in the herd perhaps reaching 40,000. The caribou are the only members of the deer family where both sexes have antlers. Their summer coat is dark; their winter fur is a light tan. In the early summer they move west. By August first they move east. These migrations are on a broad front of forty or fifty miles, not many caribou being in one group. I had seen small groups feeding around Last Lake. But they seldom stood still; they were a restless, nervous lot, seeming always to be on the move. One night an estimated 2000 caribou crossed the Sheenjek not far above our camp. Their feet pounding in the gravel sounded, as Mardy put it, like "a freight train roaring through the valley."

One day I hiked to a pass that marks the divide between the Sheenjek and the Coleen drainage. At the pass I climbed the southern slopes, looking for flowers. As I rested on a limestone outcropping, a herd of forty caribou crossed below me. They were headed east. Up ahead was a bull with head bowed under the great weight of his antlers. Lesser bulls followed. Then came the cows and the calves. Yearlings raced alongside. But every other animal followed in line, stepping in practically the same tracks as the one ahead of him. Their brown summer hair was prominent, though some had dark only along their backs. By fall a light brown would take the place of the dark color, for the whole herd and the older bulls would have strikingly white necks. This day the caribou were traveling so fast that the calves had difficulty keeping up.

These restless animals depend on lichens, grasses, and sedges in the winter; on willow and birch, grasses and sedges in the summer. This day they were driven by some great force that made this migration an integrated community effort.

This country to the east of Last Lake was good hiking terrain. Above the tundra were the knolls, thick with stands of dwarf willow and birch, which by late August turn red and yellow. The moss makes thick, moist carpets in these thickets. The crowberry and bog bilberry flourish there. Here I found the Labrador tea in bloom—a species similar to that I once found along the northern slopes that face the Arctic Ocean. On the open slopes of these knolls mountain avens and cassiope left streaks of creamy white. Alpine hedysarum added touches of violet; lousewort and arnica showed yellow; knotweed was bright

pink; the arctic lupine added bright blue; and the arctic poppy showed
gold. A mosslike silene, known as cushion pink, showed pink and rose
flowers growing on almost stemless stocks. A minute larch-leaf sand-
wort also flourished here. But what caught the eye on these knolls and
the slopes above them was the rhododendron. Some call this plant an
azalea, but its name is *Rhododendron lapponicum*. It virtually blankets
the lower hillsides of the Sheenjek Valley, turning cerise, and the air is
saturated with the fragrance of its delicate blossoms. To one who has
seen the south slopes of the Brooks Range in July, the sight and smell
of the rhododendron are never forgotten.

The slopes above these knolls are drier. But they too are green with
a nap of sedges, low shrubs, and lichens. White heather is everywhere.
Anemones grow here in white patches. Yellow cinquefoil nod grace-
fully in the wind. A purple locoweed is found here, and occasionally
a yellow saxifrage. The low evergreen shrub—kinnikinnick—hugs the
ground. So does a dwarf, rose-pink phlox. The fairy forget-me-not,
almost destitute of stems, shows cerulean blue. Camass lilies grow in
clumps.

All life on these slopes is prostrate. I came across prostrate willow
and birch that were using the south face of upturned rocks as a trellis
where they got added heat from the sun. I stopped to examine their
roots and found them running at length horizontally under the surface to avoid the permafrost. In a ravine fed by springs or on a low
spot where drainage is poor, meadow conditions exist even high in
the Brooks Range. Then the mosses and lichens are on brilliant display. Shooting stars brighten wet spots. Purple monkshood and purple
gentians grow against rich green banks. Here, too, are dainty alpine
buttercups and the familiar Jacob's ladder, two feet higher and showing
dark-blue flowers.

The higher one goes, the scarcer the vegetation. When the talus
slopes are reached, the lichens are the only plants that flourish; they
spot the rocks red and black and cover the ground in white or yellow
patches. An occasional prostrate willow has taken hold in the rocks.
Mats of the rosaceae cling stubbornly to thin soil, kept company by the
dwarf evergreen cassiope that John Muir loved so much.

One day, while hiking the ridge to the east of camp, I had left the last fingers of white spruce and came to an open, exposed promontory. I heard a deep-throated roar underground. Some great subterranean creek was rushing through the porous limestone that forms these mountains. The wind blew a gale. It was cold and piercing and brought squalls of rain. This was only the third of August, but fall had arrived. Not many days distant Keith Harringer from Fort Yukon would drop through low clouds in his Cessna plane to take us out.

Today the two short-billed gulls with their grayish youngster had taken off, heading for the south. Their departure made the camp seem lonely. Now that I was high above Last Lake, the feeling of loneliness and isolation mounted. As I turned to view the valley at my feet, it seemed that I was remote from our civilization, looking down on this earth from an aperture in the sky. There was not a movement in the vast expanse below me. Suddenly a lone caribou came out of a stand of spruce and willow, moving hurriedly toward a pass that led eastward and nibbling at low shrubs as it went. Far below on the flats, where the river runs, a moose and a calf browsed peacefully. Below the caribou but still high above camp a wolf loped leisurely along. He, too, was headed for the pass. There are black wolves in these mountains, but this was a gray one. It was a magnificent specimen. I had seen wolves before both in this country and in Afghanistan and Persia. Wherever they roam they are considered dangerous. They are fast being removed from our national scene. The Brooks Range is probably their last refuge. But even here they are hunted, a $50 bounty being on them. Why should this be? Why should man be committed to destroy this magnificent animal? These were my thoughts as I watched the great, gray wolf lope gracefully across the slopes below me.

We have some things to learn from the wolf. When wolves circle each other, threatening and growling, the less aggressive one often turns his cheek. This is not a signal to the other one to move in for the kill. The wolf who turns his cheek asks for a truce, and though the snarling continues, the truce is always granted. Turning the other cheek, the wolf teaches us, is not abject surrender but an honorable way to prevent a fight and save the species. As Lorenz wrote in *King*

Solomon's Ring, "A wolf has enlightened me: not so that your enemy may strike you again do you turn the other cheek toward him, but to make him unable to do it."

The wolf is a predator. Olaus Murie studied wolf scats collected in the Sheenjek and discovered that of forty-one samples there were thirty-eight that contained caribou. We found several kills around Last Lake. But how many wolves they fed we did not know. How many other predators, such as the red fox and the lynx, are maintained on caribou carrion left by wolves is also not known. But we have reason to think that the wolf is important to their survival.

The wolf, though fast and powerful, cannot outrun a healthy caribou. Apart from those he catches by surprise, he is dependent on cripples and on calves. Sheep also can elude him; and moose usually stand him off. The wolf does not decimate herds; he merely helps control their size, and in that way acts as a curb on the destructive overuse of the national range.

It may be necessary to control the wolf in the environment of ranges where cattle roam. But here in the Sheenjek the wolf is as much a part of the environment as the arctic ground squirrel, the ptarmigan, and the short-billed gulls. This is—and must forever remain—a roadless, primitive area where all food chains are unbroken, where the ancient ecological balance provided by nature is maintained. The wolf helps in that regard. He has, moreover, a charm that is wild and exciting. In this, our last great sanctuary, there should be a place for him. His very being puts life in new dimensions. The sight of a wolf loping across a hillside is as moving as a symphony.

The vast, open spaces of the arctic are special risks to grizzlies, moose, caribou, and wolves. Men with field glasses and high-powered rifles, hunting from planes, can well-nigh wipe them out. In this land of tundra, big game has few places to hide. That is another reason why this last American living wilderness must remain sacrosanct. This is the place for man turned scientist and explorer, poet and artist. Here he can experience a new reverence for life that is outside his own and yet a vital and joyous part of it.

ALEX HARRIS

The Last
and First
Eskimos

Alex Harris was born in 1949 in
Atlanta, Georgia, and attended Yale
University. He is a photographer,
editor, professor, and director of the
Center for Documentary Photography at Duke University. Harris has
received awards from the Guggenheim, Rockefeller, and Lyndhurst
foundations. His photographs are in
the permanent collection of numerous
museums including the Museum of
Modern Art. Between 1973 and 1978,
he made six trips to Alaska to live
and photograph in Eskimo villages.
He worked initially in the Kobuk River
region and later in the tiny villages
that dot the southern Bering Sea coast
of the state. His photographic books
include *The Old Ones* and *The Last and
First Eskimos*, both with Dr. Robert
Coles.

Tununak, July 1977

John Angaiak, Tununak, April 1976

Caribou Hunting Near Ambler,
October 1973

Louise Kanrilack, Tununak, April 1976

Nina Manegak, Newtok, April 1976

Tununak, April 1975

Schoolhouse Fire, Selawik, April 1974

Simeon Fairbanks Jr. and
Charlie Tommy, Newtok, May 1976

Newtok, July 1977

Friends Church, Selawik, April 1974

Catholic Deacons, Tununak, April 1976

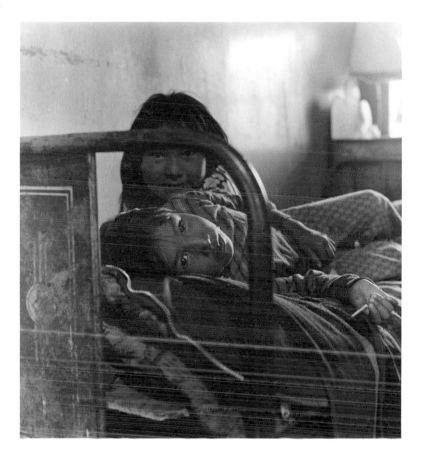

Shungnak, October 1973

Charlie Tommy, Newtok, May 1976

Graveyard, Selawik, April 1974

ROBERT MARSHALL

Toward
Doonerak

Robert Marshall was born in 1901
in New York City and attended the
New York State College of Forestry,
Harvard University, and the Johns
Hopkins Laboratory of Plant Physi-
ology. In 1924 he joined the U S
Forest Service and, until his death in
1939, served as Director of Forestry
of the Office of Indian Affairs and as
Chief of the Division of Recreation
and Lands. Mr. Marshall is the author
of *The People's Forests*, *Arctic Village*, and *Alaska Wilderness* as well
as some ninety-six shorter writings
dealing with wilderness theory and
preservation.

For seven years I had been longing to return to the arctic Koyukuk. I had been thinking of the most glorious year of my life which I spent up there. I had been recalling thousands of square miles of wilderness scenery, large creeks and even rivers unvisited by man, deep canyons and hanging valleys glimpsed from a distance but never explored, great mountains which no human being has ever ascended. But most of all I had been thinking about Mount Doonerak.

Mount Doonerak is probably the highest peak in arctic America.[1] It is the highest peak in the Brooks or Endicott or Arctic Range,[2] as it is variously called, which extends from the Canadian boundary nearly to Kotzebue Sound and divides the Yukon watershed to the south from the Arctic Ocean drainage on the North. The Brooks Range is one of the six major mountain systems in United States territory, but whereas the highest peaks in the Appalachian, Rocky, Sierra, Cascade, and Alaska mountain ranges have long since been climbed, no one is known to have ever been even part way up Mount Doonerak. Since I had discovered the mountain, had made the first map of it, and had named it during my trips in 1929 and 1930–31, I wanted to complete the job and also make the first ascent.

In addition, I was anxious to explore the uncharted and unknown sources of the Anaktuvuk River, which, by way of the Colville River, empties into the Arctic Ocean.

During the interval since my last trip to Alaska, my book, *Arctic Village* had been published. It stirred up a good deal of friendly interest in the Outside. However, because the study of this remarkable Koyukuk community was based primarily on my personal acquaintance with its inhabitants, it was very frank. Some people therefore questioned how it had been received on the Inside, even though all letters from there since the publication of the book had been cordial.

On my way back to Alaska in August, 1938, newspaper reporters from Ketchikan to Fairbanks had been asking me whether I was not afraid of being lynched when I returned to the people of *Arctic Village*. When the plane took off from Fairbanks and headed for the Koyukuk I felt mild qualms about my impending reception in Wiseman. These qualms may have been heightened by the company of three friends from the Outside, one of whom was Ernest Gruening, governor of Alaska.

They decided to take advantage of the plane bearing me and Ernie Johnson (who had been paying a brief visit to Fairbanks) to make a fleeting trip to the Koyukuk. A hostile reception would have been bad enough, but doubly so with these friends looking on.

After an uneventful flight to the Yukon—looking as muddy as the Colorado from above—and across the sources of the Tozitna, Melozitna, and Kanuti rivers, we landed on a gravel bar at Alatna. Here Ernie Johnson got out to bring the boat we were going to use up the Koyukuk to Wiseman. After a couple of hours visiting with friends at Alatna, we hopped off again for the fifty-minute flight to Wiseman.

When we landed on the Wiseman field on August 4, every Eskimo and almost every white person in town was there. Oh boy, was it great to be back! I didn't realize how much I had been missing these people until I started pumping their arms and hearing their greetings, their laughter, and their good-natured banter. "Where's your oomik (whiskers)?" "What's the matter, don't they feed you Outside, you're looking poor." "You going to write 'nother book about us?" More laughter. More pumping. Piggy-back rides to children, born since I left, who knew me already as Oomik. Lots of hurried jokes and wisecracks.

Four days later Ernie arrived in Wiseman. The following morning it was raining hard so we decided to wait another day for the water on the Middle Fork to rise and make our boating easier. As a result, I spent more than five uneventful but delightful days around Wiseman.

As a matter of fact the first impression was not delightful, for I realized nostalgically that the Wiseman of 1931 had changed. There had been more of a shift from the true frontier in the past seven years, than in the previous thirty years. Only ten airplanes had arrived in Wiseman during the thirteen months I was there in 1930–31. Now there were two or three a week. Then, only one tourist visited the Koyukuk in thirteen months. In 1937, one hundred and fifty did, stopping for just a few hours, and then going back. As a result, Wiseman was no longer the isolated community, uniquely beyond the end of the world.

Another innovation which made Wiseman part of the world was the radio. In 1931 there was only the wireless station with code reception. Now there were six radios. The first automobile had come to the

Koyukuk just before I left in 1931. Now it hauled men and supplies all summer to the two chief mining centers, six miles out on Nolan Creek and Hammond River. The rattling around the dirt streets of town never stopped now.

But the greatest change of all was the people. In 1931 sixty-two of the seventy-seven whites in the entire upper Koyukuk had come to the north country by 1911. Civilization on the Koyukuk was overwhelmingly influenced by the distinctive northern mores developed in the romantic stampedes to the Klondike, Nome, and Fairbanks. By August, 1938, twenty-eight of these seventy-seven people had left the country or died and had been replaced by forty-two newcomers to the Koyukuk of whom only five had come to the north in early days. As a result, the population of the Koyukuk, instead of having more than 80 per cent old-timers, now had half of its white people relatively recent arrivals who lacked much of the tradition of the old gold rush. Wiseman, by 1938, was no longer dominated by the pioneers of 1898.

To me it was especially saddening to find that many of those pioneers who had been among my most splendid companions seven years before, had died. When you live right along in a given environment, the deaths of friends are usually spaced enough in time to get you adjusted to them. When I returned to Wiseman, however, it was suddenly necessary to get adjusted to the deaths of sixteen white people and six Eskimos who in my mind had become an undying part of an unforgettable year.

After the first day I overcame this feeling of sadness in the throb of new life. There were eleven Eskimo children between the ages of three and seven, all born since I left, who were constantly shouting: "Give me piggy-back ride!" For all the times I obliged in the five days in Wiseman, I should have been in excellent shape for carrying 50-pound packs. There were two dances at which three little Eskimo girls aged eleven to thirteen, were among the best dancers. They apparently had a mental hangover from seven years ago, because in between dances they made me give them piggy-back rides around the hall.

One enjoyable afternoon I spent playing with the older Eskimo boys between eight and fourteen. We played a game of theirs in which you are supposed to shoot the other side by yelling "bang" and calling the name of the person you see before he does likewise to you. We had running and jumping races, and played ball with the boys' hats. They talked about school and hunting experiences. We went swimming in a frigid slough where I took colored movies of the boys who had learned to swim by the trial and error method; and then one boy grabbed the camera when I was in the water and shot pictures of me naked to the delight of the other boys.

There had been no unpleasant remarks about *Arctic Village*, in spite of the described "improprieties" in terms of Outside custom. One of the settlers, 78-year-old Verne Watts, admitted he was sore when he was quoted in his description of one girl as "so thin that a couple of macaroni sticks would make a pair of drawers for her." Another, strong-tempered Jack White, on the other hand, was delighted to find his profanity quoted and the description of his tearing off the roof of his house to evict a tenant. George Eaton, now seventy-seven, said seriously to me: "Of course, Bob, when I was saying how I'd slept with more women than any man in Alaska, I didn't expect you to put it in a book, but I'm a-telling you, it's true." Annie Kayak, a pretty young woman with two small children who came from the arctic tundra to Wiseman with her husband, Itachluk, in 1930, and whose rupture with him I had described in detail, invited me for an immense bowl of what she remembered was my favorite fruit, blueberries, and told me how much she liked the book and her eighteen-dollar share of the royalties. There were many pleasantries. One Eskimo girl, meeting me on the street one morning, laughingly quoted from the book: "If you meet an Eskimo girl in the morning she may look a little bit frowsy, but in the evening her attire, simple though it is, will be immaculate." Such a reception to a prodigal son would only be possible with remarkably honest people who do not pretend to be what they are not and therefore do not resent the truth about themselves.

Up the North Fork by Boat

In the early morning of August 10, 1938, Ernie Johnson, Jesse Allen, Kenneth Harvey, and I shoved our boat into the current of the Middle Fork for the start of twenty-nine days of exploration beyond the paths of man. We were headed for Mount Doonerak and for the sources of the Anaktuvuk.

Our rented boat was an old tub. It was too heavy for our purpose, and we soon started referring to it as "the raft," but it was the only boat available. It was 30 feet long, measured 63 inches across at the gunwale, and weighed 1,200 pounds. We had a load of 1,280 pounds dead weight, 700 pounds of us, and two large dogs.

Our journey—downstream in the Middle Fork until we reached the North Fork—was aided most of the way by a motor, although we drifted for many miles where the water was too shallow. The river was not a wilderness. Power boats had been running up and down it since 1914.

We reached the mouth of the North Fork at four in the afternoon. Here the real trip began. For six and a half days with an average of eleven and a half hours of travel per day we fought our way hundred-eighty miles up winding North Fork. We never could see more than a couple of miles ahead at a time, and usually not more than half a mile before the next bend. On the lower, relatively much traveled, river we used the motor half the time, on the upper quarter of the route not at all. By "much traveled" I mean that, in days gone by, several hundred people had been up as far as Jack Delay Pass (about halfway to the place we were going by boat); this year, it seemed, not a human being had been on the North Fork.

We traveled until after ten the first evening to make about ten miles. We were passing through a great flat, but the clouds were so low that we couldn't see much besides mud banks with spruce, cottonwood, and willow growing. It took us only a few minutes to set our 6 by 7 foot tent and have a fire going; we cooked a hasty supper and retired in the twilight of midnight.

When we awoke six hours later, the river had risen fifteen inches and had become a boiling soup of mud. Large masses of froth and sticks of wild-looking driftwood bobbed along from the sources of the North Fork. As we continued up the river we could only see occasional low mountains through the rain and fog. We watched with interest the water birds—ducks, geese, and two loons. With even greater interest we watched a piece of "driftwood" floating down the river, which suddenly turned into a yearling black bear. Harvey jumped out of the boat and waited until his feet touched bottom. Then he blazed away with his Springfield while I did likewise with my movie camera. Then we hauled the bear ashore, dressed it, and saved the skin. It provided us and the dogs with fresh meat for four days.

On the third morning, going became hard for the first time. Just below the mouth of Glacier River we battled Squaw Rapids; named after an Indian woman who drowned in its fury more than fifty years ago, before the first white men penetrated to the Koyukuk. We hauled the boat by brute force for about three miles against the pressure of the tumbling river. For at least half the way from here up we had to "line" the boat in this way. Ernie and Harvey would grab hold of the boat, one on either end, and practically lift it over the rocks where the river was very shallow. Where it was too deep to stand against the fierce current Ernie and Harvey got in the boat and pushed with poles, while Jesse and I unwound a 150-foot rope in front of the boat and then tugged with all the power we had, walking along the edge of the river or sometimes wading with the water almost to the top of our hip boots. The greatest difficulty was keeping this tow line from getting tangled with brush and snags along the shore and with trees lying in the river where they had been carried by the flood. At places the current was so powerful that for a minute or more we could not gain an inch. We would finally get the boat over the blockade and it would go a little easier for a short distance until the river halted us again. Then it would be another tug of war between two equally balanced sides. Sometimes Ernie and Harvey gave the boat a little twist and it slipped between two rocks. Sometimes the boat got crosswise with the current and had to be straightened out. Sometimes there was no solution but pull, pull, pull, and lift, lift, lift, to the limit of endurance.

Once beyond the rapids, we were at the mouth of Glacier River, first of the four main tributaries of the North Fork. Beyond here we had smooth cruising—after having spent seven hours to cover six and a half miles to Glacier River, we covered the next thirteen miles in a mere four hours.

We made camp shortly after nine at the mouth of Ipnek Creek on the west side of the river. This had been an important focal point in the Wild River stampede of 1913–1915. It was the point where the men coming over Jack Delay Pass from Wiseman crossed the North Fork and headed over a low pass into the Wild River drainage. Many decaying cabins and tent frames remained from that rush of a quarter of a century before.

On the next day smooth traveling continued. We made twenty-five miles, our biggest day of the up-river journey. Late in the afternoon we passed the mouth of Tinayguk River, the second of the main North Fork tributaries. A mile beyond, over some still riffles, was Ernie's cabin which had been his headquarters for hunting, trapping, and prospecting during most of the period between 1919 and 1931 when he was living on this lonely river. When I was there in the deep snows during the winter of 1931 the cabin was five hundred feet back from the river and out of sight, but since then a wide strip of spruce and cottonwoods had been torn out by the floods and the cabin was within plain view. We camped here and took a look at the cabin. Apparently no human being had been here since Ernie and I hitched up our dogs and drove away on March 19, 1931, but grizzlies had smashed the cabin door and torn the inside to pieces. There were old dishes scattered hither and yon and one torn 1930 copy each of the *Literary Digest* and the *Nation*. Thumbing in them I read about the growing depression.

The next morning we passed the mouth of Clear River, third of the major North Fork tributaries. It did not rain hard, but the sky was overcast most of the day. The morning was easy going, the afternoon a constant battle against the furious current and the shallow bars on either side of Cladonia Creek. Aside from this struggle, the outstanding impression of the day was the sight of a seven-mile stretch along the west side of the river, which had been burned over the previous summer, probably as the result of lightning. The destruction of the spruce and birch timber was almost complete, but even more disastrous was the destruction of moss and lichen which had already resulted in the thawing out of the ground and the opening of deep erosion gullies in the loose gravel soil.

It did not rain on the next day, but the high peaks were covered with fog until late in the afternoon. We saw four moose along the river—first a cow and a calf, then a young bull, finally a lone calf so tame he started to follow Harvey who was pulling the boat. Harvey's dog wandered off after one of the moose, and it took us nearly an hour to find him again. The river was spread out over a wide gravel flat and at places split into a dozen different channels. We had to reconnoiter ahead to keep from going up a channel from which we could not emerge. We pulled, tugged, and lifted the boat, stumbling in the rushing water all day long. All of us went in over the tops of our hip boots and got soaked. It took us nearly twelve hours to cover twelve miles upstream.

During most of the day the Gates of the Arctic towered directly to the north, as we approached that monumental entrance to the land of Mount Doonerak, our goal. When we passed through between the jagged crest of Frigid Crags towering 4,000 feet up from the valley floor to the west and Boreal Mountain rising precipitously for 6,000 feet to the east, with the two mountains only two miles apart, it seemed as if we were leaving the world of man behind and were pioneering in a trackless wilderness. This was not far from being true. We calculated that probably no more than twelve white men had penetrated the six hundred square miles of the magnificent Koyukuk country north of the Gates of the Arctic.

Next morning the wind had shifted, and it began to rain again. We pulled and tugged our way for eight and a half more hours to cover seven miles to a place where the river swung in against a low spruce bank, two miles below Ernie Creek, the fourth major North Fork tributary. It was not ideally what we wanted, because it was not high enough above the water, but it was the best patch of timber accessible from the river which we had seen all day, and the river was getting too steep and shallow to pull a ton any farther. So here, on a peninsula between the North Fork and a slough (that extended far back from the river and seemed to lose itself in a morass), hundred-eighty miles by the turns of the river above its mouth and eighty-two miles overland from the closest neighbors on Nolan Creek, we decided to make our base camp for half a month of exploration.

The Sources of the Anaktuvuk

The first task after reaching base camp was to build a cache where our extra food, bedding, and photographic equipment would be safe from the wild animals while we were away from camp for periods of a day to a week. Ernie was the architect, and he and Harvey supplied the skilled labor. Jesse did the semiskilled work while I contributed the unskilled labor. We worked on the cache for two full days, but in a pleasant, leisurely manner.

The cache consisted of a miniature spruce log cabin, built nine feet up in the air where it rested on four substantial posts. It was 5½ by 6½ feet on the outside and 3½ feet high at the front end, with a six-inch pitch to the roof. This consisted of split logs hewn into troughs to carry off the water; the cracks between them were capped with other logs having their trough on the under side. Everything which went to make the cache, except for two pounds of nails, was taken directly from the forest surrounding us.

The cache was put up on poles to keep the grizzly bear, which cannot climb, from reaching it and to exclude likewise other non-arboreal animals. The logs were fitted tightly and varied in size from six to ten inches at the small end which prevented the black bear and wolverine and the less powerful lynx, marten, weasel, squirrel, porcupine, mouse, raven, and camp robber from getting in, even if they did climb up. Without the protection of this cache much important equipment would almost certainly have been destroyed during our operation from this base.

The day after the cache was finished the weather gave promise of clearing. We crossed the North Fork in our boat and then walked to Shushalluk Creek, coming from the west two miles above, for fish and exploration. On the way we climbed an open hill, colored with the green of moss, sedge, and Labrador tea, the bright cream color of the reindeer moss, the purple leaves of the blueberries, the scarlet leaves of the Angowuk, and the brilliant red cranberries. The cranberries and blueberries were so profuse it took us a long time to reach the top of the hill.

Once there we waited while the clouds lifted off the mountains until at last we saw the goal of our expedition, the summit of Mount Doonerak. What a summit it was! It jutted so pointedly into the air that it seemed quite impossible to ascend. The northwest face, which to our vague recollection from eight years before was the one to try first, now appeared absolutely impossible. Impossible, too, was the west side, while the north face seemed to have a 2,000-foot sheer drop. We knew that the east side, which we couldn't see, was hopeless. The only chances seemed to be (1) a ridge leading up from the northwest which we could only partly see, but which we thought we remembered might be possible; and (2) the south side rising from Pyramid Creek, which apparently had never been visited. An exploration of this creek and a reconnaissance of the mountain from this side seemed the obvious activity for the morrow.

We descended from the hill to Shushalluk Creek where we split forces. Jesse and Ernie went to fish its racing waters, swollen by the days of rain. Harvey and I set out for the upper creek to map and explore it. The lower part of the stream was bounded by crumbling slate mountains, 3,000 feet high, which were gradually sliding their way into the creek. The upper part was confined by peaks of black igneous rock and already covered with early snow. The sky, to our great disappointment, had meanwhile become overcast again.

Harvey and I returned to camp at nine o'clock and Ernie and Jesse came along a short time later. The high water had practically ruined the fishing, and it had taken them four hours to catch twenty-two grayling —an almost unheard-of low in this virtually unfished country; but the fish dinner which followed was nonetheless delicious.

It was still overcast next morning, but we thought we might as well see what we could see. Harvey decided to hunt for sheep, Ernie, Jesse, and I to explore Pyramid Creek. Before leaving I examined some spruce trees about a mile beyond camp, where I found the largest tree I had yet seen north of the Arctic Circle, a spruce twenty-one inches in diameter at breast height.

The three of us stumbled along for four miles among the soft moss and clumps of sedges, until we reached Pyramid Creek. After lunch, Jesse left us to fish in the stream while Ernie and I started up the unvisited north branch.

Almost immediately we were in a deep chasm where the bottom of the valley had narrowed into a slot only six feet wide at places between the gray rock walls. There was so much water shooting through this constricted space that we had to find toeholds on the face of the cliffs. After a mile of this going the chasm widened into a valley beyond the timber zone, with rock-faced mountains on either side disappearing into the clouds, 4,000 feet above us. The few mountains whose tops we could see were black and jagged. Every mile or less, side streams came down over the rocks in great white leaps, some of the higher waterfalls seemingly pouring down from the clouds.

About four miles above the falls we were in the broad upper valley of Pyramid Creek. The top of Doonerak, directly to the north, was hidden in the clouds, but from what we could see of its lower two-thirds and from what we had seen the day before of its very crest, this seemed the most likely side on which to make our first attempt. But it had to clear!

Instead it began to rain again about the time we reached camp. This was the tenth day of rain out of eleven on this trip, and it began to be almost depressing even though Harvey had returned with a sheep and Jesse with a fine catch of grayling to brighten our dehydrated diet. It rained steadily all night and looked worse than ever when we arose late the next morning. We ate sheep meat, chatted, and read all day, and went to bed early.

Next morning at four we were awakened by Ernie who had stepped out of the tent and was saying: "Christ, boys, we've got to roll out! The river's coming into camp."

The rains of the past days had raised the river three feet during the night and a side slough from it was pouring into the fireplace. We moved everything to the two-foot higher ground near the cache. It was the highest ground anywhere around. The move proved unnecessary, however, because the river soon started to drop.

We cooked an early breakfast of sheep steak and coffee and then spent a long day in camp, alternately hoping it would clear when the sky became half blue, and fearing it would never stop raining when it became all covered with black, gloomy clouds.

When it was completely overcast again the next morning we decided we had better forget Doonerak for a while if we did not want to spend our whole trip just waiting. So we packed up bedding, dishes, extra socks, photographic equipment, and food for five days and decided to attend to the second objective of our expedition—the exploration of the never visited sources of the Anaktuvuk River.

The Anaktuvuk is one of the largest Alaskan rivers flowing into the Arctic Ocean. It does not flow directly into the ocean, however, but joins the Colville River first. The independent drainage basin of the Anaktuvuk embraces several thousand square miles and there was no record of anyone ever having been all the way to its head.

Ernie and I had probably come closer to doing so than anyone else. He had been over Ernie Pass (at the head of Ernie Creek) three different times and had descended on the Anaktuvuk side, where he had passed the main fork of the Anaktuvuk heading eastward. I had looked down into it from both Limestack Mountain and Al's Mountain—the former to the north and the latter to the south of Grizzly Creek—and had seen its headwaters disappearing eastward into limestone mountains. Now we were going to find where it really headed.

Two weeks of almost continuous rain had swollen the rivers so much that we were sure we could not ford Ernie Creek, which we had to cross two and a half miles above camp. Therefore we dragged the boat up the river and got across with its aid after two hours of hard tugging. We then tied the boat securely in a back eddy, changed from water to land travel, shouldered 30- to 40-pound packs apiece, packed 20 to 30 pounds on each of the dogs, and started stumbling our way northward through Ernie Creek valley over sedge tussocks, soggy, ankle-deep moss, and bog holes. We were all soft at back packing, so even with such light loads the going was hard. A steady drizzle all day didn't make it more pleasant. A stop for lunch at last timber was the only break in six and a half hours. We camped for the night among willows under the great black Gibraltar-like precipice at the south entrance to the Valley of Precipices which had so impressed Al Retzlaf and me on our trips up the North Fork in 1929 and 1930. Ernie had told me that in the winter following the second of these journeys, he had been calling this peak Blackface Mountain. Therefore, I used this name on my 1932 map.

While we pitched camp, we looked up at the great black rock face directly above us, but we could not see the top, because the mountain disappeared in the fog some 2,000 feet above the valley. It rained nearly all night, but our tent shed the water perfectly.

Next morning, unexpectedly, it was clearing. We could see the top of Blackface jutting almost straight into the air for 3,000 feet. On its side were many narrow ledges green with arctic vegetation, and on several of these, overhanging appalling plunges, we saw small bands of sheep moving along the cliffs.

This morning traveling was easy along the gravel of Ernie Creek up the five-mile stretch of the Valley of Precipices. I had been through this glacial gorge four times before, but its dark immensity was as awe-inspiring as ever. Underneath these great bounding walls you dwarfed into nothing.

At the upper end of this great valley Ernie Creek forks into three branches. The right-hand branch is Grizzly Creek, which Al Retzlaf and I first followed to its barren source a dozen miles to the east in September, 1930; the left-hand branch is Kenunga Creek which I first explored during the same week; and the center and smallest one is Ernie Creek itself which heads from a low pass that crosses the Arctic Divide.

Our plan was to follow the center branch, but before that I had a little piece of business up Grizzly Creek. Here was the location of my 1930 experiment of sowing spruce seeds on two adjacent plots, twelve miles north of the last timber.

Well, the seeds had not developed. My experiment was a complete, dismal failure on both plots. There was not even the sign of a dead seedling—just two patches of bare ground, marked with willow stakes set in rock. Whether the failure was due to unfertility of the seeds or faulty sowing technique or an unusually rainy autumn after sowing, which rotted them, or just unfavorable climate according to the usual theory I could not tell.

But I could not feel disappointed long, as the clouds gradually disappeared from the mountains and the great peaks of the Arctic Divide jutted all around us into the sunlight. Limestack really was a great stack of brightly shining gray lime. Alapah (Eskimo for "it is cold") certainly did look cold with its whole table-top summit covered with fresh snow.

As we climbed higher toward the head of Ernie Creek, the Valley of Precipices, now behind us, became a deeper slit in the tumbled crust of the earth. When we finally reached the height of land between the Pacific and Arctic watersheds we could see the summit of the king of all arctic mountains, old Doonerak himself. He looked more unscalable than ever from the north, with several hundred feet of precipitous summit covered with snow.

It was a superlative sight, but our greatest interest for the moment lay to the north and east where the Anaktuvuk headed. Here was a world of gray limestone precipices, among the unknown recesses of which many stream valleys vanished through deep canyons. We were not sure which of them contained our goal.

We pushed northward across the broad, low gap in the Arctic Divide which is Ernie Pass and dropped into the first valley which we had thought from the top might be the main Anaktuvuk River. It was a large side creek, emerging from a canyon world exclusively made of gray limestone, with a thousand-foot sheer precipice of gray lime rising across it—so we called it Graylime Creek. It was enticing, but we pushed on across a high ridge to the place where all of us except Jesse Allen thought the main Anaktuvuk lay, in the next valley. He was right —the creek proved to be nothing but a false alarm—so we called it Fake Creek, and climbed over another ridge.

We dropped down the easy slope on its north side to what later proved to be the real Anaktuvuk. Our immediate problem was to find enough willows for camp. We followed down the river for nearly a mile to a side creek joining from the north before we found a clump of willow brush. The biggest stems were only five feet tall and two inches through at the base. Farther down the river toward the coast the willows got much bigger, but this was the highest upstream that willows grew large enough to camp in. The nearest spruce and cottonwood were across the divide, twenty-five miles to the south.

By picking up every dry stick we could find for a quarter of a mile around, and burning some green willow when the fire was going, we managed to find enough fuel for six meals. Tent poles were harder to provide. At first we thought we would not bother about setting the tent, but then the weather began to look threatening again just before bedtime. So we slung the back end from a four-foot limestone wall, and Ernie ingeniously rigged up a fairly solid five-foot pole for the front end by overlapping and lashing together the tops of three willows. For mattresses we rolled up large mats of arctic moss.

It was lucky we took this precaution, because when we rose next morning a cold fog lay low on all mountains and light rain was falling. It was not an auspicious day to set out to find the source from where the mighty Anaktuvuk started its journey to the ocean. However, fuel was so scarce that we could not afford to hang over a day, and besides the most futile of all things seemed to be to wait for a change in the weather.

Immediately upstream from camp was a broad main valley in the center of which the Anaktuvuk flowed in a little chasm, a few feet wide and 30 to 40 feet high, where the stream was cutting through the limestone bedrock. Sometimes the water foamed over rapids, sometimes it tumbled over 20-foot ledges, and sometimes it lay in clear, deep pools where we could see a few arctic trout. After a mile this chasm ended, and the main valley turned sharply to the left.

Then we suddenly found ourselves entering a glacial valley canyon. The fog lifted just enough to show us great limestone precipices on either side of us and perhaps half or three-quarters of a mile apart. We couldn't tell how high they were, because they were still rising sheer where they disappeared in the fog, but following in our imagination the thousand or two thousand feet of straight gray limestone which we did see, they seemed to rise infinitely into a world beyond the world. Ahead of us, on the floor of the valley on this twenty-fifth day of August, was a great, unmelted field of last winter's snow. We walked six hundred yards across it, and estimated that it was nine feet deep at its deepest point.

Above the snowfield the valley bent to the left again. It was still entirely bounded by limestone cliffs rising endlessly into the clouds. Sometimes these cliffs were broken by deep gorges where small side streams also tumbled out of the mist. One such stream coming in from the left, poured down at least 1,200 feet in one waterfall after another, each of them fifty to a hundred feet high.

Just above these cascades, the main river forked. One-third of the water came churning out of a V-shaped trough which bent nearly ninety degrees to the right The other two-thirds came from a stream bending almost as sharply to the left, where it raced down a half-mile straightaway. Above this straightaway it stood on end.

This is literally true. It tumbled over a waterfall, 220 feet high by barometer reading. Above the waterfall we could not even guess what might lie. From where we stood, below, we did not see a sign of river or valley—just a few rocks and fog.

We climbed up by the side of the fall and found above it a series of igneous terraces, black and pock-marked. The creek was hidden among them. We did not try to follow it, but climbed from one bench to another until we found ourselves at the foot of a broad, hanging basin. The bottom was flat enough for agriculture, but it seemed like anything but agricultural land when it began to snow steadily as we started across. It snowed for more than an hour, though the sun shone dimly most of the time. With snow and faint sunlight, this lofty barren valley with its huge rocks which had tumbled from the surrounding mountains and with its great limestone precipices still rising infinitely into the clouds, seemed an unreal world, unvisited by human beings since the dawn of time.

Not unvisited by animals, however. We saw the tracks of sheep, caribou, grizzlies, and wolves, and several old, rotten horns of caribou and sheep. But the only living things we actually saw were one ground squirrel and one water ouzel.

At the head of this basin a large creek, with almost as much water as the main river, dropped in from the right. Like the main river lower down, it also seemed to be standing on end, so we called it Standonend Creek. Above a thousand feet of cascades there seemed to be a high, hanging valley, just below the clouds.

Our main valley again turned sharply to the left. We were now going in exactly the opposite direction from that which we took when we left camp. The upper river was making a complete circle. Beyond this next bend was a third basin, paved by deep and coarse glacial rock, with hardly any vegetation. Around us on every side towered great limestone mountain walls, their tops yet hidden in the fog. Suddenly, at the head of the valley, we realized that what we had thought was a cloud against the mountain was in reality a high glacier.

We followed up the broad basin and at the head turned some more to the left into a narrow valley bounded by rockslides dropping from the limestone walls. Half a mile up the valley ended in a wall of loose rock, 200 feet high, which had been dropped by the receding glacier. We climbed around it and found ourselves at the edge of the ice sheet. Above us was a wall of stratified ice, dirty with gravel and rough-edged rock, 50 feet high and overhanging. It was indeed the edge of the glacier, a remnant of the ice age. The river had circled around so much that the ice sheet was facing northward down the valley. Behind it and to either side, on south, east, and west, the sun was shaded out for most of the year by the lofty, closely surrounding mountains. This was the second true glacier I had seen in the Brooks Range—the other had been the one discovered by Philip Smith near the Arrigetch peaks west of the Alatna, in 1911.

We climbed on top of the glacier and stopped for an hour at the center where a pile of rock had fallen from the mountain above. It seemed to be the end of the earth or the heart of another earth as we perched on top of this remnant of a long-vanished age. Everything we looked upon was unknown to human gaze. The nearest humans were a hundred and twenty-five miles away, and the civilization of which they constituted the very fringe—a civilization remote from nature, artificial, dominated by the exploitation of man by man—seemed unreal, unbelievable. Our present situation seemed also unreal, but that was the unreality of a freshness beyond experience. It was the unreality of a remoteness which made it seem as if we had landed miraculously on another planet which throughout all passage of time had been without life. There was also the unreality of countless needle pinnacles, jutting around us through the fog, alternately appearing and disappearing as the atmosphere thinned and thickened.

It was after three when we left the glacier and started back down the valley. The ceiling had raised and we could now see the summits of most of the countless snow-covered limestone mountains surrounding us. The lower we dropped, the more enormously they towered above us. Their immense precipice faces were pitted with small lime-stone caves and pillars. Their gray and black strata were sometimes horizontal, sometimes tilted, occasionally standing on end—usually in straight lines but at several places bent into rainbow curves. Every one of the mountains had innumerable precipices, a thousand, two thousand, even three thousand feet high. It did not really matter—there were no measures in this world and after seeing the superlative so long, space began to lose its significance.

We descended to the valley below the fall and then followed the right-hand fork which had looked interesting on the way up. It did not flow in a broad valley, but in a narrow slit in the overtowering limestone crags through which the creek dropped in wild leaps. About a mile and a half up, it plunged over a hard, igneous wall, falling two hundred feet in a couple of jumps. Above this wall, tucked in among the mountains, was one of those startling high mountain valleys, so peaceful in contour that it seemed like a New England valley until one glanced up at the mountains above.

But even more startling was a find we made on the return journey. Just below the fall, Ernie who was in the lead called out: "If anyone had told me this, I'd say he was a damn liar!" The cause of his surprise was no spouting geyser or sensational natural bridge, but some lowly moose dung. However, not only was it in country along the backbone of the Arctic Divide where none of us had ever seen moose signs before, but in a gorge so rocky we would not have dreamed that moose could penetrate it.

The five miles from the forks back to camp between the immensity of the surrounding mountains were glorious. We were fresh and going four miles an hour at the end of thirty trailless miles when we got back to our tent at eight. Jesse, who had walked only to the forks in the morning, had a supper of pea soup, lamb stew, boiled dried apples, and coffee when we returned, and it made a delicious ending to a perfect day. Another fine touch was a band of seven sheep grazing on the hillside above camp, unaware that human beings, whom they were undoubtedly seeing for the first time, could be a source of danger.

We went to bed soon after supper, but I couldn't go to sleep for a while. I lay on my back and looked through the door of the tent at the foothills across the valley. I tried to reflect on remoteness and adventure beyond the frontiers, but I could not for long, because it seemed more secure and peaceful here, with three competent and devoted companions, than it did back home in the heart of Washington.

After breakfast the next morning Ernie and I walked far enough downstream to tie in on our maps the upper Anaktuvuk with the main river which Peters and Schrader had mapped in 1901 when they came over Anaktuvuk Pass from the head of the John River. The Anaktuvuk was broader and much tamer here, but a couple of side streams coming in on the right limit poured forth from wild limestone gorges. It would have been a delight to explore them, but food and firewood were both short, and we didn't want to take time either to hunt or move down river to willows for fear of being too long away from Doonerak. So we broke camp after lunch and hiked back to our camp at Pyramid Creek in an uneventful day-and-a-half journey. We walked into the teeth of a fierce rainstorm as we crossed back over the Arctic Divide. Thereafter we could see only the bases of the mountains around us and the valley floor.

We camped again in the willows under Blackface Mountain and slept snugly in our tight tent although it poured all night. When we reached our boat early the next afternoon we found it safe. It took us no more than an hour to fill a bucket with enough cranberries to last us four days, and then we loaded our stuff in the boat, shoved her off, and piled in. Under the power of the eight-mile-an-hour current and the skillful steering of Ernie, who stood in the back and guided the boat with an occasional deft push with his pole, we floated in nineteen minutes the two and a half miles to base camp at the North Fork below Ernie Creek, which it had taken us two hours to ascend.

An Upsetting Experience

The day after we got back it rained without let-up from midnight to midnight. I wrote up my notes and sketched maps from the compass bearings I had taken on the Anaktuvuk jaunt. When we went to bed we knew we might have to move before breakfast, but we preferred to wait and let nature take its course.

Sure enough, it took it. Jesse roused us at five when the rising water was reaching the edge of the tent. We moved everything to the highest ground, at the cache, where apparently no flood waters had been. Here we thought we were safe for the remainder of our stay. We passed this day marooned between the main river to the west and a roaring slough to the east, which kept us from getting anywhere in the high water. It was another day of reading, writing, talking, and loafing—a day whose peacefulness I enjoyed despite the enforced idleness.

The following morning it stopped raining, and when the water was down enough we crossed the slough with difficulty. Jesse and Harvey decided to spend the day in camp, but Ernie and I set out to explore the south fork of Pyramid Creek.

The trip was a repetition of the one taken ten days before to the forks of the creek, but now the autumn colors had deepened. Above the forks was virgin ground. It began to rain again, and the mountaintops were covered with clouds, but we could see the lower end of splendid precipices on either side. Three miles above the main forks was a second fork. The right-hand one led into a jagged canyon among the cloud-capped crags of Boreal Mountain. However, our objective this day was to explore what from the hillside above Shushalluk Creek had appeared to be a low pass into Clear River. We were especially anxious to find one, because none had ever been discovered through that rugged range which for fifty miles separates North Fork and Clear River.

We followed up the smaller left fork, which seemed to head in our direction. After a mile of dark canyon we climbed into a broad bright green basin, with gushing water on every side. It was drizzling persistently as we rose toward the skyline ahead and we were wondering whether we could see anything on the other side. We doped it out that we should connect with a prong of Holmes Creek, which we had named in March, 1931.

When we finally reached the pass, the drizzle abated and we got a fine view down into a deep creek cutting its way among the high mountains on the other side. Because of the several bends we could not quite see as far as the point where we thought it should join Clear River. But we were able to estimate the compass bearing of the lowest straightaway of the creek and to our delight found that it checked to the nearest five degrees with the bearing I had shot from the lower end of Holmes Creek in 1931. My sketching of the main forks of Holmes Creek at that time on the basis of what I saw from the mouth was consistent with what we saw from above now, so we were sure it was Holmes Creek. Sure also we were that this was a feasible pass across one of the most difficult sections of the Brooks Range. My barometer showed the notch where we were standing to be only 3,650 feet high and the going along both Pyramid and Holmes creeks was possible for either summer foot travel or dog sledding.

We descended the 1,900 feet to camp in nine miles of glowing color. I don't know any colors so varied and brilliant as those of the arctic autumn. As a background were the greens—dark green of spruce, and lighter shades of sedge, Labrador tea, *Kalmia*, and *Dryas*. This green was interrupted everywhere over the hillsides, by the rich cream color of the various species of reindeer moss. The tops of the hills were primarily a bright red from the dwarf birch. Lower down a lurid scarlet appeared in many blotches marking rocky places where the roughened leaves of the Angowuk dominated the vegetation. At other spots purple blueberry leaves gave the tint to the coloration. The valley bottoms displayed brightest gold of cottonwood and willow.

The water in Pyramid Creek had risen so much during the day that we had a hard time returning across it. Once on the camp side, we stopped among dense cranberry clumps to pick our fruit supply for the next three days. When we got to the slough next to camp the water was too high to be forded. I had visions for a moment of repeating Ed Marsan's experience many years ago on Nahtuk Creek. He had returned to camp from a hunt to find the water so high that he could not get across. So for three days his partners had to feed him by slinging hot cakes across the creek. Fortunately we were saved from this when Harvey dropped a spruce across the slough and we walked safely and dry back to camp.

Jesse shortly served us a sumptuous supper of pea soup, sheep pot roast, hotcakes, boiled apples, and coffee. We were ready for retiring comfortably to our sleeping bags, but the water in the river to the west and the slough to the east kept rising. Soon it began to trickle into our fireplace, so we moved the fire to higher ground, 30 feet away. We dug drainage ditches with a wooden shovel we had made to dig holes for the cache posts, but the water continued to rise. It was now too dark to move camp without great inconvenience. The tents, on the very highest ground between the river and slough, were still on dry land, so we decided to sleep in shifts. Ernie and I retired at eleven with our boots on. Harvey and Jesse went to bed at one in the morning. Soon water began to trickle under the tent where they were sleeping, but we did not wake them, because they were well off the ground on boughs and it wasn't light enough yet to move camp.

Shortly after three, however, it was light enough and we rolled them out. We dropped downstream about two hundred yards to a place where the ground was a little lower but where the surrounding river and slough dropped even more, so we had two feet to spare, which we felt was ample for any additional flood with the water already so high. We spent most of the remainder of the day catching up on the sleep we had missed the night before, and walking out to the edge of the river to watch the flood.

Next morning the water in the river was higher than ever. It was still raining steadily. We walked up to the point where the slough divided from the river and marveled at the colossal power of a river in flood. It was a wildly heaving, swaying, booming mass of brown, tumbling water which carried everything before it. Cottonwood trees, full of golden leaves, came churning down; clumps of willow with large sods still adhering to their roots were turned over and over by the flood and came by us as somersaulting islands; whole spruce trees, 60 feet long, went crunching by. Just above us was a point with spruce trees which I had bored a few days before and had found to be two hundred years old. We watched the power of the river beating full blast against the point where they stood, while tree after tree slowly settled from the vertical to the horizontal as the dirt was torn from around their roots until they tumbled into the water with a splash louder than the roaring torrent.

"What would a man do if he fell into a current like that?" I asked Ernie.

"He couldn't survive thirty seconds in that ice water," my companion replied.

"But if you actually found yourself in it you'd want to fight like hell to the very end. What could you do that would be most helpful?"

"Keep your head above water, float with the current, and save your strength to work yourself out on whichever side you can."

When we were not watching the flood we read from our itinerant library. Toward noon I suggested to Harvey that he walk up again with me to the point where river and slough met, to see what the main river was doing. We found that it had broken through a barrier of driftwood and was cutting a new channel headed straight for camp. Jesse whom we met on the way back told us the water had almost reached the fire and we had better hurry if we wanted any lunch.

After a hasty meal we decided to pack up, desert the country around our cache completely and move to some bluffs half a mile to the south and forty feet above the river. We could not cross either the river or the slough on foot so we pulled our boat right through the spruce forest to our cache. It had been five feet above the river when we built it, but now the water was two feet high on the poles. Our first camp was more than knee deep in water. We loaded from the cache everything we wanted to take along and then floated the boat among the spruce trees to our latest camp where we loaded the rest of the equipment. Then we let the boat down the slough, Jesse and I knee-deep in water on the bank playing out hundred feet of mountaineering rope at a time, then retying the boat by a shorter rope to bushes until we could get ready for another hundred-foot descent on the main rope. Meanwhile Ernie and Harvey were in the boat, checking its descent by poles.

When after crossing the slough we finally reached the bluffs and pitched camp on top we knew we were safe against any flood short of the one in Eskimo mythical times when the world was covered with water and the Eskimos had to take to their boats until land was finally brought back through the intervention of Toolawak the crow. Apparently some modern crow got busy during the night, because the water had dropped at least a foot by morning. The weather was still impossible for mountain climbing—the clouds hung cold and gray, less than 2,000 feet above the valley floor. We had set this as the last possible day we could wait for the weather to clear for the ascent of Doonerak. If it were still cloudy this morning we had planned to take the boat down the river. However, the water was still so high and turbulent that this was impossible. Consequently, we decided to spend the day looking for a glacier which Ernie told us he had seen ten years before while hunting in one of the numerous deep canyons emerging from the north side of Doonerak. He described the glacier as larger than the one we had explored at the head of the Anaktuvuk.

But we did not find it. There was a glacier higher up on the side of Doonerak and perhaps half a mile across, but Ernie insisted that was not the one. However, the canyons were glorious—deep limestone gorges surrounded by high limestone precipices, full of pinnacles, with tumbling water everywhere. The last one we explored had a fall which took one straight leap of three hundred feet. On the way I bored a windswept black spruce, growing on a swampy hillside, which was 6½ feet high, 3 inches in diameter, and 346 years old. Less than two air-line miles away, was a well-drained white-spruce flat which I had studied eight years before and found to contain a stand 160 years old, with sixty trees between 10 and 15 inches in diameter to the acre!

Just before we reached the last gorge, a furious blizzard struck us from the north, although it was only September 2. The driving snow hurt as it stung against our cheeks and necks. But it only lasted half an hour and was followed to our delight by the most cloudless blue sky of the trip! All mountains stood out in sharpest relief. We saw the crest of Doonerak for the third time in more than two weeks. Even though it was past our zero hour for the ascent, we decided to set out next day up Pyramid Creek to the campsite among the willows which Ernie and I had selected two weeks before as a starting point for the climb. Yet we knew that the weather, perfect as it seemed, might play us false.

It did. Next morning the blue sky was gone and the wind had shifted to the south where another storm was brewing. It had snowed on the mountains during the night and the snowline was within five hundred feet of the valley floor. Doonerak was hopeless for this year. It was time to get out.

We decided to make an easy day of it and just descend four miles down the North Fork to the mouth of Fish Creek. Here we planned to spend a day exploring the north branch of that creek which rose in never-visited igneous mountains. We knew the river was still too high for boating, but the channel which ran among gravel bars, we thought safe as far as Fish Creek.

It was snowing hard when we loaded the boat. With Ernie steering in the stern, we started down at six times the painful speed at which we had dragged the boat upstream two and a half weeks before. Several times we had to jump out and drag the boat over riffles, but otherwise the journey was peaceful. Just above Fish Creek we found that the channel had shifted 2,000 feet from the western to the eastern edge of the valley during the flood. Ernie remarked that we might as well land and make camp at the first good timber.

Then it happened.

All at once we saw that what had appeared to be an innocuous gravel bank, about 40 feet high and no different from hundreds of others along the side of the river, was not along the side of the river at all but overhanging it. The tremendous floods which had changed the course of the river by 2,000 feet pounded with full, gigantic power against the gravel bank. The force of this terrific impact had washed away the gravel from the floodline. The drop in water since the flood crest, had left a gravel bank about one foot above the river and overhanging it. The main current shot straight under this overhang, and then turned and tore right *through* the gravel bank, tunneling underneath in a 30-foot-wide passage whose end we could not see.

All of this we observed just seconds before we hit, as we streaked along on a torrent racing at fifteen miles an hour. At that stage no human power could have thrown us out of the main current. Ernie did his best, but he was helpless. Two seconds before the crash I wondered what would happen when we hit. Then I found out.

There was a frightful crunching of shattered wood as the boat passed under the overhanging bank. All at once I was deep under icy water where no light penetrated. Immediately I felt the overwhelming certainty of death. There was no reasoning in it and there was no fear, but there was no doubt either. "A man couldn't survive thirty seconds in that ice water," Ernie had said. A tunnel in the heart of the earth with perhaps no large enough exit, a chance of having your head battered against some low point in the ceiling, a fifteen-mile-an-hour current sweeping you helplessly on, rubber boots filled with many pounds of water, icy darkness . . . I didn't "think" these things, but they must have conditioned my sense of imminent death.

But other things were coursing through my mind simultaneously. They weren't thoughts that followed each other or could be listed in order. They were there all at once.

In a very practical way I was hearing again Ernie's words of two days before: "Keep your head above the water, float with the current, and save your strength to work yourself out on whichever side you can."

In a most objective way I was feeling: "What an awfully easy way to die. Hold my breath for forty, fifty, maybe sixty seconds, trapped in this tunnel, hold it till I am ready to burst, then have to let it out and it's all over."

There was one other thought I had very strongly, but I am almost ashamed to mention it, because it sounds so full of sweetness and light. I was also saying to myself: "I wish I had time to think over all the fine experiences of my thirty-seven years before dying—to have the satisfaction of recalling them just once more before I kick off."

Suddenly through my closed eyelids the encompassing blackness changed to bright light. I opened my eyes and saw instantly that I was out of the tunnel, on the left edge of the main current. I let it carry me along and saved my strength to push toward its outer edge. I worked my way to an uprooted spruce tree caught on the bottom. Beyond it the water was slack and I waded easily to shore. The tunnel, I now realized, had short-circuited a bend in the river.

I was safe, but I feared my three companions were drowned. I looked around. Ernie Johnson was just floating by, clinging to the upturned boat. A moment later he climbed on top of it. Directly opposite me, toward the other side of the river, Jesse Allen and Kenneth Harvey were being battered by the fierce current. Harvey would occasionally touch bottom with his feet, but the current would turn him over in a backward somersault. Jesse was being rolled over and over horizontally, like a barrel. Each time they would almost get control of their feet, only to be knocked down again. It was awful just to stand and look helplessly on. Finally, the current threw them both on a pile of driftwood where they managed to check themselves and gain their feet. They stood there, surrounded by water, almost exhausted, and shivering. I was afraid they might be too tired or numb to make land, but in a short time Jesse managed to stagger across to the opposite shore and to help Harvey over.

I looked down the river toward Ernie and saw the boat had grounded a hundred yards below me on a gravel bar on my side of the river. Ernie was pulling it up as far as he could to prevent it from floating away. I started to run down to help him, but my boots were so full of water, it was like lifting a ton at each step. By the time I had taken them off and emptied them, Ernie was coming up the bar. He yelled something across the river to Jesse, which I could not understand.

"How will they get across?" I asked.

"We'll forget that for the present," he said. "We've got to get a fire going as quick as possible. Jesse is going to do the same. We've got to hurry."

Then I noticed for the first time that it was still snowing, that the thermometer was around freezing, and that I was shivering furiously. We ran up on the side hill above the river till we came to a dead birch— a lucky break because birch makes particularly good kindling. Quickly Ernie ripped off a piece of bark and struck a dry match from his waterproof match case. But his hands were shaking and he couldn't get the match and the bark near each other, and the match went out. He struck another and I grabbed the bark and held it against the tiny flame. In a moment it was ablaze and then it was simple to heap on dead spruce twigs and later dead spruce limbs. Soon the fire was safely burning, not to go out until we could leave this spot nearly twenty-four hours later. Jesse and Harvey got their fire going at about the same time. It was not until the next day, when we were rehashing the experience, that I realized what Ernie and Jesse knew, that if we had not started the fires promptly we might have perished from exposure in this freezing weather.

But here we were, safe and sound, the four of us peeling off and wringing out our soaking clothes by two good fires on opposite sides of an unfordable river. We were seventy-five miles from the nearest neighbors or assistance, with a shattered boat and, so far as we knew, not another possession in the world—food, bedding, tents all gone.

"If only an ax and a gun might have gotten stuck in the boat, we could live in luxury off the country," Ernie said. "I've got a fishline in my pocket and Jesse probably has, and we can walk back to Wiseman in three days and not suffer, even if we haven't any food, but an ax and a gun would be nice."

After about an hour we were fairly well dried out and warmed up, so Ernie and I started down to the boat to see if anything could be salvaged. I have never been a dog enthusiast, but it gave me a warm feeling, to see our dogs sitting on top of the shipwreck, waiting patiently for their friends to return. We always kept them chained to the side of the boat when we were travelling on the river, and when the boat tipped the dogs had been dragged underneath it until it had run aground. An air pocket between the water and the boat must have kept them from drowning. After making the boat fast, Ernie had unchained the dogs and they had climbed on top of the boat and waited.

We reached under the boat and found that some of our possessions had neither sunk when it tipped nor floated away when it drifted down the river. The difficulty about salvaging them was that the stern of the boat was yet in two feet of very swift water, and if we tried to turn it right side up everything underneath would float away before we could grab it. Consequently, Ernie lifted the boat just enough for a few things to float out while I, standing downstream, would make a dive for a butter can or a sack of beans or the small tent or a box with shoepacs as it came floating along. By this procedure we managed to save almost everything we needed from what was imprisoned under the boat.

The prospect for the return journey now looked brighter. We found ourselves supplied with about five pounds of once-dried peas, three pounds of beans, five pounds of rice, ten pounds of flour, two pounds of saturated sugar, three pounds of salt, four pounds of butter, two pounds of coffee, two cans of dried eggs, and what had been fifteen but was now probably fifty pounds of rolled oats. This may not have been a balanced diet, but it was more than ample to get home. We cooked the oats for the dogs before leaving.

Aside from food, we saved only Jesse's and Harvey's shoepacs, everybody's extra socks and shirts, except my own, a couple of sewing kits, all film and movie magazines, which were seriously soaked, Harvey's still camera and my movie camera (which was in my large shirt pocket at the time of the upset), all three six-shooters and the ammunition for them, two fishlines, our small open tent, a piece of canvas, my field notes, Jesse's and Harvey's packboards, four waterproof bags, and, most important, fifty-five dry matches among our four match cases.

Among the more important things we had lost were all our bedding, the larger tent, all axes, Harvey's rifle and Ernie's .22 Special, Ernie's and my still cameras, all cooking utensils and dishes, my two packsacks, and the dog packs. Also all books and a barometer.

To a Nansen living two years on the ice, a Stefansson subsisting in luxury off the Arctic with almost nothing but a rifle and his own skill, to an Ellsworth wandering for months across Antarctica with almost nothing saved from a plane wreck, it would mean nothing to be left with all of this equipment in a fish- and game-filled country, only seventy-five miles from people. To me, spoiled as I was by civilization, it seemed adventuresome.

We shouted across the river to Jesse and Harvey. They wanted to wait until morning before trying to cross to our side, which was the one from which to start for Wiseman. Ernie thought he could patch up the boat enough to ferry them over. A reconnaissance confirmed that the river was unfordable at this stage of water. Jesse and Harvey had half a bar of chocolate which Jesse had in his pocket. Ernie and I, of course, had lots of food. We spent the six hours of darkness in comfort by roaring fires on opposite sides of the river.

Shortly after daylight Ernie and I started to work on the boat. It had a crack ten feet long and one-fourth of an inch wide on the side where the boat had struck the bank, and the bow was all stove in. However, with caulking cotton and some boards and nails from a box which we had saved, Ernie the carpenter deftly fixed the boat soon to leak only slowly. Then he cut an eight-foot pole from a spruce tree by pocket knife and shoved off. In less than five minutes we were all reunited on the east side of the river.

We spent most of this day finishing the process of drying out equipment, making new packsacks and dog packs out of the waterproof bags and the canvas, fashioning two pots and a griddle out of various cans, and sorting out the soaked films to see which looked like being worth backpacking on the slim chance of development.

We decided that the shortest and easiest route back to Wiseman would be over the new pass between Pyramid and Holmes creeks which Ernie and I had discovered a few days before, then down the unknown stretch of Holmes Creek, across the low pass beneath Chimney Mountain from Clear River into Glacier River, which Ernie and I found in 1931, then down Glacier River, and finally across the hills to Nolan. We moved camp that afternoon four miles back up the North Fork to Pyramid Creek. Here we found lots of dry spruce trees which we uprooted and carried whole to the fire without benefit of an ax. Harvey and I walked out to the cache to get some more sugar, a little tea, and a few dried peaches. The water had dropped five feet, but our old campgrounds were covered with up to eighteen inches of silt from this one flood. We made the seventy-five miles from Pyramid Creek to Wiseman easily in three days. We traveled every day from about seven in the morning until six in the evening, with two generous hours out for lunch. Generally, the going was good, although not as easy as on a trail. There were four hard miles of uphill work across soft moss and through brush-filled gullies to the first forks of Pyramid Creek; a climb of 2,000 feet to Holmes Pass; sedge tussocks from the mouth of Holmes Creek to Chimney Pass and for a couple of miles just before we left Glacier River; and plenty of highly adhesive mud deposited by the recent flood all the way down Glacier River. These, however, were small matters.

Our packs of course were light, ranging from 10 to 25 pounds. For

Ernie and me the only real trouble was our footgear, for we had lost our shoes and had nothing but heavy rubber boots which reached to the hips. For myself, an advocate of light footwear, this was a nuisance. However, when fording the high creeks Ernie and I had a big advantage and we would carry Jesse and Harvey across on our shoulders to keep their feet dry.

Each night we set up our small tent with the open side toward the fire, four or five feet away. After the fire had been started with spruce twigs and willows, we got our fuel by pulling dead spruce trees up by the roots. The roots gave out the most heat. The first two nights we let the fire burn down until someone felt cold enough to put on more wood. As a result we all felt cold half the night. The last night we divided into one-hour watches during which one of us would sit up and keep the fire burning all the time. By this method we were comfortable all night, except when I got overambitious toward the close of one of my watches and nearly drove everyone out of the tent by excessive heat.

Under Jesse's skillful handling of peas, beans, rice, and the improvised hotcake griddle, our meals were delicious. We ate out of coffee and butter cans with our fingers and with spoons which we whittled from alder. Harvey shot three ptarmigan, but aside from that we did not take time to live off the country.

Our trip down Holmes Creek was a real elation. From the pass to which Ernie and I had first climbed the week before, to the mouth at Clear River by which Ernie and I had mushed seven and a half years earlier, no white man had probably traveled.

Holmes Creek emptied into the lower end of the upper Clear River valley. When Ernie and I spent four days there in the winter of 1931 I thought this Yosemite-like valley with its sensational ten side canyons the most beautiful place I had ever seen. Seeing the valley now in autumn, I had the feeling of meeting the son of an old friend whom I had not seen for years. There was a strong resemblance, and yet it was a different person. Whether I preferred the valley in winter or autumn I could not fairly say, because the weather was not clear enough now, and there was no time for exploration.

The jaunt down Glacier River, almost from its source, was made enjoyable by the fresh autumn colors—the bright cream of reindeer moss, the reds and scarlets of dwarf birch and Angowuk all over the hillsides, and the glowing gold of cottonwood leaves. The willows, however, had lost their leaves, though it was only early September.

The last day we saw more and more signs of civilization—cut stumps and old camping spots littered with tin cans. We ate lunch on Yankee Creek, in a log cabin which, we discovered, old George Eaton had left just the day before. There, for the first time in many days, we prepared a meal on a stove. Ernie and Harvey, who had used up their last tobacco that morning, kept assuring me that they could go indefinitely without tobacco, all the while they were hopefully rummaging through old cans, under George's bed, and among dark corners, for some he might have left. When we saw him in town he told us he had come back only because he had run out of tobacco.

A 700-foot climb took us over our last divide at Snowshoe Pass. Thereafter we walked four miles downhill along wood roads to Nolan Creek. When we stepped up to Jack White's boiler house on the creek and were greeted by Verne Watts who was running the hoist, it was just four weeks since we had seen our last human being.

We hung around Nolan Creek until after supper, chatting with friends. We heard the news of the four weeks since we had left the world —Albert Ness having both legs broken; all of Europe mobilizing; the worst rain and floods since white men had come to live permanently in the upper Koyukuk in 1899. About Albert we were sorry; about Europe we still felt remote; about the rain and floods, we were quite satisfied. If our ascent of Doonerak was blocked and our boat wrecked, we comforted ourselves, it was only by the worst weather and the worst high water in the memory of the oldest inhabitants.

The six miles to Wiseman we walked after dark. We found that two landslides had blotted out the road for a couple of hundred feet each. In town we learned that innocuous little Wiseman Creek had broken over its banks and washed out half the gardens in town. The bridge was gone and the creek unfordable, so Wiseman was two separate cities for the night.

When, an hour later, we lay down on soft beds inside dry and well-heated cabins, the trip was indeed over. We had failed in our major objective—climbing the Arctic's highest peak. We had had twenty-seven days of rain in twenty-nine. We had lost our boat, much of our equipment, and—as turned out later—part of our pictures; fortunately not all were ruined. Nevertheless, we had explored the upper reaches of the Anaktuvuk; and, for purely a good time, it would be hard to beat our four weeks' adventure in unexplored wilderness.

Notes

1. The most recent estimates by the U.S. Geological Survey through "topography from aerial photographs by photogrammetric methods," but not field checked, of elevations of the high peaks of the Brooks Range are in its 1956 series of quadrangles. These estimates have lowered Mount Doonerak to 7,610 feet. They show the highest peaks of the Brooks Range to be Mount Isto, 9,050 feet, Mount Chamberlin, 9,020 feet, Mount Hubley, 8,915 feet, and Mount Michelson, 8,855 feet. These peaks are some two hundred miles northeast of Doonerak and are in the Arctic Wildlife Range.

2. Following a decision of the U.S. Geographic Board in 1925, the U.S. Geological Survey has used "Brooks Range" to denote the entire chain across northern Alaska from the Canadian border nearly to Kotzebue Sound as described in the text. Recent U.S.G.S. maps have used "Endicott Range" to denote that part of the Brooks Range which includes the upper Koyukuk drainage to the south and the eastern part of the Colville drainage to the north.

BILLIE WRIGHT

from *Four Seasons North*

Billie Wright and her husband Sam
became residents of Alaska in 1968,
and there they trapped, prospected,
filmed, and chronicled their life in
the wilderness north of the Arctic
Circle. She met and married Sam
Wright while attending the Unitarian
Universalist graduate seminary in
Berkeley, California, where he was
Professor of Social Ecology, and
from which she received her master's
degree in religion. Ms. Wright was the
first woman of any denomination to
be ordained in the state of Alaska.
From 1979 until her death in 1987,
she directed a global women's peace
network entitled Women To End War
in the World (WEWW) Inc.

Sound of Winter

Today Sam sets off across the creek for one of the highest peaks on the south ridge, a good vantage point from which he intends to map the contours of the lakeshore. As I bring in firewood, I can hear every crunch of his snowshoes as he rims up the slope, breaking trail, but I can't see him anywhere. When finally I catch sight of him halfway up the mountain across from me, where the spruce look as if they were only a foot tall, he is a speck against the white. The distance between us is approximately a half mile. Yet when I halloo across to him and he answers, I discover that we can talk in conversational tones and hear each other as distinctly and easily as if we were twenty feet apart.

The Eskimo hunters say that in winter, caribou can hear a man moving across the snow a mile away. All the extraneous sounds of summer that distract and confuse—wind in trees, in willow and grasses, the humming of insects, whirring of wings and the singing of birds, trickling melt and running streams—all are stilled by winter. When the thick blanket of snow and ice muffles the land, any sound breaking the silence is magnified a thousandfold.

I can hear the wings of a raven flying a mile away; its call two miles away. The song of the wolves from across the lake travels two to three miles to reach us. In winter, everything listens.

We scan the airwaves for evening news. Fairbanks disappears into wild shriekings of static, Anchorage is only a wail, the lower forty-eight a void. But a Canadian Northwest Territory station is bringing in the New Year with great enthusiasm—with shouts, applause, whistles, bells, bursting balloons, popping corks, "Auld Lang Syne" at its usual funereal beat. Provoked in thought, a kaleidoscope of past celebrations of this night, memory-hazed places, people—impressions of smoky living rooms or drafty ballrooms, of dull-eyed, thick-tongued greetings exchanged, of resolutions confessed with embarrassed laughs and crossed fingers, of individuals blurred into amorphous crowds, of worked-at gaiety with a sense of expectation betrayed somehow, of celebration gone awry, of synthetic experience.

This night, a great near-full white moon lights up the land for miles around, sprinkling many-colored brilliants across the snow. We howl to the wolves, but no answer comes back. The hard winter hunt takes them far from home territory these lean days. Long before the magic midnight number brings in a "new" year, we're in bed. Every day here new, no breaks in the continuity, no resolutions required. Awake sometime in the night from dazzling moonlight streaming in the window into our eyes. We think at first it is midday, for the moon is bright as an arctic winter day. Judging from the amount of chill in the cabin, the hour must be close to 4 a.m.

We get up for fresh-brewed coffee and supper's leftover Jell-o. Sit at the table in the light of the moon, watching the red glow from the open draft in the door of the roaring Yukon stove, talking of beginnings. The new year has arrived.

Storm

At minus forty-five, the cabin floor is frigid. We wear our warmest mukluks, indoors and out, now. The eggs under the bunk freeze.

Three days and nights of constant gale winds have changed the face of the land. All trails and paths are gone, no trace of them evident anywhere. Waist-high drifts fill the footpaths around the cabin. We dig our way out each morning. The force of the wind is so great that we can lean into it and be held. But at the same time, breath is sucked out of us.

Everything around camp is stowed safely away or tied down, but still the furious blasts rattle the glass in the window frames, shake the cabin door, tear away sections of canvas, rip loose boards and Blazo tins, sending them careening through the air. No snow falls, but the air is thick with ground snow swept up into driving sheets of stinging whiteness that race across the frozen tundra. Trees bend under the weight of the wind, leaning over several feet at each roaring blast. In summer these winds would tear the shallow-rooted spruce out of the tundra. Only the deep hard cover of snow keeps them from being uprooted now.

Wild voices seem to fill the air with shrieking, wailing cries. They will not be ignored. We are always listening—for what I don't really know. Perhaps for the momentary lull when the sound shrinks down to a muted babble. But at these moments, we listen even harder, waiting for the fury to resume, and when it does, are awed by the power the voices symbolize.

Like the Eskimos and all the wild creatures of the Arctic, we burrow into our shelter to sit out the storm. Only dire necessity could drive us outside for more than the most urgent chores. Frostbite and exhaustion are the great dangers if caught on the trail away from home in these windstorms at subzero temperatures. The recommended procedure in such an emergency is to follow the example of an old Eskimo woman heading home on foot from a visit to the next village and caught midway on the trail by one of these midwinter storms. Digging a hole in the snow, she burrowed deep enough to be protected from the wind, and went to sleep. When the storm had passed three days later, she continued on her way home.

The wind reaches us, even inside the cabin, seeping in around the chinking, up through the floorboards, along the doorjamb and window frames. All the things hanging from the ceiling beams are in motion. Icy drafts swirl about the room. The stove, stoked high, labors hard but the heat is dissipated only a few feet from it.

Over our double long johns we wear flannel shirts, wool pants, thick sweaters, scarves, but still it is necessary to warm up every few minutes by hovering directly over the stove. Feet and hands feel the chill most of all.

We wait out the storm—trying to keep warm, going to the warmth of the bed early, rising late, reading, talking, but mostly waiting.

On the fourth day, a quiet lull lengthens, silence deepens, the cabin warms, frigid drafts subside. We hurry out to do the chores before the wind returns, but when it does a few minutes later, it has lost its furious punishing power. This now is the familiar, easy wind we live with all the time at Koviashuvik.

The storm has passed.

Four and a half minutes of light added today. At midday, a bright full golden moon in the northwest sky hangs above pink-tipped peaks. The rays of the hidden sun, still low behind our horizon, reach the pinnacles for the first time in many weeks. The light slowly returns. . . .

The cold increases; the thermometer continues its downward slide below zero—minus thirty-five, minus forty, fifty, fifty-five. All the land a frozen stillness. This small cabin an insignificant speck in infinite space, too small to be glimpsed from a mile away high on the mountainside. The cabin becomes the focus of our existence, the hub from which all our forays into the bitter cold radiate out and return. An average of twenty to twenty-two hours of each twenty-four spent in this one small room. All the myriad business of dailiness taking place in twelve by twelve feet of space—working, sleeping, eating, bathing, dreaming, reading, skin scraping, snowshoe repairing, thinking, fretting, talking, relating, cooking. . . .

A friend's letter asks, "But how can two people function in that limited space? Don't you suffer from claustrophobia—from lack of privacy?" I find that I don't know how to answer the letter. It asks the wrong questions, "wrong" in that they're based on a set of assumptions that have little meaning here. The assumptions belong to life in an eight-room suburban house, not to life in a wilderness cabin.

The cabin is "shelter," in the word's most basic, most universal sense. Here, warmth, food, rest, comfort are to be found. At the same time, a paradox exists. The cabin is not a refuge from the world around it as shelter *from* something implies, but is a natural extension of the world outside it. A connection exists between inner and outer space that seldom occurs between house and surroundings in more "civilized" parts of the world, where one's shelter helps to shut out the outside, becomes a retreat from life outside, from masses of people, noise, action, mile upon mile of other such shelters—from all the surfeits of public life which invade the private life.

Just the reverse is true of our wilderness here. With a universe in which to move freely about and with a feeling of at-homeness and oneness with the world, "home" fulfills the basic needs of a place to sleep, a place to get warm, eat, move about in, a little. Not much space is required for that.

The casual visitor to the Arctic often fails to understand this spatial relationship, and the attitudes it inculcates. His interpretation of the size of the shelters, based on the status given "outside" to spacious dwellings, is that the smallness is a sign of poverty.

One of the younger, more outspoken Eskimo men at Anaktuvuk Pass told us, "We didn't realize that we were a 'poverty-stricken' village until the white men told us so." He then added with a shrewd little laugh, "Now that we know how poor we are, we want to be rich like everybody else!"

The outsider also judges the apparent lack of privacy in the arctic one-room home by his own standards and needs. He comes from a culture in which a value premium is placed on a separate room for each member of the family, in as spacious a "private world" as he can afford to rent or buy. He then sees the Nunamiut family living together quite cheerfully in their one-room house or canvas tent—parents, several children, perhaps a grandfather, aunt, niece or nephew, plus a constant stream of visitors—and, applying his own values as a yardstick, he measures incorrectly.

Missing the point that wilderness is an intensely nonpublic world, and that all of it is "home" to the wilderness dweller, the outsider is almost certain to feel that in this enjoyment of the crowded gregarious intimacy of family life, there must be less sensitivity to others, less awareness of the individual's needs and "rights," than he himself possesses.

Yet one of the most striking features of the Nunamiut is his acute awareness of the other, expressed in all his personal relationships. Although always intensely interested in other individuals, and curious about them, the mountain people do not pry. Though jokes are made about each other, a good joke on oneself is equally appreciated. To be koviashuktok, even though the concept is seldom heard verbalized, is the state most desired. If one suffers the loss of koviashuktok and falls into a prolonged period of irritability or brooding, all those around him experience the loss as well.

Untouched so far by the influences of the psychotherapeutic view of personhood, the Nunamiut family seems burdened neither with self-consciousness nor with the emotional problems commonplace among the families in the lower forty-eight.

The usual petty grievances and irritations found in all human communities are of course present: envy, competitiveness, cliquish-ness. Some larger guiding perspective in the Nunamiut life view keeps these in enough balance so that differences and quarrels are resolved, often spoken of with humor and a shrug, lived with, contained within the community. Tensions within the individual do not seem to get translated into the usual marital or parent-child conflicts.

While the concern exists that children be educated, it seems more a tribal concern for the future than the individual family's drive to see its own children learn to achieve, to compete, to be "successful" by the standards of the white world. If any "sacrifice" is made for children, it is only incidental in that the presence of the school does in part define village life. Children are otherwise treated affectionately but matter-of-factly—scolded, hugged, ignored or enjoyed, seldom indulged or "spoiled," and never excluded from the total life and activities of the entire community of families. Inquisitive and gregarious, undemanding but assertive, all the children are treated with an offhandedly casual, accepting and often amused affection by all the village adults.

Marital relationships and sexual love seem equally taken for granted. These subjects often enter peripherally into conversations. What is communicated by both men and women is that these are, of course, "good"—good in the same way as the first bright days of spring, the spring and fall migrations of the caribou, the first snowfall of late summer. Mention of any of these enjoyable matters brings quick smiles of acknowledgment and pleasure.

Despite the restricted choice of partners available in the small community, marriage nevertheless seems based on strong mutual affection, physical attraction and a conviction that marriage is a highly desirable and essential institution for both sexes. While husbands' and wives' roles and duties are in general separate and distinct, the marriage relationship provides full equality to both members, cemented by a strong bond of partnership and cooperation.

Family emotional relationships among the mountain Eskimos are so far still firmly based in a history of a very real physical dependence in which the well-being and survival of each member is necessarily rooted and nurtured.

In such an atmosphere, crowd terms like "aloneness," "alienation," "respect for the individual," "privacy" have little significance. Individuals, having no fear of losing their selfhood either to the group or to solitude, are at home and at ease with both.

One can learn from these arctic peoples, but it is the land one must look to for understanding, for it is the land that defines the size, shape and materials of the home as well as the life view of those who dwell within it.

From these assumptions, I can write about our living space; of cabins, of our cabin.

Shelters in the Arctic are traditionally an extension of the land itself.

In Anaktuvuk Pass, where no timber grows, sod huts replaced the caribou-skin tents of the nomadic life. To make the houses of sod, large slabs of moss-covered earth were stacked like adobe or concrete blocks into sloping walls, braced inside by thick willow supports and rounded over across the top to resemble a Quonset hut covered over with green turf, willow shoots, berry plants and sod. Built on the site of the removed turf, the earthen single-room house nestled low in the tundra, protected from the full force of arctic winds.

Windows, once made of bear intestines, were replaced by plastic or glass. With a stove inside, the frozen sod structures were relatively warm and dry until spring thaws brought a chill dampness inside. Then the family shifted into the white canvas tent which lets in sun and light.

A few plywood dwellings were under construction to begin replacing the sod houses on my first visit to Anaktuvuk. There was much debate among the villagers on whether the poorly insulated wooden "boxes" would keep a family warm in midwinter when winds reaching velocities of eighty to one hundred miles per hour sweep through the pass from the Arctic Ocean. With an air-freight cost of over twenty cents a pound added onto the high cost of building supplies, few families could afford an alternative to the sod igloo. Only with the assistance of public agencies can the new structures be made available to all.

In our own part of the Koyukuk, the log cabins are seldom larger than twelve by twelve to twelve by fourteen feet, slightly smaller in size than the sod huts north of timber line. The average length of suitable logs to be taken from our local spruce is about twelve feet, but the diameter of the slow-growing spruce is such that twice the number of trees are required in cabin building than farther south. To the south, timber is more plentiful, trees grow thicker and taller, trucks and tractors are available to haul and hoist; cabins are therefore larger.

One of the smallest cabins in the Koyukuk belonged to an old prospector whose gold-mining claims were located in the arid gulches of a ridge of dry timberless mountains, twenty miles south of Koviashuvik. To cut corners on the number of logs he had to drag or haul on his shoulders from the nearest stand of trees many miles away, he built a three-sided cabin backed into a hole in the rocky mountainside. Some of the local old-timers with claims on more wooded lands chuckled over this shack. "Not any bigger than a clothes closet," they said. It was not tall enough inside for its big, burly owner to stand erect. It had the essentials, however: bunk, table, Yukon stove—and a snug-fitting door to keep out cold and varmints.

Along with these essentials, an amazing amount of equipment, supplies and furniture can be crowded into a twelve-by-twelve foot area. My first impression of our cabin was not of how little space there was in it, but of how efficiently every inch of it had been utilized—ceiling, walls, floor.

Every piece of "furniture" is multipurpose. Stretched out across the foot of the big fur-covered bunk, with the window behind my left shoulder, the stove only a warm two feet away, I have the most comfortable reading couch ever designed.

The middle of the bunk is perfect for sitting cross-legged and rugging, mending, writing letters, thinking. The oilcloth-covered table is big enough for a wolf to be skinned, an afternoon's baking to be mixed, a caribou skin scraped, moose ham butchered, card games played. Two can write letters, spread papers about.

What is harder to describe is what is below and above the furniture. The wall behind the narrower bunk is covered with nails for hanging up parkys, mitts, jeans, shirts. The walls everywhere else hold shelves —shelves made of old wooden crates, roughly adzed spruce planks, water-worn sluice-box boards. On the shelves, books, magazines, film supplies, mail-order catalogues, radio, kerosene lamps, first-aid carton, rifle-cleaning kit, paints, varnish, repair kits, writing supplies, small boxes of odds and ends: replacement parts for gasoline lanterns, boot oils, sewing materials, leather thongs, playing cards, binoculars, ammunition. The wall next to the stove is decorative with hanging skillets, lids, pots, spatulas. In the "kitchen" corner, shelves under the work surface hold the large varmintproof cans of supplies. Shelves above hold dishes, cups, smaller supplies, spices. What can't fit on a shelf hangs from the ceiling. With its many hanging items, the entire ceiling looks like an old general store in a farm community on the midwest plains. Lines strung between the big spruce beams hold sweaters, eight pair of wool mittens and gloves, six pair of leather and canvas work gloves (all clothes pinned to the lines), wool socks, extra blankets, towels, flour-sack dishcloths, wool scarves, ermine and squirrel pelts. From nails driven into the beams every two feet hang lanterns, cameras, two big kettles, tools, plastic bags of sourdough bread, of instant soups, bags of yarn, bags of rags and scraps of fur, coils or rope, wire, boots and mukluks.

Over the two-foot-wide "aisle" in the center of the cabin hang the wet things: dripping mukluks and mitts, laundered clothes, defrosting moose or caribou. There is also room in the aisle for dancing.

Under the bunks, a warehouse of things: a carton for our clothing— our "chest of drawers"; cartons of stored summer clothes and boots; two of my rugs-in-progress in heavy plastic bags to protect the wools from nest builders; a wooden toolbox (working with metal tools that have been left out in subzero cold can tear flesh from the hands); cartons of papers; work files. Under one end of the table, a twenty-five pound tin of flour, another of sugar, a fifty-gallon box of instant milk. Everything else that is not regularly needed and that will not suffer from freezing goes into the dogtrot or the cache.

In the cabin is all that we need—roughly in order. Still, to a visitor fresh from "outside," it would look cluttered beyond belief, as the homes of the villagers looked to me the first time I visited and wondered how they would ever be able to locate anything in the casual jumble of clothes, toys, furs, supplies, cookware, dishes and food. In one way, the confusion of things in the sod huts and tents was less noticeable than that in some equally small log cabins because there was less clutter of furniture. Some of the dwellings had a folding chair or two. But most sitting was done on fresh willow boughs spread on the tundra floor, or on the family bed, a pile of caribou skins and blankets raised off the ground by a pad of cut willow boughs, and filling the entire space across the back wall.

With no timber for furniture building, and furnishings flown in from outside exorbitantly costly, one very sensibly improvises better answers: wooden boxes and crates become supply cabinets; a piece of plywood or lumber boards nailed together, set on wooden boxes, makes a low table. The sheet-metal stove, also set low, rests on four tin-can "legs."

Out front, a new snowmobile may be parked beside the villager's house. Inside, however, only surface variations mark a change from the old nomadic way. The atmosphere of the villagers' homes always seem snug, homelike, comfortable, busy, welcoming. But in the absence of many material goods, of chrome and plastic, of foam-stuffed upholstery, nylon carpets and power appliances, the casual visitor may miss the richness of what the people created and communicate of "home," and see only poverty.

With wood available to the log cabin builder in the timbered areas of the range, furniture is more readily constructed. Much of it is crude, jerry-built; some, made by sourdoughs with carpentry skills and hours of leisure in the long night, lovingly crafted.

Most of the old cabins in the Koyukuk were built by lone men for their own occupancy. Women were not in the picture. Many of the old prospectors were spartan in their needs and tastes. They were here to get the gold out of the ground. Everything else was a waste of time and energy. Others of the old sourdoughs imported curious mementos from "home" into the arctic frontier. In one of the rotting old cabins which belonged to a lone prospector at Jim Pup, there is an enormous, elaborately wrought, brass-plated double bed. The springs are rusted through; the mattress shredded, carried off by birds, voles and squirrels for nests. But the big golden bed still stands among the collapsing log walls and sinking floorboards. A long and expensive journey by sea freighter, river boat and dog team brought that monument of "civilization" into the Koyukuk wilds.

The early gold seekers prospecting the wild creeks of the Arctic were in the tradition of all frontiersmen. Some came for adventure, and quickly satisfying the craving in the dramatic climate, among their burly cohorts, grew restless and moved on to new horizons. Some came to escape unpaid debts, a nagging wife, dull job, law-enforcement agencies. Most came to get rich quick in order to go back to wherever they had come from with the gold fruits. Most returned home instead on borrowed fare. Few came in search of a "home." But those few who remained did so because they were caught, not by the dream of the "yellow stuff," but by limitless sky, the thin lonely night cry of the wolf, endless ridges of horizonless mountains, the mysterious arctic winter twilight.

I think of my friend Jan in her eight-room suburban house . . . and I see her "confined" within walls, ringed by a narrow moat of carefully cultivated green and a six-foot-high fence. I try to imagine her in a one-room cabin or sod hut, ringed by infinite universe. The universe can be frightening if one is closed off from it too long. Many have lost connection with it.

Were I to return to the city now, I suppose that my perspective would be forced to reverse itself. Remembering the jangled sounds, the crowds, the cement canyons, the cold steel, glass, neon, the grime and thick air, the hurry, the search for green or a glimpse of sky—where can the need for space be satisfied? Or the need to move about easily, take one's time, enjoy the walk, smell the fresh natural smells of clean earth and grass, move about the places of people without tensions and fears? No; like Jan, I would be forced to disconnect myself from the world, to find a shelter closed off like a fortress from what lies beyond the walls—a place that offers nurturing of the inner life, provides some respite from the din and freneticism of crowds.

I do not know what the answers are. The alternative to city-suburb is not the wilderness for more than a very few people. Not only is there not enough wilderness left to absorb more than a very few, but once the wilderness is invaded by the many, it will no longer be the wild.

The great ecologist Aldo Leopold and many others have stressed the need for wilderness as a laboratory, a living example of the land in a natural ecological balance. The concern has been repeatedly expressed that soon there will be no land left that has not been manipulated, cultivated, exploited, changed by man's hand. Perhaps the wilderness needs also to be protected as a laboratory in human values, a place where the land, not man, is allowed to determine in large measure the human relationships to nature's ecological balance—a place where man discovers firsthand the kinships, harmonious interdependencies, the essential connections of all life systems.

While broad institutional answers which may yet prevent us from destroying the planet or our own humanness on it are being sought —or ignored—or rejected—we individuals might begin by making our own individual choices, taking our own individual actions toward these answers.

A letter to Jan ends:

The value study has led us to a choice. When the "year" is up, we will remain here in the wilderness. Build our own small cabin on one of two silvery, rushing creeks that tumble down from the white peaks into the deep waters of this mountain lake. When the sun returns in the spring, we'll begin to explore the territory along the two creeks and decide whether to build on "Holy Moses" or on "Last Chance" Creek, both obviously, perhaps prophetically, named by two old prospectors.

But we're after a different gold. It can't be found by "going back" to old frontiers, although this is what some of our friends "outside" will believe our decision represents. But no one moves back in time or space to what is past.

The present frontier, for all of us, is the crucial one. It has to do with the life quality that the Nunamiuts are in the process of losing as that dinosaur of old and outlived frontiers, "progress," continues to gobble up and to devastate the planet, along with the uniqueness and diversity of all its human inhabitants.

That amorphous quality is still here in the smiles and nods of these inland people, in their recognition and acknowledgment of the "good" in merely being alive. The frontier we are all on at present is where commitment to that "good" is to be discovered.

Here, the value of one's own life is a prerequisite for hope in the future. Here there is a conviction that life is better than anti-life and that a concern for others is expressed in the acceptance of one's own responsibility for answers. . . .

. . . at Koviashuvik, which might be—anywhere. . . .

Learning to recognize the limits of subzero cold is like exploring an alien environment. The fine line of safety can be crossed over without warning. In the minus forties, I go to the cache and without stopping to think take off the arctic mitts to work only in my wool gloves. All the body heat is sapped swiftly from my hands by the frozen supplies handled. Within two minutes, I can no longer hold onto anything and my fingers feel burned.

Rushing back to the cabin, I immediately immerse my hands in hot water. The pain is excruciating but reassuring as normal sensation slowly returns.

End of January

We have not seen the sun for more than two and a half months. Today Sam calls me outside at about noon, and bets fifty cents that the sun will reach the cabin in less than an hour. Each day the line of light has crept across the land, coming closer and closer to the cabin. We see it moving. The golden color, like a white-frothed tide, slides down the slopes, over the northern end of the plain of the frozen lake, reaches the tip of the small island, creeps up the mountainside to touch treetops behind the camp. But in the south, toward Jim Pup, where the sun itself will have to clear the mountain peaks before it can strike our camp, there is no sun. Not today. Our camp remains in deep blue shadow, encircled by distant golden light. In two days. . . .

Minus Sixty

The hint of promised sun holds no warmth. These days are bitter cold. The thermometer slides steadily downward, reaching minus
forty-five, then minus fifty, fifty-five, and holds at minus sixty degrees
Fahrenheit. With the wind stilled, there seems at first to be little difference between the more familiar minus forty and forty-five and this
new low. But after only a couple of minutes outside, beneath a cold
white aurora, I sense the difference. Exposed face skin instantly grows
taut, numb. Hands and feet begin to sting and grow numb, even in
heavy mitts and arctic footwear. The frigid air hits the lungs with a
jolting, savage bite. To remain inactive for very long at these temperatures could result in freezing to death. Men can and do survive in this
severe cold, but survival is borderline. No room for miscalculation or
error. But one never really gets "cold" in this extreme, subzero cold.
One stays warm or dies.

Today the cabin looks cluttered. It is too small, too confined. The blue-
shadowed world that we have lived in for months now seems permanent. The cold, wearing, wearying, eternal.

Just once I'd like to race out the door fast and far over the tundra
without first having to put on six layers of footwear and strap myself
to clodhoppers called snowshoes! I feel snappish, claustrophobic, irri-
table, trapped, which means a full-fledged first attack of Cabin Fever!

And for Cabin Fever there's no remedy but bootstrapping.

After sawing two big logs with the Swedish bucksaw, and stacking
them onto the woodpile, and panting furiously from the exertion at
minus forty-eight degrees, it's very nice to come back into a spacious,
well-ordered, cheerful little cabin. The fever has passed.

Visitor

Stepping out of the cabin to do our chores this morning, we come
face to face with a great white wolf. He stands fifty yards away, silently

watching. His yellow slanted eyes glitter; he does not move. We do not move. We three seem frozen together in a fragment of time, like a stopped frame of movie film, action jammed midaction. On a faint stir of wind, I can just smell his wild smell. His yellow eyes do not waver. He still does not move. We wait. His stance does not change, but a sudden tension enters it. Still watching, his yellow eyes fixed steadily on us, he takes a few steps; the hairs on the back of his neck are up, the tail up, ears alert. His body begins to draw itself together, shoulders hunching, the fine deep ruff of thick white fur across his back rising as he walks slowly, watchfully away, and disappears down into the creek bed. . . .

Return

By late morning, light has almost covered the land.

By noon, the moving edge of gold has reached three-quarters up the plateau, sweeping steadily on toward our camp. I will make no bets against the sun's arrival today! Mukluks go on to be ready to dash outside, if, today . . .

At twelve-thirty, the tops of the spruce just below the cache catch golden fire. The blue-black winter look of spruce turns warm green in an instant. I thought the trees were black because they were frozen. It was the absence of sunlight.

We hurry outside, and the whole world lights up.

The great bright glow moves surely, steadily, across the limitless snowfields. Reaches the woodpile behind the cabin and turns the stacked split logs a warm tawny yellow. Touches the back corner of the cabin roof and turns a long blue icicle into a glittering diamond dagger. The paths around the cabin fill up with brightness. The cabin is bathed in light.

Sun pours over our camp as, above the mountain peaks toward Jim Pup, the fiery globe itself appears in a blaze of hot gold. Sunlight now embraces all the frozen land. Sun warmth strikes our faces in a sudden gentle blow. We lift them to the light, dazzled, blinded. Shout greetings to the sun as if welcoming an old friend who has been missing too long.

Raise our arms and reach toward the source of warmth, toward the light which wraps around us, and everywhere, blue snow now gold-warm and splashed with a skyful of dancing brilliants.

A strange and joyful madness erupts in our camp. And we dance a lunatic, gleeful jig round and round the cabin with our boots making the music as they clump over frozen snow with drumming, bassy, crunching sounds. We come around the cabin corner and meet our shadows, seen for the first time in seventy-seven days. Elongated and distorted by the low-in-the-sky midday sun, our shadows start a contest in mugging and jumping and dancing, and I wonder why elsewhere shadows have come to belong only to children!

Dashing into the cabin for a camera, I'm stopped at the threshold by the newness of an interior aglow with yellow brightness which streams in through the frosted windowpanes, spilling over onto the oilcloth on the table, reaching out in golden fingers to probe the farthest, darkest, coldest corners behind the bunks.

The sun crawls along the white mountain crest for two, four, five minutes—which stretch to a precious ten. We are content to stand in its warmth, quietly watching the landscape of our journey through the universe as our planet, on which we have passage, tilts its range of mountains up into the sky and slowly covers the great glowing circle.

The sun is gone. It does not reappear today, though we see its bright rays above the ring of mountains as they glide on past it. Tomorrow its passing will take longer, and still longer the following day, until long sunlit days of spring will become the arctic day of summer and the world will be light, both day and night.

The blue shadows of sunlessness resettle over the land. There is a different quality in the vast white sweep of frozen mountains and valleys —or is it in the way that we now look at them? The long arctic night of winter is past. The sun has returned, a miracle. At Anaktuvuk Pass, as at Koviashuvik, and in all places where the sun's absence has been most deeply felt, its return today was greeted as it has been for centuries, with smiles and joyful greetings and uplifted faces. Our sun has at last returned.

A Giant Reflector

The sun has been back only a few days. Although it is still low in
the sky and its warmth feeble, we're already troubled with sun glare.
A letter from Dishu warns to be careful of snowblindness as the sun
returns.

She writes, "You better watch out eyes getting burned, sun coming
back. Potato poultice good. Cover eyes with potato if you get snow-
blind." I hope instant potatoes will substitute.

Apparently the unfiltered sun's reflection off the snowscape burns
right through the eyelids. Caught out without sunglasses, rubbing soot
on eyelids and around the eyes is helpful—or a pair of crude goggles
with narrow eyeslits cut into them can be carved out of wood. Meanwhile, sunglasses go back into parky pockets as part of our trail emergency equipment.

Weather, raw and uncertain. Erratic winds and skittish temperatures,
as if the return of the sun had triggered quiescent forces into uneasy,
conflicting motion.

Mail day today, and here at the cabin it is minus forty-five at noon.
The winds blow hard, first from the west, then the north, then from
the camp itself, in swirling clouds of ground snow as if wind were being
created right here on the premises.

Right after breakfast, Sam heads down to the shore to wait for Daryl,
who finally arrives at about three o'clock, with light to spare. He is
airborne again almost immediately. His rushed departure must be due
to the extreme cold of today—and the cold is always most severe down
in the bowl of the frozen lake where the coldest air sinks and winds
from the Arctic Ocean sweep through the pass from the north and over
the open plain of lake ice.

When Sam returns with the mail sack tied to his packboard, his red
wool face mask is white, coated over completely with a thick layer of
ice crystals. Hanging up the frozen mask to defrost over the slop pail, he

rubs his face briskly. A bitter day at the shore: minus fifty-six degrees at the shelter when he left. Daryl stopped only long enough to pass the mailbag out the plane door, grab the outgoing one and take off.

Coming up the trail, the wind was head on, sharp as a knife, Sam adds. Halfway up, he realized he'd better put on the face mask. Now, as he turns toward the lantern, I see a small patch of yellowish white on the soft flesh just above his cheek. The rubbing has reddened the skin around it, but the mark remains white, a sign of frostbitten flesh.

The danger of frozen skin is one of the primary reasons why the "buddy" system is recommended for arctic travelers. In subzero temperatures, especially with winds, exposed skin freezes without warning, without even the knowledge of its owner. Once the skin is frozen there is little to be done out on the trail. The danger in stopping to build a fire in order to thaw out is that thawed skin is highly susceptible to refreezing. This more drastically damages already damaged tissue. Whether surface tissue has suffered frostbite, or fingers, toes, hands or feet have deep-frozen, it is wiser to leave them frozen and to continue on to camp to avoid the danger of thawing-refreezing. Rubbing the frozen limb or skin with snow was commonplace treatment until fairly recently. Its effect was just the reverse of what was intended. Toes and fingers were unnecessarily lost in the "treatment." The current recommended procedure on reaching a warm shelter is to immediately immerse the frozen area or member in hot water. As the frozen part warms and thaws, there is also a general loss of body heat from cooled blood circulating through the body. Alcoholic drinks, which give an illusion of warmth, actually lower body temperature, and should be avoided at this time.

Sam is fortunate to have escaped with such minor frostbite but another problem has also been created by the bitter cold of today. His body temperature returns to normal, but his feet remain numb. Stripping off the layers of mukluks, felt boots, wool socks, we discover that his feet also show signs of frostbite. The lines of white around the heels and across the toes match almost exactly the outlines of his snowshoe straps. Snow must have accumulated and packed down under the straps, then frozen to an icy ridge. During his long hours out in the intense cold, the ice penetrated all the protective layers of footwear to freeze the skin beneath.

I brush aside an uneasy recall of tales told of isolated arctic wilderness dwellers who have been forced to amputate their own fingers or toes, and in some desperate cases, a hand or foot, to stop the spread of gangrene, which can be the aftermath of deep freezing of the flesh.

In seconds, the metal washbasin is filled with boiling water from the teakettle, cooled down with snow water to a temperature Sam can bear to hold his feet in. Every few minutes, more hot water is added. Thawing frozen skin is intensely painful. But the treatment begins to work. Feeling and color slowly come back into all the toes but one. That and the heel skin remain discolored and numb.

Considering today's temperature of minus fifty-six degrees, and a wind of at least ten mph, maybe more, the chill factor reached down to at least a Fahrenheit temperature equivalent of eighty-five to ninety degrees below zero. Luck has been ours this day, really!

We have done all we can. Sam dries his feet and gets into warm wool insulated socks, settles down with another cup of steaming coffee, and then we remember the unopened mailbag.

Today the news from "outside" seems irrelevant. . . .

The bitter cold of the day holds into the night.

By evening, all wind motion has ceased, leaving a vacuum which seems gradually to fill with a new, strange and massive kind of silence. The night has never been this still.

Despite the roaring fire, tonight the cabin is cold: continual unrelenting cold. All the window glass has disappeared under dense coats of ice. We hang blankets over the windows, but chill cuts through the heavy wool. The cardboard insulation covering the log walls is heavily stippled with ice crystals. Small icicles form long fringes along the corner shelves of the "kitchen." Our washtub snow-water storage tank across from the Yukon stove is frozen solid, radiating a wide circle of frigid air out into the room. We use the ulu to chip out chunks of ice to fill the teakettle. The filled teakettle seems to cool the stove, to radiate its own cold waves.

We turn in two hours earlier than usual to try to escape the inescapable icy pall that has permeated the cabin, crawl into bunks not half warm enough tonight, with their sleeping bags designed for sub-zero weather and their piles of furs and blankets. We take turns reading aloud to distract ourselves, holding the book in mittened hands, but fingers stiffen quickly and the unrelenting presence of the arctic cold overshadows any meaning of the pages' words of elsewhere. We blow out the lantern and burrow deep into the bunk, fighting to relax against the tension prolonged chill brings. Time suspended. . . . Our own interior heaters, well stoked with caribou fat, begin in the snug enclosures to warm us at last, the warmth held inside the den of the sleeping bags.

The tension of cold dissolving under the comforting, reassuring waves of warmth, from deep down in our secure burrow we listen to the mammoth stillness that is the crash of silence, the sound that is frozen sound at minus sixty-five degrees Fahrenheit.

Two hours of direct sun today. Only a little more than a week since it returned. It rides higher in the sky each day—rather, earth tips on its axis a little more each day. Morning light now arrives close to 6 A.M., usually in a "painted desert" sky of fluorescent reds and yellows! Twilight falls between 4 and 5 P.M.; our "day" seems long.

Winds and temperatures continue to vacillate from day to day. There seems to be no stable plateau in the weather. A week ago, minus sixty-five degrees; three days ago, minus thirty. Yesterday, up to minus five —and today, sliding back down to minus twenty. And still the erratic winds, suddenly shifting direction, unpredictable.

A parky squirrel poked its head up through the snow this morning. He sat there in the mouth of his tunnel, just dug out from his burrow, unmoving, fixed, as if he'd fallen sound asleep in the sunshine. A blast of icy wind suddenly swept across the snowfield, leaving a wake of snowclouds. The moving mists engulfed the squirrel. In a flurry of swirling crystals, he dropped instantly from sight.

Sun or no sun—he must be as confused as I!

Thirty feet below the cabin, the tracks of a lone caribou where it paused to paw down through the snow to reach the lichens, followed by the tracks of one large lone wolf. In the wolf tracks, a large snowshoe hare's bounding prints, which look like those made by a three-legged creature, and following the hare, one very small ermine trail.

What words are right for snow?

A fresh snowfall. Sun bright and hot by early afternoon, when it reaches its highest point just before slipping again behind the peaks. The snow cover changes under the sun's few hours of heat. The top layer has begun to thaw, and the smooth iced surface we are accustomed to turns to a consistency resembling melted marshmallow. The snowshoes sink down almost a foot deep with each step. Without snowshoes, boots break through even the crusted layers below, and a leg can unexpectedly get jammed down in a hip-deep hole in the snow. Getting out of the trap without injury is as tricky as summer tussock-hopping across an arctic bog.

Wrestling the sled, even unloaded, through the soft stuff calls for all one's endurance and patience. Now the sun replaces the light of the long arctic night to determine when we do our chores. Travel and sledding are best done early in the morning before the sun has had a chance to soften the surface snow, or a few hours after the sun has disappeared, when cold and wind have had time to refreeze the surface.

As I come to know the myriad kinds and conditions of snow, English words for them become inadequate. To be able to use the Eskimo terms would be helpful. The many dialects of the Eskimo language seem to be deeply rooted in the special ecology of the Arctic. Unwritten and unrecorded until recent years, Eskimo is spoken language with the emphasis on action words, rich in descriptiveness and immediacy, or present tense.

There is no single Eskimo word to represent "snow," for in the Arctic there is no such thing as just "snow." Instead there are terms for "new snow," "old granulated snow," "very old granulated snow next to the ground," "snow to be gathered for water," "snow spread out," "snow that is drifting," "snow like salt," "snow newly drifted," "snow piled up near the bottom of a hill," "snow mixed with water," "snow on clothes," "it snows," and so on. In all of these terms there seems to be no root word for "snow."

MARGARET MURIE

Geese

Margaret Murie was born in Seattle, Washington, and attended Reed College, Simmons College, and was the first woman graduate of the University of Alaska in Fairbanks. Married to biologist Olaus Murie, she was honored in 1976 with a Doctor of Humane Letters degree from the University of Alaska for her life-long work in the cause of conservation. Mrs. Murie is the author of *Two in the Far North*.

"Will you love me in December as you do in May?"

Jess was standing on the decked-over bow of the scow, poling and singing. He had a very nice high tenor voice. I love to sing too. We both knew hundreds of songs, and I really believe this saved our sanity, our friendship, and the success of the expedition. Down on the floor of the scow, just behind Jess, the baby and I spent our days now in a four-by-four space under the light muslin-and-netting tent a field naturalist friend in Washington had insisted we take along. Life from June 29 on would have been fairly intolerable without it. Here in this space were the baby's box, beside it Olaus's collector's trunk, and, piled on the trunk, all the baby paraphernalia and other small articles needed during the day. My stool was set in front of the chest, beside the box. And that was all; this was our world. By leaning forward and putting my eyes close to the netting, I could catch glimpses of the outside world. It remained unvaried for five weeks: Jess's booted legs, the tip of the red-painted bow, a green blur of grass and willows on the shore, maybe a bit of sky. Sometimes I caught a view of Olaus, trudging along on shore, the line over his shoulder. He was "pulling her by the whiskers," as the trappers say; Jess, experienced with the pike pole, leaned his weight on every stroke in a steady rhythm, all day long.

So we slid along, and sang song after song, and estimated our progress, trying to pick out landmarks from the Geological Survey maps. But the Old Crow throughout its middle course has no landmarks; just high banks, brown stream, green shore.

Variation came when Olaus would signal frantically from shore. The song would stop in mid phrase. Then we would quickly haul up the canoe, and both men would get in and push off, after a flock of flightless young geese which by now would have taken fright and would be beating furiously through the water. By this time I would be out on the bow, pole in hand. "If we're gone too long, try to get to shore where you can hook a willow, and wait for us"—the parting shot as canoe, men, and geese disappeared around a bend upstream.

It was fortunate that the Old Crow *was* a sluggish stream. The scow drifted now toward one shore, now toward the other. I wound the bandanas tighter over my shirt cuffs to keep mosquitoes from crawling in, tied the strings of the head net tighter about my chest, leaned on the pole, and waited. If the slow current took us close to shore, I reached out and caught a branch with the hook. Then it was just sit there on the bow and hold it. If it were near Martin's mealtime and he began to call and fret, I could only pray that the bird banders would appear again sometime.

In ten minutes—or an hour—they would come, bringing a new story. "Hey, you should have seen your husband up there in the mud, trying to catch up with an old goose before he got over the bank." Or: "Jess should have been a football player; he made a peach of a flying tackle after two young ones. Well, that's six for us already today."

Sometimes the canoe would come in fast, sliding up to the scow, and Olaus would reach over and dump a gunny sack at my feet. "Don't worry, they won't hurt one another. We're going after another bunch up here."

The banders' advantage was that in these weeks the adult geese had shed their wing feathers and the young had not yet grown theirs, so that all were flightless.

One hot day the sack contained six full-grown but flightless geese. For forty interminable minutes I drifted, and poled, and watched the river in vain for the canoe, while those poor creatures never stopped squawking and wriggling. It was a big surprise for me when, after finally being banded, they all went down the stream again honking furiously, and unhurt.

Lunch was more ordeal than pleasure during these weeks. The men would try to build a fire for tea, but the willow, so much of it green, was poor fuel. Some days we merely went ashore with the tin grub box and ate a bowl of stewed fruit or tomatoes with pilot biscuits or cold sourdough pancakes and a bit of cheese. Bowl in hand, you loosened the string of the head net, poked the spoonful of food into your mouth, and quickly let the net down again. It was the same with all the bites. Even so, there'd be a few bugs to squash inside the net when lunch was over! This was merely taking in fuel for energy; it was no social hour.

Down in the tiny haven on the scow I heated mush or tomatoes or a bit of gravy on the Sterno outfit for Martin. He never came out of there until we camped at night. That is why we had to let him crawl about the tent as long as he liked in the evenings, and why Olaus romped and played with him every night. It was his only exercise during those five weeks.

Olaus has a biologist's scorn of allowing anything biological to disturb him. All creatures are a legitimate part of the great pattern he believes in and lives by. He ignored the mosquitoes with a saintly manner that made me furious at times. But one day he paid!

He and Jess had been chasing a long white-fronted goose for a long time. As it was the first white-fronted goose of the season, it was worth a lot of time and effort. Olaus finally went ashore under a steep mud bank and waited for Jess to drive the goose to him with the canoe. From across the river, where I had hooked a willow, I watched the play. The goose swam upstream, Jess after it. Just as he came close enough to hope to turn its course, the goose dived. Jess waited and watched. As soon as the goose came up he paddled hard, trying to get ahead of it and force it to swim toward Olaus. The goose dived.

This went on for a half an hour. Every line of Jess's figure as he swung the paddle expressed determination; even under his head net I could see how his long jaw was set. The goose seemed fresh as a daisy. It rose each time with a quick sidewise glance at the canoe and a Bronx-cheer kind of honk.

Once she came up very near the scow. Jess came tearing past, talking to the goose. "God damn you, I'll get you if we have to go clear to the canyon together!"

Away they went around the bend; Olaus waved to me from across the stream, the kind of wave that said: "This is a funny life we're in, isn't it!"

Then the goose came swimming back again, paddling furiously, honking a little anxiously; right behind her Jess, also paddling furiously. And this time she decided shore was the place.

Olaus had lifted his net to watch the performance, and had also taken off his gloves—something Jess or I would never have done. Now he had to freeze into position, for the goose had begun to wade ashore at the spot where he was crouching. It padded determinedly up the bank. Suddenly it became aware of the figure there and hesitated. "Onk?" it questioned, and waited, watching Olaus. Then it put one web foot forward in the mud. "Onk?" again. Olaus didn't dare move an eyelid. Mosquitoes were setting in black clouds on his face and hands.

Out in the stream sat Jess, at ease in the canoe. Now it was his turn; he could make all the noise he wanted; he had forgotten his awful anger at that goose. "Heh, heh, heh," he said in his high-pitched voice. "How you like the mosquitoes, eh? Nice comfortable position you're in, isn't it?"

Olaus kept silent; he was as determined to get this bird as Jess was. The bird took another very tentative step, looked at Olaus, and asked him again: "Onk?" No answer. From out on the river: "Boy, don't you wish you'd kept your net on! How long d'you think this will take? Watch her now!"

The goose took three steps; it was feeling the nearness of the overhung bank and safety above it. Like a fox drawing his legs up imperceptibly for a pounce, Olaus moved his feet, so carefully. "Onk?" Spring! Pounce! He had it round the body by both hands; they were sliding down the slippery mud together, and Jess was whooping: "Hang on, don't let her slip—I'm coming! How do your mosquito bites feel? Boy, don't anybody ever say anything to me about foolish as a goose; they're about the smartest damn critters you can find!"

They were slow, strenuous hours, chasing geese like this. Yet practically every goose we saw was caught and banded. Either the Old Crow had been much overrated as a nesting ground or something strange had happened in 1926, for we never found the "hundreds of thousands" someone had described to the powers in Washington. The days were hot and muggy, and we felt almost a claustrophobia down there between those steep banks of thawing Pleistocene mud, in a steaming, whining breathless world where insects were in full command. We human creatures were saved from insanity and death only by a few yards of cheese cloth and netting and leather. Sometimes the shield felt pretty thin. We longed for a breeze with passionate longing and welcomed a hard shower, because it downed the hordes for a while; and at least it substituted the sound of water for that other perpetual sound.

"Notice how much lower the banks are today? I think we're getting into different country." Olaus, always hopeful, always optimistic, was poling today.

Jess was on the line, over on the lower shore. His answer was prompt: "Can't be different country any too damn soon for me."

Five o'clock—the banks still lower, a clear sky. "Hey, Mardy, feel the breeze?"

I scrambled out from my "hole." What a feeling! Moving air! I looked up; the solid cloud of spiraling insects was gone; the wind had dispersed their formation, broken their absolute control of the land. "Can't I go ashore and walk a little? Martin's asleep."

I fell into step behind Jess, shoulder under the line. "Sure a lot more current here," he said. "Maybe we are getting into something different; even that old mud bank over there is pretty low. Looks as though it ends up ahead there. What's that?"

A dull boom, like a distant cannon shot, from upstream. "D'you hear that?" Olaus yelled. We threw our utmost into pulling, peering upstream. "Be a good joke if we found people up here after thinking we were the only ones in creation."

"I don't think it sounded like rifle fire exactly."

"Could some party have come over from the Arctic? You said it was only about eighty miles in a straight line now."

We rounded the next bend. "Boom!" Right there, near us. Then Olaus shouted, pointing; ripples were running out against the current in one place. In the mud bank on the opposite shore we saw a great lens of dirty brown ice. We watched. Crash! A big piece of ice suddenly dropped into the water, a rending, a crash, and a splash. Here was the exact northern shore of that ancient lake; the Pleistocene ice was being defeated by summer sun and the modern stream.

Suddenly Jess threw up his arm with a shout: "She's clear!"

I dropped the line and rushed to the very edge; there on our side was clear, shining beautiful water. As though sighting a new planet, we looked down into the bottom, into the beautiful yellow gravel. Then we looked across, and halfway over, there was the dark line in the stream where the Pleistocene mud was still falling off with the ice.

"Come on," Olaus shouted. "Let's get above that mud. Look, it's flattening out up here. We *are* in different country."

A mile above the lens of ice we made camp, to the accompaniment of that cannonading; it exploded regularly, every two minutes by the watch. We had, in the space of a few moments, emerged into another world. The gravel bank was low to the stream, flat as a floor, dotted with all manner of brave arctic bushes and flowers. Better yet, there was a breeze blowing, and best of all, we were on top of the world; we had come up out of weeks in that Pleistocene hole.

We threw off our head nets, gloves, and heavy shirts, and stood with the breeze blowing through our hair, gazing all around. We could see, far out over miles of green tundra, blue hills in the distance, on the Arctic coast no doubt. This was the high point; we had reached the headwaters of the Old Crow. After we had lived with it in all its moods, been down in the depths with it for weeks, it was good to know that the river began in beauty and flowed through miles of clean gravel and airy open space.

Latitude 68 degrees, 30 minutes.

We had a paradise camp for a few days. The men went out in the canoe and explored the river upstream. It became shallow rapidly, and they satisfied themselves that there were no other goose grounds. Martin had a heavenly time, turned loose in the air and sunshine. He had long since learned that gravel hurt his knees; he did not crawl, but walked on all fours like a cub bear. Here on a long leash he explored, crawling right over the low bushes, playing peek-a-boo behind them, scuttling away like a laughing rabbit when someone "found" him.

Jess caught some eighteen-inch grayling the very first night in the clear pools just above camp. The baby stood at my knee and kept begging for another bite and another bite while Jess kept saying: "It can't hurt him; it's good for him," till we realized he had consumed a whole big grayling.

Jess is a real fisherman, and getting these beauties, our first fish in weeks, lifted his spirits a little. But he was experiencing a letdown of sorts. He was drawing away from us, into himself. After all, I don't know how one could expect a trip of this kind to be all sweetness and light unless the personnel were recruited in heaven. Plenty of things could have affected Jess. Olaus and I were together; we were content; his Clara was miles, weeks, months, away from him, and she was to bear their sixth child in August before he could be with her again. Then his motorboat had let him down. Every one of those slow miles up the river since June 29 must have reminded him of how easy it all would have been with that engine. And now after the tremendous effort was over and we had reached the headwaters—well, there had to be a letdown.

It was hard having Jess lost to us. He became a very polite stranger. At meals: "No thank you," instead of "Couldn't eat any more of the stuff!" "Yes, please," instead of "Hey, Mardy, you going to eat all the stew yourself?" He was even more polite to Olaus. They were really on the outs. Before, they had been two old pals on a trip together; now Jess was a stiffly polite employee; Olaus was the boss.

It was good that, while Olaus explored, Jess went fishing. I didn't blame him for needing to get away by himself.

Three days' respite from the mosquitoes; then it was time to turn south, back into the mud, and brown water, and clouds of insects. We all worked at sorting and reloading the outfit, in polite formality. The baby's little nook was placed amidships now, to make room up front for the rowing. The handmade oarlocks were put in place, then the two long oars, which had been made from two spruce trees.

On that last evening, after the baby was asleep, Olaus and I slipped across the river in the canoe and climbed up onto the tundra. It was ten o'clock, July 26. The sun had just slipped below a distant blue ridge, but bright saffron light filled the northwest; the rest was pale blue. It was still daytime, but that very still, strange, exhilarating daytime of the arctic summer night, which can only be felt, not described. Here the flowing green-bronze tundra stretched as far as we could see—to the north, a few short ranges of hills; far to the south, rising pale blue off the flatness, the Old Crow Mountains again. In the morning we would be turning toward them.

We stood there for a long time, just looking. This might be our farthest north, ever. If we could only take a giant step and see the Arctic shore; we were so near.

Then our eyes came back to the near tundra, the velvety sphagnum hummocks, the myriad tiny arctic plants gleaming in the moss, in the golden light. The Labrador tea had gone to seed, but its sharp fragrance filled the air. In a tiny birch tree, a white-crowned sparrow, the voice of the arctic summer—"You will remember; you will remember," he sang.

Borders

Barry Lopez is the author of *Arctic
Dreams*, *Of Wolves and Men*, and
several story collections including
Desert Notes, *Winter Count*, and
*Giving Birth to the Thunder, Sleeping
With His Daughter: Coyote Builds
North America*. A contributing editor
to *Harper's* and *North American
Review*, he is the recipient of the
John Burroughs Medal and an Award
in Literature from the American
Academy and Institute of Arts and
Letters.

In early September, the eastern arctic coast of Alaska shows several faces, most of them harsh. But there are days when the wind drops and the sky is clear, and for reasons too fragile to explain—the overflight of thousands of migrating ducks, the bright, silent austerity of the Romanzof Mountains under fresh snow, the glassy stillness of the ocean —these days have an edge like no others. The dawn of such a clear and windless day is cherished against memories of late August snow squalls and days of work in rough water under leaden skies.

One such morning a few of us on a biological survey in the Beaufort Sea set that work aside with hardly a word and headed east over the water for the international border, where the state of Alaska abuts the Yukon Territory. The fine weather encouraged this bit of adventure.

There are no settlements along this part of the arctic coast. We did not in fact know if the border we were headed to was even marked. A northeast wind that had been driving loose pack ice close to shore for several days forced us to run near the beach in a narrow band of open water. In the lee of larger pieces of sea ice, the ocean had begun to freeze, in spite of the strong sunlight and a benign feeling in the air. Signs of winter.

As we drove toward Canada, banking the open, twenty-foot boat in graceful arcs to avoid pieces of drift ice, we hung our heads far back to watch migrating Canada geese and black brant pass over. Rifling past us and headed west at fifty miles an hour a foot off the water were flocks of oldsquaw, twenty and thirty ducks at a time. Occasionally, at the edge of the seaward ice, the charcoal-gray snout of a ringed seal would break the calm surface of the ocean for breath.

We drew nearer the border, wondering aloud how we would know it. I remembered a conversation of years before, with a man who had escaped from Czechoslovakia to come to America and had later paddled a canoe the length of the Yukon. He described the border where the river crossed into Alaska as marked by a great swatch cut through the spruce forest. In the middle of nowhere, I said ruefully; what a waste of trees, how ugly it must have seemed. He looked silently across the restaurant table at me and said it was the easiest border crossing of his life.

I thought, as we drove on east, the ice closing in more now, forcing us to run yet closer to the beach, of the geographer Carl Sauer and his concept of biologically distinct regions. The idea of bioregionalism, as it has been developed by his followers, is a political concept that would reshape human life. It would decentralize residents of an area into smaller, more self-sufficient, environmentally responsible units, occupying lands the borders of which would be identical with the borders of natural regions—watersheds, for example. I thought of Sauer because we were headed that day for a great, invisible political dividing line: 141 degrees western longitude. Like the border between Utah and Colorado, this one is arbitrary. If it were not actually marked—staked —it would not be discernible. Sauer's borders are noticeable. Even the birds find them.

On the shore to our right, as we neared the mouth of Demarcation Bay, we saw the fallen remains of an Eskimo sod house, its meat-drying racks, made of driftwood, leaning askew. Someone who had once come this far to hunt had built the house. The house eventually became a dot on U.S. Coast and Geodetic Survey maps. Now its location is vital to the Inuit, for it establishes a politically important right of prior use, predating the establishment of the Arctic National Wildlife Refuge, within whose borders it has been included. I recall all this as we pass, from poring over our detailed maps the night before. Now, with the warmth of sunlight on the side of my face, with boyhood thoughts of the Yukon Territory welling up inside, the nearness of friends, with whom work has been such keen satisfaction these past few weeks, I have no desire to see maps.

Ahead, it is becoming clear that the closing ice is going to force us right up on the beach before long. The wedge of open water is narrowing. What there is is very still, skimmed with fresh slush ice. I think suddenly of my brother, who lives in a house on Block Island, off the coast of Rhode Island. When I visit we walk and drive around the island. Each time I mean to ask him, does he feel any more ordered in his life for being able to see so clearly the boundary between the ocean and the land in every direction? But I am never able to phrase the question right. And the old and dour faces of the resident islanders discourage it.

Far ahead, through a pair of ten-power binoculars, I finally see what appears to be a rampart of logs, weathered gray-white and standing on a bluff where the tundra falls off fifteen or twenty feet to the beach. Is this the border?

We are breaking ice now with the boat. At five miles an hour, the bow wave skitters across the frozen surface of the ocean to either side in a hundred broken fragments. The rumbling that accompanies this shattering of solid ice is like the low-throttled voice of the outboard engines. Three or four hundred yards of this and we stop. The pack ice is within twenty feet of the beach. We cannot go any farther. That we are only a hundred feet from our destination seems a part of the day, divinely fortuitous.

We climb up the bluff. Arctic-fox tracks in the patchy snow are fresh. Here and there on the tundra are bird feathers, remnants of the summer molt of hundreds of thousands of birds that have come this far north to nest, whose feathers blow inland and out to sea for weeks. Although we see no animals but a flock of snow geese in the distance, evidence of their residence and passage is everywhere. Within a few hundred feet I find caribou droppings. On a mossy tundra mound, like one a jaeger might use, I find two small bones that I know to be a ptarmigan's.

We examine the upright, weathered logs and decide on the basis of these and several pieces of carved wood that this is, indeed, the border. No one, we reason, would erect something like this on a coast so unfrequented by humans if it were not. (This coast is ice-free only eight or ten weeks in the year.) Yet we are not sure. The bluff has a certain natural prominence, though the marker's placement seems arbitrary. But the romance of it—this foot in Canada, that one in Alaska —is fetching. The delightful weather and the presence of undisturbed animals has made us almost euphoric. It is, after days of bottom trawls in thirty-one-degree water, of cold hours of patient searching for seals, so clearly a holiday for us.

I will fly over this same spot a week later, under a heavy overcast, forced down to two hundred feet above the water in a search for migrating bowhead whales. That trip, from the small settlement of Inuvik on the East Channel of the Mackenzie River in the Northwest Territories to Deadhorse, Alaska, will make this border both more real and more peculiar than it now appears. We will delay our arrival by circling over Inuvik until a Canadian customs officer can get there from the village of Tuktoyaktuk on the coast, though all we intend to do is to drop off an American scientist and buy gas. On our return trip we are required by law to land at the tiny village of Kaktovik to check through U.S. Customs. The entry through Kaktovik is so tenuous as to not exist at all. One might land, walk the mile to town, and find or not find the customs officer around. Should he not be there, the law requires we fly 250 miles south to Fort Yukon. If no one is there we are to fly on to Fairbanks before returning to Deadhorse on the coast, in order to reenter the country legally. These distances are immense. We could hardly carry the fuel for such a trip. And to fly inland would mean not flying the coast to look for whales, the very purpose of being airborne. We fly straight to Deadhorse, looking for whales. When we land we fill out forms to explain our actions and file them with the government.

Here, standing on the ground, the border seems nearly whimsical. The view over tens of square miles of white frozen ocean and a vast expanse of tundra which rolls to the foot of snow-covered mountains is unimpeded. Such open space, on such a calm and innocent day as this, gives extraordinary release to the imagination. At such a remove —from horrible images of human death on borders ten thousand miles away, from the press of human anxiety one feels in a crowded city— at such a remove one is lulled nearly to foundering by the simple peace engendered, even at the border between two nations, by a single day of good weather.

As we turn to leave the monument, we see two swans coming toward us. They are immature tundra swans, in steel-gray plumage. Something odd is in their shape. Primary feathers. They have no primary feathers yet. Too young. And their parents, who should be with them, are nowhere to be seen. They are coming from the east, from Canada, paddling in a strip of water a few inches deep right at the edge of the beach. They show no fear of us, although they slow and are cautious. They extend their necks and open their pink bills to make gentle, rattling sounds. As they near the boat they stand up in the water and step ashore. They walk past us and on up the beach. Against the gritty coarseness of beach sand and the tundra-stained ice, their smooth gray feathers and the deep lucidity of their eyes vibrate with beauty. I watch them until they disappear from view. The chance they will be alive in two weeks is very slim. Perhaps it doesn't exist at all.

In two weeks I am thousands of miles south. In among the letters and magazines in six weeks of mail sitting on the table is a thick voter-registration pamphlet. One afternoon I sit down and read it. I try to read it with the conscientiousness of one who wishes to vote wisely. I think of Carl Sauer, whose ideas I admire. And of Wendell Berry, whose integrity and sense of land come to mind when I ponder any vote and the effect it might have. I think of the invisible borders of rural landscapes, of Frost pondering the value of fences. I read in the pamphlet of referendums on statewide zoning and of the annexation of rural lands, on which I am expected to vote. I read of federal legislative reapportionment and the realignment of my county's border with that of an Indian reservation, though these will not require my vote. I must review, again, how the districts of my state representative and state senator overlap and determine if I am included now within the bounds of a newly created county commissioner's territory.

These lines blur and I feel a choking coming up in my neck and my face flushing. I set the pamphlet on the arm of the chair and get up and walk outside. It is going to take weeks, again, to get home.

CLARA FOSSO

Alone With Death on the Tundra

Clara Fosso was born in 1888 in Long Lake, Minnesota, and, following her graduation from the University of Minnesota, moved to Teller, Alaska, where she and her husband, a Norwegian Lutheran minister, worked as missionaries from 1917 to 1920. After Teller, they moved to Wisconsin and Minnesota, returning to Alaska in 1930 to live in Ketchikan. Mrs. Fosso died in 1966.

Oluf and I had spent our first year of marriage as young missionaries at the Teller Lutheran Mission. We were in our second year of adjustment to the Alaska "sourdough" way of living when the "flu" came. Our baby boy had been born in July and this was November. Fortunately, Jorgine Enestvadt, a government teacher who had spent the previous twelve years teaching the Eskimos, was with us. She knew not only the nature and customs of the Eskimos, but also what was necessary for us to do to prepare for a secluded and "snowed-in" winter.

Secluded it was, for it was ninety miles by dog-trail to Nome and fourteen miles to Teller, the nearest trading post. Teller was populated by about twenty white people and some natives. We, at the Mission, had no communication with these places for in 1918 radio was something little more than a dream.

Four Eskimo children and Isibruk, a feeble minded girl of about thirty, lived with us at the mission. A quarter of a mile away was a group of igloos housing about one hundred Eskimos and there were scattered igloos along the coast.

Negotiations were then in progress to end the bloody battles of World War I when the scourge of influenza, even more ravaging and extensive than the war, had begun. Spanish influenza, as it was called, not only encircled the earth through the temperate and warm regions but also reached its demon claws into some Arctic areas, often claiming as much as three-fourths of the Eskimo population wherever it struck.

Did the "flu" germs fly in the air? I think we have good proof that they did not. Families who had no contact with the sick did not get the "flu." Such a one was the Dunnak family. When this Eskimo family was approaching the Winfield Store at Teller to trade their fox-skins for white-man's food they were met with a shout, "Everybody 'peelak' (sick). No come or you 'peelak' too." Bewildered, the Dunnak family turned in their tracks, returned to their igloos in the hills and lived on Eskimo food that winter, but contracted no influenza.

Likewise, to the north of Teller, the native villagers of Shishmaref were warned of the many deaths at the neighboring settlements—the Teller Mission and the Cape Prince of Wales. As cautious and wise Eskimos, they set up a day and night vigil to prevent dog teams from entering or leaving the village. Shishmaref was spared the scourge of the deadly "flu" bug.

We had no such warning at the Teller mission. It was a Sunday in November. The little chapel was filled. This meant no sitting room on the floor or seats. Welcomed to the services were two native visitors who brought greetings from Nome. They reported, "Much peoples come from outside (states) on Victoria (steamer). Peoples much 'peelak' (sick)."

Special joy and friendliness were felt in the little chapel as we partook of holy communion. I remember, too, at the close of the service that old man Kinauquak rose and said, "Please, Man of God (missionary), give sermon over again."

Rather surprised at such a request, the missionary asked, "Did you not understand it?"

Kinauquak answered, "Ili kans mik (thank you), me remember all, but Emaklena—him late—him need hear, too."

The missionary responded, "Kinauquak, maybe you tell him."

True Eskimo hospitality reigned that afternoon as they joined in feasting on reindeer meat, Eskimo hot cakes, blueberries in seal oil, and tea. Then followed the usual songfest and discussion of the morning sermon. The tardy Emaklena was not left unenlightened. The Eskimos are truly a friendly lot with much love and concern for one another.

I do not recall what became of the visitors but the "flu" germs they brought were bent on their deadly work. On Monday, calls came for the missionary to visit sick natives. Tuesday, Mrs. Neelak died. The five Eskimos in our mission and the missionary became ill. We did not know what the sickness was. Whatever it was, it seemed to affect its victims in three different ways; some the brain, some the lungs, others had intestinal trouble.

Jorgine, the baby and I were still well. Fearing that we might also become sick, however, my husband determined to go for help. Though feverish and somewhat delirious, he hitched up the dogs and drove the fourteen miles to Teller. He returned with the word that the situation there was no better than ours. They promised only that someone would visit us up at the mission as soon as they were able.

As he unhitched the dogs after that strenuous and futile attempt for aid, he looked up to see a staggering form through the tundra twilight. It was Alaluk. A woman reared at the mission, she spoke fluent English. "We are in need of spiritual help. Will you come with me?"

The missionary's answer could only be, "I will come."

The two figures staggered back to Alaluk's igloo. There, lying on a cot, was a very sick child. The father, Anakartuk, was huddled and shivering beside a cold oil-drum stove. All of the store of driftwood had been burned. It was cold, but somehow a strange light and warmth filled that room as they read together the twenty-third psalm and joined in prayer. The three then staggered the quarter mile back to the mission with little Florence on a sled. The three year old lay two days unconscious with what appeared to us to be a brain fever when death relieved her.

Two days later Anakartuk, too, passed on. Alaluk, an expectant mother, developed pneumonia. About two o'clock one morning I heard Jorgine come down the stairs. Suspecting something was wrong, I met her in the kitchen. She said, "Alaluk thinks her baby is coming and wants me to get Angak." Angak (the old woman) was an Eskimo midwife.

"With all the loose dogs around it's too risky for you to go alone this time of night, so I'm going with you," I said. She tried to dissuade me, saying it would be tragic if the two of us didn't return, for the dogs were panicky from hunger. We couldn't spend our time arguing so we armed ourselves with a flashlight and a stick and set out into the stormy night, making sure to follow the edge of the tundra.

Crawling through the long dark passageway we entered the igloo, finding there as many people as there was space for them on the floor. We had to call out our errand and someone raised up and pointed Angak out. I think I can still hear the snoring, moaning, and groaning in that igloo on that weird night. We found Angak underneath a reindeer skin. After much persistence we were able to help her into her mukluks and the outer parka. Crawling out through the passageway went very well, but we had gone about twenty steps down a bank when she fell down and again I had to persuade the ardent Jorgine before she would agree to return poor Angak to her bed of skins. Angak had the influenza and it took all our strength to get her back into the igloo to her deathbed. After that night's experience Jorgine, too, became seriously ill with double pneumonia. Alaluk's baby was not born and a few days later, after expressing her content to join her husband and child in death, Alaluk said goodbye and thanked us for what we had done.

Just previous to Alaluk's passing, Isibruk had also died. She was a moody person (about 30 years old) who either cried or laughed all day long and required much care during the day. She told me she was going to be with Jesus and that he had paid for her sins.

I could without help drag these bodies into an unfinished part of the upstairs. Alaluk's body was the fifth and last to be so stored. Little Florence's remains had been placed in an outdoor storeroom. She was the only one to lie in a coffin which my husband had been well enough to make and even cover with cloth. However, as I retired one evening, I discovered that seepage from the corpses had penetrated through into our bedroom. This meant moving our heavy home-made bedstead into the living room near Oluf's cot. Two weeks later we were able to remove the dead and place them in Alaluk's igloo.

Because of his trip to Teller, Oluf had a serious relapse, so for three weeks time I was the only person walking. Each day more and more sick people were added to our number at the mission until I wondered what spot the next one would occupy. It was a long cumbersome stairway when it came to making the many daily turns with fuel and care of the sick with no toilet conveniences. I was not a muscularly strong person, but I do believe that superhuman strength was given me to lift tubs of coal as I was hauling fuel to run six stoves at thirty-five degrees below zero. The November daylight at Teller Mission is hardly four hours long, so I worked into the twilight to finish my outdoor chores. Besides hauling coal and tending stoves I had to chop ice in a creek about 30 yards away and melt it for drinking water. For wash water I would cut the snow with a saw and carry the chunks into an oil-drum connected by pipes to the cook stove. "A wonderful invention," I thought, for the snow melted and hot water could be taken from a tap on the oil drum. When these tasks were being done, a tub of dog-food was cooking on the stove. There were seventeen dogs to feed. I climbed to a loft over an outdoor storeroom to get dried salmon and blubber which I supplemented with the cooked meal. On my way to the doghouse many hungry Eskimo dogs which had torn loose from their stakes would lurch around and follow me as they smelled food. At first, as I entered the doghouse, some of our own dogs showed vicious teeth when I came to feed and water them. Malemutes have much respect for their own master, but it takes time before they will adopt a new one. However, after a week or so, a few tails even wagged as I made my daily turn.

The long Arctic nights dragged on and grew longer and deeper. Although the mission home was filled with people, I was alone. There was no one to converse with. My husband was deliriously driving dogs in his sleep. The sick were constantly moaning and groaning. Outside, the loose wild dogs howled like wolves.

One night, after the nightly rounds of my patients and caring for the baby, I fell exhausted on the bed. I was sleeping heavily when a dog howling close to the window startled me. I jumped up and talking to myself, I asked, "Is this real or only a bad dream?" Seeking an answer, I stepped out on the doorstep from which I could look out over the frozen sea and into the heavens where the moon and stars shone on glistening snow when nights were clear. But what was this? I stood awed by the splendor of an immense curtain of gorgeous rainbow colors hanging from Heaven to the sea and swaying from side to side. "Is this the Lord's return?" I pondered. I stood dazed in expectancy. The bitter cold soon made me aware of the reality of my situation and I went inside fully assured that God was still on His throne and that I need not despair. I was not alone for He was with me.

A few days later I noticed great improvement in all the sick. It was a happy day for me when others began to walk about. Some of the Eskimo children began to do little jobs. Then my husband and later Jorgine were able to be about. They acclaimed me a good doctor and nurse. Could it be that epsom salts and camphorated oil were efficient remedies for "flu"? They were all I had.

When people from Teller finally were able to visit us, they hesitated, watching as they approached for smoke from our chimney before they ventured to rap on our door. Needless to say they were shocked at what had taken place but happy to see that some of us were still alive.

Later, another scouting party came from Teller to help us. One day was spent shooting the loose dogs and looking for signs of life in the igloos. One place had as many as twenty-five dead bodies. Alaluk's igloo in which the dead from the mission had been placed struck them with a scene of horror. Dogs had broken in and eaten them leaving a gory mess of human bones. They could only gather the remains into sacks.

Another igloo had had its "seal-gut" window in the roof broken. As the party of men looked down through the opening they saw several corpses. Much snow had drifted in. Luckily, one thought he saw something move in the corner of the igloo. As they shouted down, three frightened children popped from under the deer skins screaming. They virtually had to be captured for they seemed to be in a wild stupor. The children had kept themselves alive on a package of oatmeal. When brought to the mission they were like hungry animals and had to be spoon-fed for fear they would overeat. Their coal black hair was gray with lice. We trimmed it short and applied the usual ointment. This became most routine from day to day.

In another igloo, a girl was living all alone with the rest of the family dead around her. She couldn't tell how long they had been dead.

In an outlying settlement four children were found alive, several adults having died. All the wood and everything in the igloo that would burn had been used for fuel. The children had kept warm in their bedding of skins. The little girl of seven years had saved her baby brother's life by keeping cans of milk thawed by their body heat.

These and other children increased our mission family to forty-six orphans. Only eight grown-ups were left in the nearby settlement. To supply bedding for our big family the missionary made several trips to the village, gathering the skins from under many bodies. A trip to Nome with two dog teams for clothing had wonderful response from the army base there. Soldiers' uniforms were made over for the boys. For the girls we made over clothing from other sources to fit them.

Never have I known sorrow and joy to mingle as they did on that Christmas of 1918. We enjoyed Christmas with the usual broomstick made into a Christmas tree by threading dwarf-willow boughs through holes in the broomstick and winding green paper. Cranberries and pop corn were strung and candles added for light. After singing carols we closed our program with "In the Sweet Bye and Bye" in the Eskimo language as it had been translated by Anakartuk.

After Christmas, seventy-six bodies were hauled as wood on dog-sleds and placed side by side in a long trench steamed out of the frozen tundra with mining machinery to a depth of six feet. Burial services were later held at the graveside attended by the children and a few grown-ups. The missionary and wife from Mary's Igloo, who had gone through a similar tragic experience in their village, were also present.

It was at this place that bodies were exhumed recently by medical researchers. The bodies, lying on solid ice, were found to be well enough preserved to provide specimens for an attempt to isolate the influenza germ.

Can we hope that the scourge of influenza, so fatal and destructive to human life on the Eskimo tundra, may still become a benefit to humanity by helping to eliminate one of mankind's most dreaded diseases? Then my memories of those grim days alone with death on the tundra will be adorned with a flower of hope—that because these died, others in future years may live.

JOHN MORGAN

Letter
From Wales
(Alaska)

John Morgan grew up in New York
City and has been the co-director of
the writing program at the University
of Alaska, Fairbanks, since 1977. His
books of poetry include *The Inside
Passage*, *The Bone-Duster*, *The Arctic
Herd*, and *The Cyclist*.

Here at the tip of the Seward Peninsula, where it points west into the Bering Strait, an arrow in the shack that stands as the village post office also points west. Neatly hand-lettered it announces: "Russia, 30 Miles."

Partly to verify this fact, the other day I climbed the steep ridge that rises to the southeast behind the straggly double line of houses along the single dirt street that constitutes the Eskimo village of Wales, Alaska (pop. 130). It was a warm day, near fifty, sunny, and the wind which usually blows in a confusing, gusty, shifting fashion was temporarily calm. I followed the small stream that provides summer water for the village up to its source in a tundra spring. Snow buntings flitted around me, individually curious but cautious in groups, each warning the others not to get too close. Among the dark gray rocks I caught a fleeting glimpse of a bulky arctic hare. Two hours out of town, climbing toward the bright sun, as I neared the ridge-line there appeared on a farther ridge a large silver dish, rivaling the sun: an Air Force radar station, staring west.

I sat down on a boulder and turned that way myself. The village had disappeared below, and I looked out on the Bering Sea. To the north, more water: Kotzebue Sound and the Chukchi Sea. Mid-water, on this unusually clear morning lay the two Diomedes: islands separated by less than three miles, yet one full day apart. Little Diomede, part of Alaska and the U.S., is situated on our side of the International Date Line. Big Diomede, against which the smaller island is a dark silhouette, lies on the far side of the line, a day ahead of us. It belongs to the U.S.S.R.

Still farther off, about fifty-five miles from where I sat, I could see through haze the dim outline of the Siberian Coast.

I was, in effect, looking through time, into tomorrow, looking ahead by exactly one day, and I was somewhat reassured that the far coast appeared innocent, peaceful, reassured though I knew there would be large silver dishes out there staring back over here at us; and beyond the radar stations, missiles too, much like our own. But from the unusual vantage point I had, it was as easy to look back as ahead. For, if archaeologists are correct, the spot where I was sitting, sipping a six ounce can of Dole's unsweetened pineapple juice ($.57 at the Wales Native

Store), looked out on the route of crossing of the first people ever to set foot in the New World. And not just men had crossed here, but mastodons, mammoths, the hairy rhino: here lay the landbridge, here the crossings wave upon wave, Siberians moving east, animals first, then man. Indians, Eskimos.

In addition to its Eskimos, Wales is home to a handful of Caucasians and a Philippino-American couple who manage the naval weather station. Most of the Eskimos are out of town now, gone "camping" thirty miles to the northeast, where, at camp, they follow traditional ways; hunting, fishing, gathering berries. Those currently in town seem to wish they weren't—they feel the pull of the camp—but they're here usually out of a sense of responsibility to their children: school started this week. The kids having a good time out at camp will be falling behind in their schoolwork. Talking the other evening to my host, Walter Weyapuk, I could sense his hopes for his daughter Leah. A high school graduate himself (as is his wife, though this is not at all common in Wales), he patiently coached the bright, round-faced, smiling girl with her math and writing.

Walter is the postmaster (Wales, AK 99783). Compact, with a black wispy beard, a black moustache, he smokes as he talks, his hair shoulder-length like mine, a digital watch on his wrist. There's a mound behind the village, he tells me, a designated "Historical Site." Another village once stood there, its people in friendly competition with the people of Wales. But as time went on, feuding developed, fighting maybe; anyway, the ones over there picked up and moved. They went up north to the village of Point Hope. When Walter Weyapuk left Wales to attend high school, his roommate came from Point Hope. They compared notes and found that the two village traditions agree on this point.

The Weyapuks, Walter, his wife Flo, Leah, and an adopted two-year-old son, much-loved Michael, occupy a three bedroom prefab house provided by the Bureau of Indian Affairs. Now, Eskimos aren't Indians, but at $35 a month, they'll take the house. Many other families in town have identical dwellings, and those who don't usually live worse. This place is comfortable, even if it isn't quite secure against the arctic

winds. Its kitchen—a common feature in the village—has two stoves
and no refrigerator (the enclosed front porch serves well enough for
that). Two stoves because, should the village generator conk out, a
back-up heat source will be needed.

Yes, there's electricity, but no plumbing. The BIA-provided bathtub
serves for storage. I noticed that it currently contains a basket filled
with dirty laundry, two large bags of Friskies Dog Dinner, several rolls
of paper towels, a rusted two gallon can, cables, some boxes of Pam-
pers, a rug, and a fancy oval Cardin make-up box. For a toilet, the
now-traditional "honey pot"—a covered plastic bucket with a toilet
seat above a disposable plastic bag.

I've felt a lot of different things in the three days since I flew in
from Nome. The plane that brought me, a rickety six-seater provided
by Forster Air Charter, followed the coastline for the last half hour no
more than 100 feet off the water. Along the way we saw five or six dead
walruses on the beach, and each time my pilot moved in closer, hoping
to spot one with tusks. No luck—they'd already been removed. I'll ad-
mit I was scared as we banked steeply around those rocky points of
land that jut out into the sea—scared but exhilarated. And I was feeling something else, something more disturbing—separation anxiety, I
decided it was. It was like being sent away to camp for the first time.

In Nome I was told it would be rough, that I would see some disturbing things, some things that would disgust me. I haven't found it
that way. Look, I'm from New York: what could be rougher than that?
Still, my moods here fluctuate, intense interest giving way to periods
of intense boredom. The thought of living here—no movie house, no
tv for God's sake!—horrifies me at times. At other moments it seems
perfectly natural. The Weyapuks' extended family—the grandmother
(a distinguished village elder), the many uncles and cousins—takes in
a good percentage of the population here, and reminds me in some
ways of my own large New York Jewish family, with similar tensions,
intimacies, rewards.

In many ways Wales is much less cut-off than I'd expected. Radio,
telephone, mail service, cb, hi-fi all connect it to the fast-moving world
out there. "I collect albums," Walter tells me. "I can pick up the phone,

call Anchorage, and have the records I want in five days." His latest shipment just came in: Linda Ronstadt, Billy Joel, the Stones ("Emotional Rescue"), Eagles, Lipps Inc. "The Greeks Don't Like No Freaks" gloats on the hi-fi, as we sip tea, munch on pizza, thumb through *Newsweek*, a Sears catalog, the *National Enquirer*. All these reach Wales, and more.

And yet it is *not* the same. Walter tells me about the spring hunt. First whales (beluga and bowhead), then bearded seals, then walrus, each for a period of weeks coming up the coast on their annual migrations. This spring—much excitement—for the first time in ten years the village got a bowhead, a small one, thirty-five feet. When that happens, everybody in the village gets some, everybody eats better. With chicken at the village store going for $7.50 apiece, subsistence hunting is no joke.

Still, the Weyapuks do vary their diet with an occasional chicken, beef (generally cooked as soup), with pizza (the Chef Boyardee pepperoni mix costs $3.02, but if you live here you get used to the prices). My first meal in town was bearded seal with onions. For dessert, "Eskimo ice-cream": reindeer fat and sugar whipped up over salmon berries. The dried seal was milder than I'd expected, the salmon berries crisp and sweet; I went easy on the ice cream.

The other day Eric flew in. Tall, bearded, white, a man of the Sixties, casual in manner but intensely talkative, driving. From Milwaukee originally, he's lived in Nome the past six years, travels around to villages buying up ivory (walrus tusks, whale bone, fossil mammoth and mastodon tusks), carved and uncarved, buying it up for resale in Nome. I suspect some of the stuff he buys comes from that mound behind the village—not strictly legal trade. Eric is happy to spend $100 to get here, confident of turning a good profit in Nome.

He cuts overhead, I'm told, by bringing in booze and selling it to a few reliable customers. The night he spent here was the only time I've seen a drunken Eskimo in the village. As that old man weaved his way up the street, children were called in to the homes. Eric is also blamed for the break up last year of a marriage. Again it was booze.

But it would be wrong, I am aware, to idealize Wales and blame its problems on outsiders. The occasional drowning or hunting accident, the drinking and drugs, the too frequent suicides—these are not all imports from Nome. One hundred thirty people on a sandy spit of land reaching into an arctic sea—what a fragile enterprise at any time of year! And when winter closes in with roof-high drifts, sub-zero cold, and nearly continuous dark, who'd blame the whole town for folding up and moving elsewhere?

Wrong again. Those are my white-man's natural assumptions, but in fact not winter but summer is the alien season here. Oh, the few warm perfect days of continuous sunlight are appreciated, but except for fish-camp the residents of Wales find summer boring. There's just not that much to do. The kids play soccer and climb on the roofs. The adults play pinochle, pool (in the Village Association rec hall), and visit back and forth. Winter brings snow-machines, ice-skating, downhill and cross-country skiing, dog sleds. Chop a hole in the ice and drop a line. Remembering keenly, Walter tells me how he contrived a twenty-foot-long snow tunnel from the post office door out to the street last winter. Snow is the Eskimo's element.

I'm here on a rural orientation program from the University of Alaska where I teach. Just whose orientation is involved is not exactly clear, but I dutifully pass out the stamped postcards I've been given addressed to the Office of Admissions and Records. The villagers can write for information. Natives make up about ten percent of the students at the Fairbanks campus, well below their proportion in the state population. I find, however, that the people of Wales are well aware of the University: the chairman of the Art Department, Ron Senungetuk, comes from Wales. Walter Weyapuk asks me somewhat wistfully if it's true that it takes four full years to get a degree. It's just too long to be away from the village, where he is an important member of the Council and the Board of the Village Corporation. Since the Native Claims Settlement Act, the village has had to manage large sums of money. The new general store was built out of these funds, but in general, Walter says, the older people just want the money kept in a bank. He would like to see more spent on improvements: a better generator, perhaps, or plumbing.

Besides Walter, a number of kids—teenagers—seem genuinely interested in the university. But whether interested or not, the villagers all seem puzzled by my presence. Archaeologists have been here to study their mound and anthropologists to study their traditions, their *way of life*, but I am neither of these. I shrug, smile, repeat the words, rural orientation, and try to explain.

One feeling I neglected to mention before, but it comes back to me strongly as I sit here on the ridge looking out over all that land and water—is privilege. What an honor to be able to fly into this village, be met at the airstrip and welcomed into a home. I pay my way of course, but that's not the point. It's so easy in this day of mass culture to lose all sense of the particularity of your own personal experience: how little we do that isn't equally available to everyone we know. But this is certainly different and enriching. My strongest regret, I find, is that I can't stay longer and spend some time at the fish-camp. The impact of Western culture is recent, subsistence hunting thousands of years old.

Yesterday, a flock of cranes in a lopsided V flew over, honking, coming from Siberia. Someone ran out of a house and fired a shot at them right in the middle of the village. I'll take that away with me, along with all the bones that litter and for me symbolize the elemental nature of the place: whale bones, seal bones, scattered vertebrae and ribs—bones of all sizes going back to the sand. On one doorstep the skulls and tusks of half a dozen walruses.

And I'll take this—a yellow Bombi Bombardier towing a flatbed trailer. On the flatbed a green metal boat with two outboards. In the boat, brown plastic bags loaded with supplies, and four people sitting up there, two with holstered pistols. A large tan dog is handed up to them and eagerly joins their company, as they set off in high spirits for camp. One of the men in the trailer is white: someone who stayed.

I feel I could stay too, but I know I won't. A question arises: I've taken no snapshots, what can I bring home with me that will inevitably remind me of this place? The shells on the beach—some are beautiful —and the driftwood, sure I've collected some, but these are much like shells and driftwood from any beach, only more plentiful.

I know what I want. Behind the Weyapuks' house, discarded among sandgrass, there's a large whale vertebra from that bowhead they got last spring. It must be twenty inches across the beam, a rich creamy brown, and nobody seems to claim it.

The morning I'm to leave the weather turns bad. A strong southeast wind, heavy fog. The whitecaps are up. KNOM announces that a Wien Twin-Otter has taken off for Shishmaref, Wales, Teller, and back to Nome. No mention of my Forster Cessna. It seems touch and go as I lug my suitcase, my sleeping bag, my whale vertebra—I seem to need another hand for all this—out to the hangar, a quarter of a mile from town. I watch the fog and mist lift, then come back heavy. I hear a drone. It's the Twin-Otter taxiing up the runway. I'll get on if I can. But it turns out to be mostly for freight and full-up. Then, as they're about to take off, they pass the word that's just come in by radio: my charter is on its way.

I have at least an hour's wait. My thoughts move forward and back, but already my experiences here are changing, acquiring a frame, becoming dreamlike. I don't feel I'm losing them, I feel they're going deeper. Last night I stayed up till near two a.m. and wrote most of this article—just a snapshot, really. I can't claim more for it than that. Others will have to do the sociology, the economics, the political structure of the place. They will see Wales, perhaps, as a problem to be solved, and solving it will come away with answers of a much more positive sort than any I've acquired.

What can I do? I'm just a tourist after all. I love the place, but I can't stay. Yesterday I asked Flo Weyapuk about the vertebra, whether it would be all right to take it. She shrugged and said, a bit puzzled, a bit amused: "You found it. It's yours."

JOHN HILDEBRAND

Fables

John Hildebrand was born in 1949 in Royal Oak, Michigan, and attended the University of Michigan and the University of Alaska in Fairbanks where he also taught for several years. Mr. Hildebrand is the author of *Reading the River: A Voyage Down the Yukon,* as well as numerous articles and short stories. He has been teaching at the University of Wisconsin–Eau Claire since 1977.

The weather only worsened. The quick, lightning-shot storms of early summer were gone, replaced by a misting, wind-blown coastal weather that steadily ground me down. After the first hour at the throttle, I put on a wool sweater, then added a heavy woolen overshirt, a windbreaker, and finally a rubber rain poncho. Still, I felt chilled to the bone. A monotonous gloom settled over the day. The more I stared over the bow at the bobbing horizon, the less distinct it became—grey river, grey sky.

For a hundred and fifty miles below Kaltag, the Yukon flows through deserted country with no intervening villages and very few fishcamps. It is a perfectly bleak terrain, a Euclidean landscape of bald headlands and muskeg swamps, all sharp right angles and planes. Across the river, the Kaiyuh Flats stretch in an unbroken line of alder and willow, while to the west a stark range of coastal hills soars above the river, their summits disappearing into the thick cloud ceiling.

The river was a mile and a half across, split into channels by wooded islands that went on so long I often mistook them for the shore. I kept to the leeward side and ran below the terraced banks, dodging in and out of the wind. Crossing an open stretch between islands, the canoe would buck in the whitecaps, climbing a green swell only to pitch forward when the bottom of the wave dropped out and drenched me with spray.

Late in the day, running in a light rain, I startled a flock of sandhill cranes on the point of an island. The birds nest in the Flats and were gathering now in large numbers to prepare for their autumnal migration south. A rush of grey wings, a few tentative hops, and the cranes went aloft with a great clangor. They flew across the river at a slight incline —long necks extended, legs trailing—breaking into three flights against the backlit sky. Then they headed back, circling to gain altitude. Higher and higher, the cranes kettled into the sky, a great wheel turning on the axis of the clouds.

Not being a naturalist, I'm interested more in my own species, but traveling through a long stretch of unpopulated wilderness I often wondered where all the game was hiding. Except for the occasional moose or black bear tramping along the beach, what wildlife I'd glimpsed on this journey had been in the sky above or the river below. These great migrations went on for the most part unseen. The birds and the salmon I did encounter always seemed to be in a crowd, always in a hurry, and always headed upriver. As the long summer days dwindled, I often got a sinking feeling that I was going in the wrong direction.

After ten hours at the throttle, I killed the engine and glided onto a sandbar, a tear-drop Atlantis recently emerged from the falling river. Without the outboard's constant droning, an immense silence settled on the water, broken only by the interior ticking of my own brain. I sat on a log in front of a driftwood fire, my heels dug into the sand, and watched the brown river steal past without a sound. In the west, beyond the headlands, a dull light was dying.

All day I had passed no other boats and seen no tents in the woods along shore. Only the land itself seemed alive—trees bending in the wind, the fluid movement of the river—all part of a world that lives and breathes without men. In such a landscape, who wouldn't feel peripheral and alone? Perhaps to make the land less lonely, Natives had invested the natural world with spirits, believing that animals and even plants possessed something like a soul. Setting off on a hunt, a hunter might address his quarry in song so that his prey, when he encountered it, was more than a stranger. The soothing words also assuaged any lingering guilt he might have felt at stalking a fellow spirit. Even the animal's death was governed by ritual and social obligations. I remember a Yupik Eskimo from the delta, a bright student and natural leader, who grew unaccountably glum and anxious during his wife's first pregnancy. Later he explained that he had failed to share the first seal he had killed with the rest of the village, as was the custom, and so he'd been worried that if his wife bore a son, the boy would be physically marked by the father's transgression. His wife delivered a baby girl, as it turned out, so the matter was laid to rest.

I don't know how much currency that view of the world has in villages today, or how long such beliefs can withstand the onslaught of daily soap operas and satellite-beamed golf matches. It's easy to lament the passing of such traditions even though I cannot bring myself to believe that animals have spirits. If we were ever on speaking terms, we've

long since forgotten the words or run out of things to say. When I've
brought a deer down in the woods and crept up to finish the job, following the wounded animal's hemorrhagic breathing, the last thing I'd
want to do is speak to it, or worse, have the deer speak back. Still, the
tribal hunter rarely felt lonesome in the woods, which was how I felt at
the moment. Marooned on this sandbar, I hungered for conversation,
for contact with a soul other than my own.

Swimming out of sight, great schools of whitefish and salmon keep
their own company in the river. Beluga whales sometimes lose their
way in the labyrinthine channels of the Yukon Delta and stray far upstream searching for an outlet to the sea. The 19th century naturalist
William Healy Dall mentions a white whale being killed a few miles
below Nulato, at least four hundred miles from saltwater, its appearance an ominous sign to the villagers of something clearly out of place.
But I think such a visitation would be marvelous. Out on the river
in the twilight, the canoeist feels something rubbing against the hull
as if he had run aground. Looking over the side, he sees a ghostly
shape breach the surface, exhaling mist from its blow hole. The head
is pale and fetal, eyes set back beneath the high, intelligent forehead,
the mouth a droll curve. Beluga and river traveler stare at each other
across the vast evolutionary gulf. In a high-pitched tremolo, the whale
speaks. What it asks is how to get home.

Through the rain, I saw a steamshovel, monstrous and wet, scoop-
ing gravel from the beach. The huge mechanical jaw hovered above a
dumptruck as though about to devour it, then unclenched, emptying
its load with a resounding crash so that the truck bounced twice. I followed the dumptruck up a puddled road past new frame houses built
on pads of gravel torn from the same beach.

Grayling was the only village I'd seen along the Yukon that did not
overlook the river. A half mile back from the beach, it occupied a
flat tongue of land flanked by birch-covered hills. Behind some trees,
a helicopter was landing and taking off with a jet-age whine. On the
front porch of the Native Store several loose-limbed teenagers stood
out of the rain and looked me over.

Off the river, I was quickly reduced to the role of tramp, dependent upon the charity of others and, in bad weather, the shelter of public buildings. So I went to mail a letter at the small post office. The mail plane had just landed, and the tiny foyer was jammed with people. The postmistress stood on the other side of an open dutch door dispensing mail. She wore an oversized cardigan sweater and a crumpled man's hat, set cockeyed on her head, that gave her a coquettish look. By the time I bought my stamps, everyone else had left.

"You look like you've been standing in the rain all day."

"More like three days," I told her.

The run-off from my rain poncho made a small puddle on the floor. I must have looked pathetic.

"Wanna come inside and warm up? I've got a stove in the next room. I'll put on some tea."

She held the dutch door open for me, then locked it shut. "So we won't be disturbed." From behind, the postmistress had a sweet, girlish figure, but her plucked eyebrows and smear of lipstick on her mouth made her look closer to forty. She'd made cozy quarters for herself adjacent to the mail room. There was a big potbellied stove and a television set blaring a game show. She'd decorated an entire wall of the room with pictures clipped from fashion magazines. Cover girls in various stages of cleavage and soft-focus lovers in fragrance advertisements stared down approvingly, although I imagined Grayling offered few opportunities to test out the wisdom of *Cosmopolitan.*

"Why don't you take off your wet clothes," she suggested "and I'll get us something to eat."

She disappeared out the back door while, a little uneasily, I stripped off my rain suit and layers of wet wool setting them beside the stove where they began to steam. Down to jeans and a t-shirt, I turned around to find the postmistress smiling at me. She'd returned with a loaf of spongy bread and a tin of cocktail sausages to eat with our tea. The room was already stifling, but the postmistress stoked the stove for my benefit until I felt flushed from the heat and the rose-scented cloud of her perfume.

Behind the stove was a wall map of Alaska. Tracing my finger down the Yukon River, I was perplexed at not being able to find Grayling on it.

"That's an old map," she said. "This place wasn't even a village until twenty years ago."

The people at Grayling had once lived far up the remote Innoko River at a place called Holikachuk. Since salmon didn't migrate up the Innoko, each summer the people would travel to the Yukon by way of an interconnecting slough to fish. In the early Sixties, the BIA convinced the people to move permanently to Grayling where they would be less isolated. Now nobody was left at Holikachuk.

"I'll tell you something if you promise not to laugh," the postmistress said huskily. "A long time ago, maybe a hundred years ago, people who were living way up the Innoko River killed a shaman. Before that shaman died, he told them that one day there would be no one living on the banks of the Innoko."

She pulled back a little. "Maybe you think that's a stupid story, but it's coming true! Nobody lives at Holikachuk anymore or at Iditarod or Flat. That leaves only Shageluk. And a lot of people are dying of cancer at Shageluk."

I didn't laugh.

"It's still pouring outside," she said, munching on a sausage. "Do you like games?"

After lunch, she brought out a Scrabble board. The television set still blared unwatched in the background.

"P-E-R-T," she said, spelling out each letter as she laid the little wooden tiles down on the board. "A triple word score. That's eighteen points!"

In no time at all, she was trouncing me. But then she came up with words I had never thought of before: hyphenated terms and misspellings and her own original compositions. But I didn't want to seem rude by pointing these out, especially since it was still raining.

While I tried forming a word on the board without vowels, a teenage boy came by (her son?) and gave me a hard-eyed look. When he left, I said I had to be going.

The postmistress pressed my knee warmly between hers.

"Are you married?"

"Yes," I lied. The funny thing was that I was a better flirt as a husband. A married man on the road is apt to act like a conventioneer, safe in the knowledge he has a home to go back to, while the single man knows he has to lie in whatever bed he makes for himself. I didn't want to wake up to any family scenes, besides being too much a coward for this.

"Then maybe you can give me a little advice on married men," the postmistress said. "There's this helicopter pilot who's a real fox!"

I told her I was the last person to ask for romantic advice. Putting on my damp clothes, I thanked her for lunch and headed out to the rain.

She asked where I was headed next.

"Anvik."

She laughed. "That's a wild place! Two families got into a shoot out not too long ago in Anvik. They call it Dodge City!"

It was thirty miles by river to Anvik. The rain had stopped, but a mist hung in tatters over the low mountains separating the Yukon from Norton Sound.

The Anvik River came in from the west behind a long point of land. I motored up the clear, dark tributary until I came to a village sheltered in the lee of a wooded bluff. The small houses hanging on the hillside and the damp smell of woodsmoke made me think of Appalachian hollows and feuding families locked in a deadly crossfire.

The Anvik general store had a plank floor and shelves stocked with hardware and a few groceries. When I asked the manager about the gun fight, he said the quarrel began over salmon stolen from a fishwheel. He was young and blond, and I could see he didn't want to talk about it.

"Things have quieted down since the shooting," he said. "One of the people is in jail. Nobody got killed. Someone just took a little buckshot in the hand is all."

He was less interested in Anvik's recent doings than in the safely distant past. From the backroom he returned with a cardboard box and set it on the counter. The box held a collection of Indian artifacts:

milky blue trade beads from Siberia, bone awls and combs, serrated ivory arrowheads, crescent-shaped slate ulus, or women's knives, and a bear-tooth pendant.

The storekeeper had found these things across the Anvik River on a point where the old village had been. As the Yukon ate away at the riverbank, it exhumed old graves, spilling bones onto the beach, as well as possessions placed with the dead to sustain them in the afterlife. Just the other day the storekeeper had seen a coffin hanging over the river, ready to drop, and surmised a double burial since it held two small skulls. He was quick to point out that he never disturbed the bones that tumbled onto the beach, only the trinkets and tools buried with them. Otherwise they would be washed to the sea.

"I'm only keeping them temporarily," he said, "until the village gets around to building a proper museum."

He replaced the lid on the box.

"If you're really interested in the past," he added, "you ought to talk with my in-laws."

The storekeeper's wife made a telephone call, and a few minutes later her father came to fetch me. He was short and slight and walked with such economy of movement as to appear weightless. Joe Jerrou lived a short walk from the store in a frame house with sturdy, dark furniture and a needlepoint sampler on the wall. His wife Alta was waiting for us in the livingroom. She wore a high-collared blue print dress, sturdy black shoes, and rimless glasses. A tall and graceful woman, she was old enough to have grown up speaking Ingalik Athabascan and now taught it to children in the village school so the language wouldn't disappear entirely. She spoke with the slow solemnity of her years.

"There was a trail to Saint Michael when people used to trade with the Eskimos for seal skins and seal oil for their lamps," she said. "The Indians always went to the coast in the spring when a crust covered the snow. They traded wolverine and wolf skin and 'made things' like wooden bowls and snowshoes. The Eskimos also liked the punk that grows on the sides of birch trees. Indians took baskets of it over, and the Eskimos mixed the punk with ashes to make a chewing tobacco."

The winter portage followed the Anvik River to its headwaters, then went over the divide to the Golsovia River and down the coast to Saint Michael. It was the same route used by the Russian creole Andri Glazunov when he crossed from Norton Sound in 1834 to become the first white man to lay eyes on the Yukon River. The last time anyone from Anvik crossed the portage to trade with the Eskimos was in the late 1920's, although ten years before the route had been used regularly.

"The village used to be on a point across the river," Alta said, "until the mission built the church and the people started coming over. I attended the mission school but I didn't live in the boarding school because I lived right here in Anvik. The boarding school took in children from up and down the river, mostly orphans."

Joe Jerrou excused himself to get his hearing aid. When he returned, he recalled seeing the first plane to land in Anvik, a biplane that skidded onto the frozen river on skis and brought a precious cargo of smallpox serum.

"That was the first plane I ever saw. The pilot had to stay two days because a thaw made the ice too sticky for him to take off."

Two years before, Anvik had been hard hit by a devastating influenza epidemic. The outbreak came in late April while snow still lay on the ground and the Indians were preparing to leave for their spring camps.

"I was a little girl then," Alta recalled. "When the flu came, people scattered. Some of them made another village two miles below Anvik. Others just lived in the woods along the river. A lot of people died. They'd come down with the flu, then catch pneumonia, and die. Afterwards the mission school took in many orphans. In June a hospital boat came down, but by then it was too late."

The epidemic struck particularly hard at the elderly and those already weakened from tuberculosis. As many as four or five people died in a single day. Because the ground was still frozen and most of the men sick, coffins were heaped upon a scaffolding until graves could be dug.

"Doctor Chapman did the best he could with the medical supplies at the mission," Alta said. "But he wasn't an M.D. He was a doctor of divinity."

She was six years old when John W. Chapman left Anvik after a life-

time as its missionary. A picture of Chapman's son and successor hung
on the Jerrou's livingroom wall. He was, she said fondly, the image of
his father.

John Wight Chapman was a soft-spoken New Englander who had
served his Episcopal diaconate in New York City before embarking
for the Bering Sea under the direction of the Domestic and Foreign
Missionary Society. On June 26, 1887, Chapman landed on the rain-
drenched coast at the old Russian fort of St. Michael to begin his
efforts. Walking on the beach a few days later, he chanced to see a
squad of marines from the revenue cutter *Bear* escorting the shackled
murderer of Bishop Seghers aboard. The Catholic missionary had been
killed in his sleep by his lay assistant, now a baying lunatic. It was an
inauspicious beginning.

Chapman and another missionary, Rev. Octavius Parker, purchased
an old boat and hired a steamboat to tow them through the boggy delta
and upriver to Anvik. Approaching the Ingalik village, Chapman saw
old men sitting on the cutbank, hands drawn into their parka sleeves,
watching impassively. "Something of a sense of loneliness came over
me," he wrote, "as I landed among a strange people, who spoke or
understood hardly a word of English."

"Ingalik" was a term given the Athabascan Indians of the lower
Yukon by their Eskimo neighbors; it meant "louse-ridden." The Indians
called themselves Deg Hit'an, or "the people from here." At the time of
Chapman's arrival, they lived in underground hovels, relished spoiled
fish-eggs, and bathed in urine. They believed that when a man died
his soul journeyed underground to a village of the dead located in the
mountains at the source of the Yukon. Thus they regarded the pale
strangers coming into their country as reincarnations of their deceased
ancestors who had somehow lost their way.

After the first winter in Anvik, Chapman and Parker moved the mission across the Anvik River from the village to be more autonomous.
For thirty yards of ticking, fifty pounds of flour, and some tea and sugar,
they purchased land at the foot of Hawk Bluff. Indian families were
not allowed to live on mission land unless they converted and paid a

yearly rental of one dollar. The Anvik River then became the dividing line between the "mission Indians" and the unreconstructed, a wide Jordan between heathen and saved.

Parker departed the second summer, leaving Chapman on his own. He stayed more than forty years. He built a church and a boarding school but, despite the steady trickle of Indians across the river to the mission, he felt himself losing the battle for souls with the village shamans. How was he expected to compete with men who conversed in dreams with animals or rescued the sun from being devoured by an eclipse?

To make his case, Chapman undertook to learn the Deg Hit'an language. He found an extensive vocabulary that wedded the Indians to their country and particularly to the great river running through it. To fix their position, for example, the Deg Hit'an chose from a string of riverine adverbs corresponding to our cardinal directions. Thus, there was *ngido'* for "downriver," *ngine'* for "upriver"; *nginiggi* for "back from the river," and *ngitthing* for "to the river."

With the help of an Indian named Isaac Fisher, Chapman began translating the legends and stories told in the *kashime*, or men's house, to pass the long winter nights. It was not an easy task. He wrote: "The one word which translates 'I thank thee' is an example of Ten'a spelling. It is *hoxwoqourcrigudastcet*. A page of this writing has something unfamiliar about it at first." Chapman found in the Deg Hit'an genesis a Creator specified only as someone being above. The first of his creations was a porcupine, followed by a white bear, a man, and a brown bear. Afterwards, the Creator retreated to a distant heaven from which he punished people for wrong-doing by taking away their food. A more vital character was Raven, who is called *Yoqgitsi* or "Your Grandfather." Always wandering and hungry, as well as over-sexed, it is Raven who introduces confusion into the world and makes death permanent by blazing a trail for the dead to take so that they do not return in spirit form. Chapman may have searched in vain for moral equivalents to the Gospel, but what he preserved was the face of a culture he had dedicated his life to undoing.

A hazy sun had broken through the clouds when I left the Jerrou's. Walking along the riverbank, I found the prim New England chapel with its white belfry and shake-covered walls that Chapman had built in a style to remind him of home. The mission boarding school next to it had fallen on harder times. The three-story building was painted chocolate brown, the windows boarded-up, and a sign hanging over the door said Whitey's Cafe & Pool Hall.

At the store, I'd bought a copy of the folktales collected by Chapman and recently retranscribed by Deg Hit'an speakers, Alta Jerrou among them. Sitting beside the old church I read the book into the late afternoon. The stories were marvelous, full of humor and wisdom, with characters certainly truer to Indian life than the cruel savages of Jack London's fictions. They spoke of a life spent in the woods and on the river in a constant search for food. The plots were a curious blend of the mundane and the fantastic: a jealous wife who transforms herself into a brown bear to destroy her unfaithful husband, a lonely spinster who hears a singing fish and realizes too late it was a man, a mother's-boy who refuses to marry until he's forcibly "tickled"—a euphemism for rape—by two old hags called "the Dog Sisters." (Since men and beast share souls, characters change form as easily as slipping an animal skin over their own.) One story put me in mind of the box of relics at the store. A young girl who lives alone with her grandmother unearths a string of beads from an abandoned village. She brings it home to her grandmother who guesses where the beads came from and instructs the girl to return them. The next day the girl goes down to the river to fetch water and meets a man driving a big sled. She gives the beads back to a sleddriver who turns out to be the ghost of her dead grandfather.

I thought of the stolen beads as I trolled slowly off the point of the old village looking for the exposed coffin the storekeeper had mentioned. But I never saw it. Perhaps the coffin had already tumbled into the river and begun a new journey.

ROGER TORY PETERSON
AND JAMES FISHER

Tundra of the Emperors

Roger Tory Peterson was born in
1908 in Jamestown, New York, and
attended the Art Student's League
and the National Academy of Design.
His awards for his lifelong work in
conservation and ornithology include
the William Brewster Award, the John
Burroughs Medal, the Geoffrey St.
Hilaire Gold Medal from the Société
Nationale d'Acclimation de France,
the Audubon Medal, and the Medal
of Freedom from the United States
Government. His many books include
*A Field Guide to the Birds, A Field
Guide to Western Birds, A Field Guide
to the Birds of Britain and Europe,
A World of Birds, A Field Guide to
Wildflowers, Birds of America,* and
Penguins.

James Fisher was born in 1912 in
Clifton, England, and worked as an
editor at William Collins Sons & Co.,
Rathbone Books, and Aldus Books
Ltd. His books include *Wildlife Crisis,
The Migration of Birds, The Birds of
Britain, A History of Birds,* and *Zoos
of the World.*

Wild Alaskan peaks, deep under snow and glacial ice slid beneath our big airliner. Had anyone ever set foot on these mountaintops, we wondered? Except for parts of arctic Canada, Alaska is certainly the wildest remaining part of wild North America.

We would reach Anchorage in an hour, so we dug out our notebooks and brought the bird list up to date. Vaux's swift on the Olympic Peninsula had been our last new bird—Number 497. Our running total now equaled Guy Emerson's record. We had, in just over ten weeks, seen as many species north of the Mexican border as anybody had ever previously seen in a year. Anything from now on would be a new record.

The crucial bird—Number 498—came shortly after we reached Anchorage. Flying overhead near the airport was a short-billed gull. We sent Guy Emerson a telegram informing him that he had lost his throne as champ of the bird-listers.

Our stop at Anchorage was just long enough to get oriented before taking one of the Alaskan airways to the outpost town of Bethel on the Kuskokwim. Here we bought provisions for a week's stay on the tundra. Coca-Colas, we noted, were still with us at this arctic outpost. This enterprising beverage quenches the thirst of a continent; but whereas the Mexican Indians at Xilitla pay three or four cents a bottle and drink it warm, the Eskimos stick a quarter in the slot and get theirs ice-cold from the big red refrigeration machine.

The small plane that we chartered at Bethel would safely carry only 1000 pounds, including the four of us and our equipment—no more. We did some quick figuring: Finnur Gudhmundsson weighed 280 pounds; James Fisher, 230; I weighed 200, and Bill Cottrell is a good-sized man. The four of us weighed nearly 900 pounds—and my camera equipment weighed 50. This posed a problem. We had our camp gear—and the two big boxes of food. Jimmy Hoffmann, our pilot, figured we could make it if we took fuel only for the outward trip; he would take a chance on picking up gas from the Eskimos at New Chevak after he had dropped us. It was an uncertain moment when our small float plane, heavily laden, faced the fresh breeze on the Kuskokwim and took off for the abandoned village of Old Chevak.

We had been unable to find Old Chevak on any of our maps. In fact, we couldn't even find New Chevak, but Hoffmann, who had been making this run for eight years, knew exactly where they were. As we flew over the tundra we could see why this country was still inadequately mapped. Rivers looped back upon themselves like tortured snakes, complicated, braided rivers that meandered among a million potholes, ponds, and lakes. Finnur Gudhmundsson said it was the most exciting-looking terrain he had ever seen. Here one could still have a lake or a small stream named after him. Niall Rankin, the British bird photographer, came here on a goose chase in 1951; now a stream in the heart of the black brant grounds is known as "Rankin's Slough."

As our plane sped along we tried to spot birds below. They seemed few at first, but with each mile as we approached the coastal marshes the frequency of ducks, geese, swans, and cranes increased. An hour later, when we came in for a landing, James pointed excitedly to a Sabine's gull as it swept past our windows. Soon we felt the broad pontoons hit the water and we taxied up to a slight rise on the tundra where stood a one-room wooden building. This was Old Chevak, or what was left of it; for the Eskimos now had a new town, a few miles distant. This forlorn building, which had been the old Russian church, was to be our headquarters for a memorable week.

June 24–July 1

When the Cessna lifted from the water and roared off, the four of us—Finnur, Bill, Roger, and I—gazed after it rather soberly. Jimmy Hoffmann promised to be back on July 1, but we knew that if the fogs rolled in from the Bering Sea we might be stranded for two or even three weeks, with food for only a week.

Our home was to be the old church, which at the time of our visit was inhabited by Matt Peterson and his young assistant, Jack Paniyak, trained Eskimos employed by the Fish and Wildlife Service on goose counts and goose marking. In the old days the Chevak Eskimos used to drive the geese across the tundra—when they had big goslings and were in their flightless molt—and net them in thousands for food, a method of wildfowling known also to natives in northern Canada and Siberia, and in Iceland, where it became a great art in the Saga Age.

These tundras between Chevak and the Bering Sea have been called the greatest goose nursery in North America. Influential conservation organizations have made representations to the U.S. Department of the Interior, urging that this area be set aside as a federal refuge, but so far this has not been done. However, in 1937 about 6800 acres round Hazen Bay, about twenty miles south of Chevak, was made a refuge. Paul Adams, with his headquarters at Marshall on the Yukon (less than an hour away by float plane), is the manager. During our stay he brought a cheerful plane load of ecologists for a night's visit on their return from an air survey of the musk ox herd on Nunivak Island.

"Had a bit of trouble on the way," said the pilot. "Snagged a hole in the hull, landing on a lake. Paul had to lose his aluminum cigarette case—it was the only thing we could find to patch it with."

"Matty and Jack will look after you," Paul Adams told us. "They'll show you the geese," and they did. For eight days we lived in their two outboard dinghies, and enjoyed fine weather (with the exception of one rather awful day) and were out fourteen hours a day and splashed through bogs and ate like hogs and slept like logs. Finnur had a permit from the Fish and Wildlife Service to fill some gaps in the collection of his National Museum of Iceland, and was busy preparing specimens while we cooked and wrote and slept. He was nearly always first afield in the morning, with Bill Cottrell, having the time of his life. Bill did more pure birding than the rest of us, for he was unencumbered with gun or camera. He was the notebook king. Roger's silhouette, as he stalked over a distant tundra, was a queer five-legged animal as he trailed his big movie camera and tripod at the ready.

The slow winding rivers of our journeys, the Kashunuk, the Kikleevik, and the Lingliquak, meandered through a flat green tundra. Afloat, we could seldom see about the banks, which were aproned by mudd-quaggy and adhesive. When we climbed the higher, drier banks we looked over an eternal expanse of green and brown: grass, creeping willow, crowberry, bearberry, cornel, and Labrador tea. Clumps of cotton grass waved their silky tufts in the bright clean air, and Jacob's ladder, big and bold and blue, was in full flower. It was a glorious garden of arctic plants, this summer tundra-delta, and stiff with northern birds, so that never for a moment were we out of sight or hearing of crane, goose, duck, or wader. Everywhere Lapland longspurs, in full black-throated breeding dress, dropped their pretty notes; they seemed to be the dominant songbirds, although the lisping of savannah sparrows was heard frequently, and occasionally a redpoll would fly by.

The great permafrost maze of grassy marshes, moors, tarns, lakes, sloughs, and rivers is a paradise for wildfowl and waders such as exists in few other places in the world. In sheer variety and numbers it beats anything in the glorious tundras under the central icecaps of Iceland. Its only rivals are the alluvial deltas of the Athabaska and Mackenzie in Canada's northwest, or the great northward flowing rivers of Siberia.[1]

Just back of the old church, on a dry hummock raised a few feet above the surrounding countryside, was the cemetery of the dead Es-kimo village. Here on the tundra the permafrost forbids any digging and the Eskimos bury their dead above the ground. Wooden crosses at their heads, the coffins sprawled about the top of the hummock. Some had disintegrated and a whitened skull or femur or humerus marked the grave spot. The newer coffins were covered with canvas painted white, which caught the eye even farther off than the church.

Near the cemetery a hen willow ptarmigan tried frantically to dis-tract us from her brood. We frequently came upon these white-winged arctic grouse as we explored the creeping willow swards and the bear-berry moors. A short-eared owl, which haunted the cemetery in its search for voles, also had a family nearby, a half-dozen golliwogs in a grass-lined nest. Short-ears we saw quite often, but never a snowy owl. This was not a lemming year.

Waders of a dozen sorts were nesting, singing, scolding wherever we went. The air resounded to the whickering of godwits—the Pacific race of the bar-tailed godwit, an Old World bird that invades the New only in western Alaska. Excitable, and inquisitive, these cinnamon-colored birds with long, slightly upcurved bills followed our movements across the tundra like village dogs inspecting a stranger. The air was full of the lovely rippling trill of the dunlin, reminding me of certain summer moors in north England; and Finnur thought of Iceland. Roger picked up the sky-larking male in the bull's-eye of his camera gun and followed it in slow motion across the sky, closer and closer until it nearly filled the picture, at which point it was joined by its mate. Quivering on parachute wings, the pair sank gently back to the marsh a few yards away, their mutual display imperishably recorded.

Along the edges of the tarns the little western sandpipers fluttered and twittered, running, raising their wings as banners, then flying up into quivering dunlin-like display flights with their high bubbling notes. Pectoral sandpipers, like large streaked stints, and black-bellied plovers in full nuptial dress, pale above and black below, we found only on the drier ground. Ruddy turnstones on the drier tundra inland gave way to black turnstones downriver. These dusky turnstones, new to me, were among the most numerous waders. Several times we saw curlews that we suspected might be the rare bristle-thighed curlew (which Arthur A. Allen found nesting less than 100 miles northeast of here), but we listened in vain for the plover-like notes that distinguish it from the ordinary Hudsonian whimbrel. Unexpected were a flock of four Hudsonian godwits—obviously wanderers, for this rare wader is not known to breed in this part of Alaska.

Spinning on the dark mirror of every pool were northern phalaropes, slight swimming waders, subtle in their breeding dress. They were whirling about, dabbing nervously for tiny unseen prey, wickering musically, and pursuing each other in endless courtship chases. The phalaropes are waders in which the role of the sexes is largely reversed, for when the larger, more richly-colored female has laid her eggs, the modest male has all the duties of incubation. Only on the tundra do the phalaropes have much to do with the land; most of their year is spent on the sea, on the oceans south of the equator. Occasionally we found a red phalarope, in full deep-russet dress, so unlike the gray phalarope we sometimes see in passage in England, and which is the same species in winter feather.

Down the Kashunuk River, Matty and Jack, the Eskimo boys, had established a field camp under the guidance of Paul Adams, with a decent big tent stretched over a wooden framework—comfortable quarters from which to do their job of assessing the goose population. On our way downriver to this camp we ran a gantlet of waterfowl such as I had encountered but once before in my life. Only at Myvatn in north Iceland had I seen as many species of nesting waterfowl in one day. We scored 16 species in Anatidae in the Chevak tundras all together, and more than once saw 13 or 14 in a day.

This was the week of the big hatching. Everywhere geese were convoying their fuzzy goslings to the water. There must be survival value in this simultaneous hatch; the predators—particularly the glaucous gulls—cannot make the inroads that they would if hatching took place over a longer period. Once the young have grown a little they are fairly safe. Often as we went downriver we would slow up to avoid disturbing a family of cackling geese caught in midstream. These diminutive Canada geese, hardly larger than mallards, would sort themselves out: the goose leader in the crouched position, neck stretched forward, the goslings, sometimes as many as seven, wobbling behind her, the gander bringing up the rear, neck erect, head aggressive. On reaching the muddy banks they would scuttle up with some difficulty, flapping their wings to keep balance. These cacklers were very courageous in defense of their young, and allowed us to come within easy photographic distance. To repay them we tried to get the photography over as quickly as possible, and we always saw to it that the family was totally united, with the glaucous gulls out of reach, before we left. The big gulls were always overhead seeking what they might devour, waiting their chance to snap up goslings separated from their parents.

It was on the Kashunuk River that we met the noble goose we had come so far to see—the emperor goose. You must go to western Alaska to see this white-headed, scaly-backed bird. Seldom does it winter outside the Aleutian chain, and its summer grounds are confined to the deltas of the Bering Sea. It may be one of the few species of wild geese that Peter Scott has never seen wild, but he finds little difficulty in breeding it in semicaptivity in the fine collection of the Wildfowl Trust in Gloucestershire.

In nature the emperor does not look quite as neat and shiny as it does on the Severn Grounds, because, like many swans and geese in the North, it picks up iron stains from the soil. We saw lots of emperors, and all of them had their white heads stained orange or rusty. We met them on the river, and often beside the boggy tundra pools, walking with their new broods in the rushes with their feet awash. Their goslings were gray, almost greenish-gray in general tone, much more like the goslings of the black brant than the brown goslings of the cackler. We could usually spot emperors some distance away by voice before we could see them. Their rather hoarse, far-carrying, two-syllabled calls (like a very deep pink-foot) kept finding them for us.

While we were still among the cacklers and emperors we came upon our first black brant, leading parties of greenish goslings on the rippling waters of the gray river. They growled as we approached. Only once did we hear the ordinary winter voice of the brant, the *cronk cronk*. Mostly they talked to each other with this guttural voice. A large population of black brant breeds between Hooper Bay and the south entrance to Baird Inlet—that is, in a smallish area of coastal tundra centered on Hazen Bay and the Chevak marshes. Downriver from the camp we were in the heart of their nesting grounds.

In 1950 David Spencer, Urban Nelson and Winston Elkins, making counts by plane, found that the tundras between Chevak and the coast supported about 130 nesting waterfowl to the square mile, of which 60 percent were cacklers, 20 percent black brant, 10 percent emperors, 5 percent white-fronts, and 5 percent pintails. Inland from Chevak the density goes right down to 17 waterfowl to the square mile, and these marshes are dominated by ducks: American scoters (30 percent), scaup (17 percent), pintails (15 percent), lesser Canada and cackling geese (14 percent), white-fronted geese (6 percent), old-squaws (5 percent), and lesser numbers of swans, mallards, baldpate, teal, and others.

All our way down to Matty's camp we kept on landing, staggering through the prehensile mud, to gain some green marshside with its families of cacklers and emperors, with the clanging of cranes in the background, and the distant belating of Wilson's snipe, and the laughs and scolds and complaints of little colonies of Sabine's gulls, and the lovely aerial songs of the waders. We often cut off the motor, to drift down upon a Pacific loon fishing in the middle of the channel, or to listen to the bubbling quacking of a red-throated loon going downriver on its way to more marine feeding grounds.

Female Pacific eider ducks waddled across the mud flats with their peeping ducklings hard at their heels. We never saw the king eider; it passes the coast only on migration. But the rare Steller's eider, with its white head and red breast, was about in small numbers. Finnur marched over acres of boggy tundra not far from the sea until he had found a duck incubating her eggs. It was a little bird compared with the big dark Pacific eiders that were nesting all around. Farther inland we occasionally saw female spectacled eiders, with a curious ghost of the bright "spectacles" of the male, but nowhere could we find a drake. They were probably all down at the club, having done their duty for the season, for drake eiders take no part whatsoever in the management of the family. On a little pond near Matty's camp we found a female with two tiny dark babies clinging to her apronstrings. We tried to herd the little family into camera range, Roger on one side of the pond, Finnur and I on the other. Jack Paniyak, with his strong Eskimo sense of humor, doubled up with laughter at the sight of the three large forms (certainly the three largest ornithologists in Alaska at the time) that were gesticulating like wind blown scarecrows, all because of one little duck and her brood. But this was no ordinary duck. None of us had ever seen a spectacled cider before we came to Chevak.

Wherever we went we found those curious anomalous sea predators, the jaegers, which we in England call skuas. On pointed falcon-like wings they hunted over the tundra. Scarcely ever did we look up without seeing a parasitic jaeger with its three-inch tail-points, or a long-tailed jaeger with ten-inch tail-streamers. There was no evidence that either of them did any harm to the ducklings or goslings, but once while we were watching a leggy young western sandpiper only a few feet away, a long-tail swooped from the sky and carried it off.

To me, Sabine's gull was the real surprise; this pretty little gull with its forked tail and bold triangular wing pattern was one of the commonest birds. I had always thought of Sabine's gull as one of the most northerly of all high arctic species—and one that nested in single pairs or small numbers, often taking the protection of an arctic tern colony. But here it was a dominant bird, breeding in scattered colonies, without much sociability and with communal display-grounds of a rather desultory kind round the muddy edges of the pools. Here the gulls quacked and laughed and pattered about in their hunched displays, made agitated choruses with their mates, took off, circled round, strafed and dive-bombed us—behaved almost exactly like the black-headed gulls back home in England.

On the 27th of June we ran the fifteen or twenty miles down to Hooper Bay and eight or ten miles up from the bay to New Chevak. At a bend in the river before we reached Hooper Bay we stopped at an Eskimo fish camp. All the men were away in their kayaks, except for a deaf mute. He couldn't speak, but was eloquent, nonetheless, as he showed us in graphic mime how to hunt a seal in winter. The women were running the camp, splitting dog-salmon for wind-drying, sewing clothes for their children. They came out of their store-bought canvas tents and paraded their children for us when they saw Roger's movie camera. They were smiling and jolly and, sure enough, put on a dance. It was a pretty good one, but not nearly as good as the comic dance two of the girls did when we were offshore on our departure—a priceless imitation in dance mime of Roger's business with the movie camera.

The wind was whipping over Hooper Bay as we sliced into the open water and cut across to the mud flats of the Lingliguak, a river of interminable bends. The village of New Chevak was on a hill and in full view during the last long miles of our voyage, but time and again, as we headed straight upriver toward it, we would find ourselves swept by yet one more long meander, in the opposite direction. The motor blew a gasket when we had two miles to go, and it was quite late in the afternoon when we eventually stepped ashore in the modern Eskimo village.

New Chevak is built on a modest escarpment of nearly a hundred feet, which gives the village a wide view over the tundra, and on clear days, even a sight of the Bering Sea. Chissicking along the steep bluff was a reminder of home, a yellow wagtail, one of the handful of Old World songbirds that spills over the Bering Strait into Alaska. We saw an arctic redpoll in the low willow scrub, and there was even a little tree by a lake where we found pectoral sandpipers nesting—a tree with bushes beside it enough to support a tree-sparrow territory.

Matt's brother, Charlie Peterson, was the village chief and storekeeper. With the utmost cheerfulness he offered us a roof for the night, for our outboard motor had given up the ghost. He gave us the liberty of the village store and as many new store blankets as we wanted. We slept through a comfortable night, bought some thick flannel shirts from Charlie in the morning, and enjoyed a terrific breakfast of bacon and eggs out of the refrigerator, and airborne bread toasted in an electric pop-up toaster. Such was Eskimo civilization, Alaska, 1953!

How different things were for the great pioneer birdman E. W. Nelson when he first explored this area in 1878. He sledged in when the geese were gone, though he learned from the Eskimos the first news of the greatest goose ground of North America. He left St. Michael, nearly 200 straight miles to the north, with the Yukon fur traders Charles Peterson, an ancestor of the Charlie Peterson who was now chief of New Chevak. On his way, below the Askinuk Mountains, Nelson stayed the night in an earth-covered hut, less than four feet high in the center, and sloping on every side. "The floor was covered with a deep layer of garbage, giving rise to a horrible stench, while about the low platforms on the sides crouched a number of pasty-faced children and sickly-looking elders, a litter of puppies were snuffing about among the wooden dishes in the farther end of the place. A large cake of ice served as a window in the roof, and everything bespoke of the most abject filth and poverty."

We did not stop long enough at New Chevak to learn much about Eskimo life today. Many of them were still living in barabaras, the primitive half-underground turf houses, but a number of wooden houses had gone up and a warehouse and a new school were being built. Some of these Eskimos, I thought, are more American, now, perhaps than Eskimo—with the very American idea that they can do it better than Father did.

The home of the affable Charlie could not be called typical. Obviously he was a very successful businessman. He even possessed a two-

way radio and a Burroughs adding machine. He was the owner of three
or four boats, including one shallow-draught cabin boat and half a
dozen outboard motors. We looked rather enviously at his new outboards, for we knew there was little chance of getting our big motor
going again, and that we would have to rely on the tiny spare one-
horsepower motor to see the big dinghy back.

On our interminable journey back to Old Chevak, which took us
close to 15 hours, we were chilled to the marrow by the damp and cold.
The temperature was around 40 degrees. Two kayakers on their way
to their salmon nets paced us for the first three miles. Their kayaks
were of traditional design, but whereas one of the Eskimos was in skin
dress, with hooded parka, the other wore store clothes. The picturesque
Eskimo is rapidly losing his cultural identity.

An arctic weasel started out of a hole in the riverbank as we slowly
passed by, and slipped along the bank and over the rim. A little flight
of whistling swans came overhead. We never found a whistler's nest,
but many small parties were flying round the tundra. Incidentally,
whistlers don't whistle with their wings as do the big mute swans. At
the end of Hooper Bay a tern flew over the boat, giving us just enough
time to confirm it as the rare Aleutian tern and not the arctic tern,
which lives up and down the tundra rivers.

Except for this one miserable day, we had many long, happy hours
in the field. Finnur, who was busy preparing specimens, was excused
meal duties, and somehow Roger never came in for more than the tail
end of washing up. Bill and I did most of the catering. Once we pulled
Finnur's leg, for Finnur, though a great tea drinker, likes his weak. "Is
this all right?" I said, as I added water from the kettle. "Too strong," said
Finnur. "Still too strong." "Well, this then?" "Still too strong." Eventually I got it right. "Ah," he said, "that's just how I like it." It was not
until after the meal that I broke it to him that the brown color of the
fluid derived from a natural infusion of fresh-water plankton, mainly
copepods, and that there were not any tea leaves in it at all.

On the last morning, Roger and I spent hours with the old-squaw
ducks on the pool back of the church. It was extremely difficult to
count the newly hatched ducklings; they kept diving, bobbing up, div-

ing again, scuttling down to the other end of the tarn, hiding in the reeds. But eventually the mother got used to us, and disclosed fifteen youngsters. There are records of old-squaws having laid fifteen eggs or even more, but these are rare. When we showed Peter Scott the movies afterwards he said, "Oh, it's pretty certain, though of course unprovable, that you've got two broods there; it's a very common thing among the sea-ducks—the pooling of broods, under one joint mother-cum-fostermother."

We were still watching the old-squaws when a humming in the sky announced the return of our plane. We were ready, all packed up, gear rolled up on the bank, goodbyes said to Matty and Jack. Jimmy Hoffmann waddled the machine onto the mud like a swan. It was with real regret that we carefully stepped through the mud to the ladder and climbed into the Cessna's cabin. We took off down a straight stretch of river, cleared the bend by a smallish margin, and roared off to Bethel, across the fantastic mosaic of unmapped land and uncharted water that forms what we are now quite prepared to believe is the most bird-rich tundra in all the arctic world. It had been a wonderful week. We had learned a great deal about birds, quite a bit about mud, and not enough about outboard motors.

Note

1. Herbert Brandt in one season listed 86 species in the Hooper Bay area, not far from Chevak. Our own week's list of 52 included neither the sea nor the mountains. Other Alaska lists are: Cape Prince of Wales, 79 (A. M. Bailey); Point Barrow, 60 (McIlhenny). Few Greenland tundras can raise more than 36 species, seabirds included. A few other tundra samples are: Perry River, Canada, 44 (Peter Scott); central Iceland, 29 (Fisher, Gudhmundsson, Scott); Baffin Island, 30 (Soper); Spitsbergen, 28 (Fisher); Novaya Zemlya, South Island, 33, North Island, 25; Franz Josef Land, 21. Siberian deltas would run between 30 and 40. So we were privileged. Our tundra at Chevak was a super-tundra.

PETER MATTHIESSEN

Oomingmak

Peter Matthiessen was born in New
York City in 1927 and was educated
at Hotchkiss School, Yale University,
and the Sorbonne. As a naturalist-
explorer, he has been a member of
several expeditions to remote areas
of the world. Mr. Matthiessen was one
of the founders of *The Paris Review*,
and his books include *At Play in the
Fields of the Lord*, *Wildlife in America*,
*The Cloud Forest: A Chronicle of
the South American Wilderness*, *The
Shorebirds of North America*, *Blue
Meridian*, and *The Snow Leopard*,
which received the 1978 National
Book Award.

At Nunivak Island, lost in the cold ocean mists of the Bering Sea, wind and rain give way rapidly to each other. The sun rarely penetrates the mists, and soon retreats before the rush of sea fog, as if uncertain of its authority in this melancholy place.

The Bering Sea is little more than a great bay of the Arctic Ocean, and both its Alaskan and Siberian coasts, laid bare of trees by permafrost and wind, are polar in their composition. It is the meeting of Arctic waters with warm air masses from the Pacific that breeds the chronic overcast and fog, and hides from view an island which, in a more temperate place, would be one of the most beautiful in all the world.

Nunivak, like all the islands of the Bering Sea, was a high plateau in the great land bridge that once connected Asia with America. Mammoth and saber-tooth, deer and bison, bear, wolf, wolverine, and man were among the large Eurasian mammals that crossed this bridge and spread southeast across the American continent. These creatures abandoned Nunivak before the waters rose again to separate it from the mainland, and the island, lost in northern mists, was known only to Eskimo peoples who came there in crude open boats of skin to hunt the creatures of the sea and ice. The Eskimos still cross rough shallow seas to Nunivak, and a few hundred live there all the year.

The musk ox on Nunivak are the only musk ox in Alaska, and in 1957 I made a vain attempt to see them. In that year, I was doing a survey of the rare and vanishing wildlife of North America, and was travelling around the Territory with pilots of the Fish and Wildlife Service. The game agent-pilot for the Yukon-Kuskokwim deltas met me one windy day in Bethel, on the Kuskokwim, and we flew downriver toward the sea. Everywhere across the estuary of the Kuskokwim, white tents and drying racks of bright red salmon meat, signalling the summer fishing camps of Eskimos, spun up at us out of the fogs. We meant to cross that day to Nunivak, but the mists deepened as we went along, trapping us finally at Quinhagak. We had been there three days, eating the last pickled pigs' feet of the local missionary, before the fog lifted and allowed us to take off for Nunivak a second time. The coast line was so clear that the white heads of Emperor geese could be picked out against the tundra, but the weather hung in a dense wall just off the shore. We circled and probed it, drifting northward, and finally put down at the salmon station at Akulurak, where the great Yukon, flowing north and west up out of Canada, empties at last into the ocean. Somewhere behind us, south and westward, lay an island of great shaggy beasts that I had missed my chance to see.

A second opportunity to visit Nunivak came this year through the kindness of John Teal, an Arctic ecologist and anthropologist whom I had accompanied on an earlier expedition into the Northwest Territories. Like Vilhjalmur Stefansson and other authorities before him, Teal is convinced that the musk ox is a potential domestic animal and that it could do much for the economy of the North, not as a food source (though Stefansson, in his travels, subsisted for long periods on a musk ox diet and found it excellent) but for the wool of its undercoat. This has been shown to be superior to cashmere. Compared to the goat, which supplies but three ounces of wool annually, the musk ox is prodigal in its shedding, and about six pounds per animal, each summer, is scattered on the winds of the northern barrens. No systematic harvest of this wool has ever been attempted, and "qiviut," as it is called, remains best known to amateurs of the crossword puzzle, since it lacks a "u" after its "q." In years to come, qiviut may well become as celebrated as vicuña.

The object of the expedition sent to Nunivak in 1964 by the University of Alaska and the Institute of Northern Agricultural Research was the capture of a number of young musk ox calves, to form the nucleus of a permanent domestic herd. The calves would be transferred from Nunivak to an experimental farm at the University of Fairbanks, where the buds of the dangerous horns would be removed and the animals hand-raised systematically. (For example, the musk ox cow which in the wild throws one calf every second year would be encouraged to wean her yearling before rutting season and thereby make herself available for annual reproduction.) If all goes well, the Fairbanks herd will one day supply the breeding stock for herds established elsewhere in the North.

Meanwhile, the animals roamed uncaptured. Furthermore, as the

members of the expedition convening in Anchorage knew, the musk ox
are large, sharp-horned, and tenacious in defense of their young. Also,
they are scattered wide on a remote waste of boggy tundra, many miles
from the small airstrip on a roadless island shrouded almost permanently in mist. Hence there seemed to be every likelihood that their
freedom would continue and in the beginning, as things turned out,
it did.

From Anchorage there is no road westward, and it remains a frontier town. Despite its efforts at Main Street respectability, and town
chimes that play *Some Enchanted Evening*, it still has pawn shops full
of guns, hides and snowshoes, and saloons jammed with Indians and
prospectors (no longer gold but oil). Violent death is not an unusual
event in Anchorage, and its jail is full of wild young men. The town
has a striking location by the sea, on a plateau surrounded by mountains, and despite its recent earthquakes, its prospects are immense.
But domesticity is soon to come. Its novelty stores will no longer sell
small moose droppings made up as earrings, and it will be just another
provincial town to which zoning came too late. I was happy to see
Anchorage again and glad to leave it.

On August 3rd, the expedition flew west in an F-27 cargo plane of
Northern Consolidated Airlines. The forward half of the compartment
held the equipment, which included a canoe and a 1200-pound tracked
vehicle lent by its local designer to help solve calf-transport problems
on the tundra; the after half contained the personnel. Northern Consolidated serves the bush country to the south and westward of Anchorage and Fairbanks, including such localities as Red Devil and King
Salmon, Eek and Flat. Like all Alaskan airlines, it is accustomed to
flying under minimal conditions, and the third of August was no exception. The plane rose from a rainy field into dark swirling mists, as the
slaty beaches of Cook Inlet surged and vanished; it climbed as rapidly
as possible, to clear the jagged black-white wall of Alaska Range. The
mountains were crossed at sixteen thousand feet and never glimpsed.

West of the Alaska Range lies a vast spruce bog that subsides in
turn into bare tundra. Here the great Kuskokwim River breaks from the
forest and rolls unimpeded to the sea. The trading post and depot of

this region is the Bethel Mission, now called Bethel, where the plane made a mail-and-cargo stop on the way to Nunivak. Bethel, a sprawl of shacks, mud and rusting oil drums, dumped from the sky onto the barrens, has its admirers, but neither Teal nor myself, who had been here before, could be counted among them. We were in dread that bad weather would entrap us there, perhaps for days. But the overcast was high at Bethel, and we headed west after an hour, none the worse for our short stay.

The delta region between Bethel and the sea is a lacework of shallow ponds. The ponds loomed and vanished in the shifting mists, giving way at last to the gray metallic seas of Etolin Straits. Flying conditions at Etolin Straits, which resembles the English Channel in both width and rudeness, are notorious. The smoky haze of sea and sky mix treacherously in the wind, and the rough shallow chop that blows across the sunken land bridge would smash a ditched sea plane in a few minutes.

The Eskimo settlement on Nunivak is located southwest of Cape Etolin, on the north coast; its harbor is formed by the mouth of the Mekoryuk River. The Eskimos say that there has always been a village at Mekoryuk throughout the memory of mankind, and, despite the iron hand of missionaries, it remains the North American Eskimo settlement where the aboriginal culture is most intact. Skin parkas and mukluks are still sewn and worn, walrus skulls with gigantic tusks cure on the roofs, and sled dogs are tied to stakes about the beach. Red salmon meat cures on long racks, reindeer sinew dries on doors and walls, and a new skin kayak, gleaming ivory in color, is stretched on its frame behind the huts.

However, the kayaks are fast being replaced by outboard skiffs, and the dog teams by the snow sled, and Mekoryuk's young men go away now to the mainland, protesting the mission ban on dancing, drink and smoking. Mekoryuk itself, where the white man has built his air strip and his generator, where fields and beaches lie submerged in the inevitable heaps of rusting oil drums, could be a shanty town almost anywhere on earth. Its approaches, from land, sea, and air, are all depressing. Yet the people live much as they have always lived, trapping and fishing and hunting the whale and seal that pass on their migrations and the walrus and polar bear that drift down out of the Bering Straits on the floes of spring.

We left Mekoryuk in small fishing boats as soon as we could get them loaded, taking advantage of a rare calm in the Bering Sea; we would make our base camp at Chekeesiweek, now called Nash Harbor, down the northwest coast. It was six P.M., but there would be daylight for a few more hours.

A wind came up as we reached the open water, and as the boats rounded the bleak point made by a peninsula and a rock islet, the tide rip was so violent that our tracked vehicle burst its lashings on the cargo skiff, which was forced to retreat and take shelter behind the point of the peninsula.

The canopy frame and a strip of gunwale had been broken. It was raining, and the sea was rough, and night was falling, yet the Eskimos remained cheerful. Peter Smith (like most of the people of Mekoryuk, he has taken a western name) sawed and hammered his repairs right on the spot. Eskimos are resourceful carpenters and mechanics, and carry tools wherever they go. They are small, sturdy, well-set men, and their economy of motion is a thing to watch.

Eskimos are rarely upset by small emergencies, having been tempered by the North to constant vigilance. Thus they accept philosophically and even cheerfully what would strike most of us as constant hardship. The Eskimo stands quietly, and though his own language is rapid and guttural, he speaks English carefully, in a slow sweet voice. He is, all observers agree, a generous, merry, most impressive race of *Homo sapiens*, one of the most likeable men on earth.

One of the few chronicles of Nunivak in the world's literature is the report of a recent military survey. Its anonymous author, with a squad of soldiers, had walked the coast of the whole island, guided by Charlie Spud, one of the fishermen who came out with us from Mekoryuk. The lieutenant's reaction to the natives is the sole spontaneous note in an otherwise dry, dutiful account: "The people also are a happy jovial-type race. The cheeks of many are rosy and when someone with their appearance gets a smile on his face, you are almost forced to feel good." Peter Smith was smiling a great part of the time; perhaps he was thinking of his favorite meal, which he described as "salmonberries, milk and chicken."

The boatmen had the cargo lashed and the skiff underway within the hour. We rounded the point and met the tide rip again just as darkness came. Overhead, in all directions, black cormorants and puffins flew, whirring around their sea rock like huge bats started from a cave.

All this time it had been raining, and as darkness fell, it began to rain in earnest. With the rain came cold. Huddled in the cabin of the first boat, we peered out through the gloom at the silhouette of the steep coast, rising and falling with each roll and pitch. An islet was passed to which three musk ox had wandered on the winter ice; the Eskimos said that the beasts would die there, for there was no water. We sighed and yawned. A following wind blew the exhaust through the dripping doorway, fouling the close air, and the night dragged on; the boatmen were grunting with fatigue. We arrived at Nash Harbor after seven hours in rough seas, but as it was pitch dark and low tide, we could not go ashore until daylight.

The high cliffs guarding Nash Harbor are broken by a half moon beach that separates the sea from a tidal lagoon. At the inland end of the lagoon a stream pours down from the plateaus of the interior, and at the seaward end, a narrow channel cuts through the beach into the bay. Above the channel lies an abandoned village, a sagging conglomeration of shacks and native sod huts. With its small wood door in the side of a grassy mound and its tin chimney, the sod hut looks much like the cozy dwellings of woodland animals in old-fashioned books for children.

Toward four A.M. the helmsman drove his boat—it banged on rocks all the way in–through the low surf at the inlet, and moored it in the channel below the village. An old school house and storage shed recommended to Teal for expedition use had been torn down, and the whole place seemed half sunk away in the tall rye grass which rings the island shores. We moved our gear under tarpaulins and set up tents, and, having made coffee, looked for places to lie down, for nobody had slept. Three of us crossed the channel by canoe and made our way past a graveyard of skinny crosses to a lone shack overlooking the half-moon beach. The shack contained one ancient bunk, a reindeer robe, some rotted salmon and waterlogged provisions, and primordial damp. We curled up where we could and fell asleep immediately.

The crosses near the solitary shack marked the graveyard of the abandoned settlement; beside the crosses were the mounds of a dead village wiped out by flu a half century before. Those killed by flu were placed in a single hut, which was then demolished. Harold Weston, an Eskimo hunter camped at Nash Harbor, did not know which of the many mounds was the common tomb.

Harold Weston was staying at Nash Harbor with his wife Birdie and a little boy, curing the seal skins taken in the spring; his wife gathered wild celery and sheep sorrel and red mushrooms. "Everything here to eat," Harold said enthusiastically. In the afternoon, he went back into the lagoon to spear the dark flounder that came in with the rising tide, and the next morning he went out hunting sea birds. In Alaska, according to Federal law, "Eskimos and Indians may take, possess, and transport, in any manner and at any time, auks, auklets, guillemots, murres, and puffins and their eggs for food and their skins for clothing . . ." They also can and do shoot reindeer.

The huge reindeer herds are owned by the Bureau of Indian Affairs, which directs the herding and harvest until the day—it may never come —when the Eskimos forsake the existence of the hunter for a pastoral life, and take over the animals themselves. While the reindeer program is a worthy one, so little effort has been made to set up good markets for reindeer venison—which is excellent—that only a small percentage of the multiplying herd is harvested, and the natives are given work for an all-too-brief period in a project that might easily support the entire island.

Harold Weston and his wife Birdie, and the little boy of six or seven whom they call Rex, waited over another day, packing away skins and utensils. The Eskimos are notoriously unpossessive about wives and children. "He is not my son," Harold said of the boy. "A friend gave him to me." Like the people who had seen us off from the beach front at Mekoryuk, Harold was much amused by the tracked vehicle and by our plan to take its young from the large dark beast with downswept horns and shaggy hair that the Eskimos call the Bearded One, Oomingmak. The people of Nunivak fear Oomingmak and leave him alone.

We arranged with Harold to use his sod hut for drying clothes. In this cold place, wet clothes are a constant problem. The Eskimo sod hut, largely underground, is a dank place when no fire is tended, but most are fitted out with stoves made cleverly from oil drums, and are readily fueled by oriental driftwoods that spin slowly northward on the currents out of Asia and litter the beaches of the Bering Sea. In all the huts, Eskimo utensils were in evidence; carved net floats of wood, old handmade flensing knives, an unfinished axe-blade of black stone, scalskin mukluks, dried grass for basket-weaving and mukluk insulation, a fish spear with a four-pronged point carved beautifully of walrus ivory, a heavy wood harpoon with a bone point. Two sealskin oil bags, tied off at neck and limbs, glistened and stank along one wall. All of this was privately owned, but Eskimos do not fear that property will be taken, nor do they object to the possibility that another may find use for it.

"Do not break much," Harold said, and departed, smiling. He got into his outboard skiff with the hearty little boy named Rex and the inscrutable Birdie, who wore her best seal-gut rain parka with red trim. They headed eastward, down the raining coast.

The wild musk ox, *Ovibos moschatus*, is one of the rarest of large Ice Age mammals left on earth, and it is also one of the most controversial. Since the existence of this "buffillo" was reported first in 1689, by a traveller in Canada named Henry Kelsey, it has been called the most dangerous big-game animal on earth, and the most timid; inedible and delicious; intelligent and stupid. Its common and scientific names (*Ovibos moschatus* means "sheep-cow musky," though it is neither sheep nor cow, nor has it musk glands), are erroneous from start to finish, and until recently, no two authorities could agree on what it really was. In its appearance, as Kelsey suggests, it is most similar to the bison, and mammalogists, for many years, placed it accordingly among the bovines. But paleontologists, working with its bones, re-

lated it to the sheep and goats. As late as 1955, in fact, in a French
volume devoted to mammalogy, O. moschatus was referred to as both
the Bovinae and the Caprinae. Recent tests made by serologists have
borne out paleontological opinion: despite its faint resemblance to a
bison, O. moschatus is of the Caprinae, one of the last of a great Ice
Age family of goat-antelopes that includes the European chamois.

The musk ox was once a circumpolar species, common on Arctic
and sub-Arctic tundras all across the world. In the time of the glaciers,
it ranged south as far as France, where it was recorded in the cave
paintings. Like many other Old World mammals, it spread across the
land bridge at the Bering Strait, and it vanished entirely from Eurasia
even before the Stone Age was at an end.

In North America and Greenland, its numbers declined with the
coming of the white man. The last musk ox native to Alaska were
slaughtered by the whalers a century ago, in the vicinity of Wain-
wright. Farther east, an estimated six hundred were shot down for food
by Peary's expeditions alone. Fifty years ago, driven to the bleakest
reaches of the Arctic, it was on the point of trailing its ancient relatives
into the abyss of extinction.

Today the musk ox is confined to remnant populations in northeast Greenland and Arctic Canada, with transplanted herds in Norway,
Spitzbergen, and Nunivak. The Nunivak herd of approximately four
hundred and eighty has grown from a group of thirty-three Greenland
calves released in 1930.

In the old days, the capture of musk ox was a simple matter. The
animal hunter merely hied himself to the nearest herd, shot down the
adults, and took away the calves; eight adults killed for three calves
taken was considered a fair average. There is now an understanding
among zoos throughout the world that no musk ox will be purchased
or exhibited, but a person wishing to inspect a musk ox may visit the
Vermont farm owned by John Teal. The one specimen in the latter place
is descended from a group of seven calves captured in 1954 and 1955 on
the Thelon River Sanctuary of Northern Canada. These captured were
permitted on the understanding that no adults would be killed, and the
calves were taken only after a long series of failures had made clear that

musk ox are far-sighted and swift of foot, much more than a match for sheep dogs, lassoes, and the kinds of corrals that can be constructed in the wild. Musk ox, after centuries of wolf defense, are expert at killing dogs (a dog that got loose once at Nash Harbor did not survive the night). They are too dangerous to approach with a lasso, and they splinter all but the sturdiest enclosures. The one method of capture that proved to be both merciful and effective was to drive the herd into deep water, where the panicked animals would permit the seizure of their young. This technique, which we meant to apply on a much larger scale at Nunivak, would not be simple in open country, working with animals so fast that airplanes are required to herd them. The airplanes were due in a few days.

On August 4th, camp was set up, and the next day was spent in reconnoitering a musk ox band near a pond five miles from camp. Three cows and three calves were led by a large bull, and we lay on a hillside opposite and watched them graze. Beyond, toward the sky, two other bands were visible, rising and falling from our view.

The day was cold and windy, and in the late morning and through the afternoon, the wind was accompanied by rain. But in the rare iron gleam of sun, the tundra was fired by a brief fierce beauty. In this rolling treeless world one can feel all the immensity of upland tundra, mile upon mile of natural rich pasture. The grass glistened and glowed with rose root and dwarf fireweed, bluebell and the striking monk's hood, inset in shimmering green beds of cloudberry and moss and equisetum. A flock of ptarmigan, flared by a jaeger, rose in a ball and broke apart across the hill, and cranes on long black-fingered wings bugled sadly across the wind, and in the bunchgrass hummocks at our feet, the lemmings darted.

Musk ox at any distance are impressive. In this monotone landscape without shadows, they appear much blacker than they are, and big as bison. On the hill opposite, the wild-haired bull leapt and pranced in agitation at our coming. The musk ox has acute sight and sense of smell and hearing: the animals were aware of our distasteful presence two miles off, across a valley.

Musk ox, approached, will graze a while in studied calm, as if em-

barrassed by the intrusion and affecting to ignore it. In just such a way
the animals in this herd continued to feed as they drifted northward
toward the sea. Three of us cut down into the valley and up again,
fanning out behind them, while the others formed a line along the cliff.
The plan was to practice herding them, using hand-signals and three
walkie-talkies. Teal was uphill on my left—we were still below the
animals, which were out of sight—and before long I heard him yelling. I ran toward him, rounding a steep grassy bank, and found myself
face-to-face for the first time with the Bearded One.

Backing the cows against the bank, Oomingmak turned his attention from Teal to myself. He was a very big beast with heavy skirts
of dark brown hair and a hoary saddle mark and a bold boss of horn
across his brow—bulls and cows are all but indistinguishable behind
their skirts, but the horns of the cows do not meet upon the brow—
and he was snorting and pawing and rubbing his muzzle on his foreleg,
which among musk ox is a warning. This performance, at point-blank
distance, commanded my instant respect. Following Teal's example, I
yelled as loudly as I could and waved my arms. Then the band wheeled
in one hairy commotion and rushed up over the bank and galloped
away toward the cliffs, the calves hunkering along right in the middle. Backs rising and falling on the grass horizon, long hair blowing,
they seemed to flow across the wind, moving with a grace and speed
astonishing in such a heavy animal.

They overran our trap and paused finally at the cliff-edge, hundreds
of feet above the sea; there we managed to cut them off. Oomingmak
backed the cows into a circle, all horns outward, calves squashed in
the middle. This is the classic musk ox defense, which proved useless
against men armed with rifles or even spears, but serves the musk ox
well against unarmed creatures, including wolves. Every so often, a
calf would be squirted outward by the pressure of shifting bodies, and
would instantly make a run-and-squeeze to force itself back into the
center. The restless cows seemed confident that they could break out
through us, but every time one ventured forth, Oomingmak butted her
back into place so violently that large sheds of qiviut blew on his horn.

The band circled slowly, studying each of us. When we got too close, the adults pawed and snorted. So long as a respectful distance is maintained, the cows will rarely leave their calves to press an attack, but rutting bulls have no such inhibitions and are not predictable. Since we could not attempt a capture, we did not force the issue. We turned our faces into a whipping rain and trudged back towards Nash Harbor. Musk ox are intelligent enough to be perplexed, but they wasted little time in glaring after us, and before we were out of sight, began to feed.

According to the Eskimos, June and July on Nunivak are all that might be wished for in the way of splendid weather, but the same is not true of August, when musk ox calves become old enough to be taken from their mothers. The wind and rain persisted, day after day. In the first week of Nash Harbor, a blue sky appeared just once, during the supper hour, only to be swept away during the night by the depthless and overwhelming grays cast up by the cold seas. Our airplanes, had they appeared, would have been grounded by low ceilings and violent winds, which were reported at Mekoryuk in gusts of fifty miles per hour, and meanwhile, some discouraging experiments with the tracked vehicle, now called the Pig, had confirmed the Eskimos' chortling faith that such a machine would prove no match for the bogs, eskers, boulders, and volcanic outcroppings of their frost-heaved tundra.

Not that it was difficult to pass the time. The old village, in its dramatic location in the corner of land, sea and sky, was a storehouse of odd details, and the buried village across the narrow channel, the one wiped out at the turn of the century, was full of crude artifacts. The silver fish in the swift water of the channel were pursued skillfully with wet flies by Chauncey Loomis, our cameraman, and even I, using cruder techniques, caught four Dolly Varden trout one evening in the space of a few minutes. On most days, we could take enough of these big sea-run fish to feed the camp, and at this season, the females all bore golden roe, which was fried for breakfast.

On the headlands that rose like battlements on each side of the bay were the graves of hunters. These rectangular stone coffins were roofed with heavy timbers to deter foxes, and alongside two of them were laid ancient shotguns with twin hammers. By a third, incongruous on a high hill, lay the rib of a whale. These graves overlook the sea.

Large yellow poppies hide along the cliff edge, and there are strange rock cairns, like sentinels. These were built up long ago, for they are hoary with hard lichens, and they were used, said Peter Smith, to keep hunters of another time from falling from the cliffs in time of mist.

Most of the time, the distances were empty; the only creatures constantly in view were birds. Half-grown loons and oldsquaw ducks and pintail swam on every pond, and the sandpipers and golden plover were already assembling for migration. Strings of black brant crossed before the snow-patched buttes, and there was a flock of white-fronted geese on the delta pond of the next stream to the eastward. The stream bed there maintained the only trees on this part of the island, a thin string of dwarf willows, six to eight feet high. From the stream banks, spawning salmon could be seen, huge dying fish scarred with white fungi, waiting in pools for a rise in water that would let them proceed upstream. Merganser ducklings, scampering on the white water of a shallows, passed the warped skeletons of last year's fish, oblivious. In a nearby ravine, crouched out of the wind, a crippled reindeer was fair game for the wolf that on Nunivak would never come.

Awaiting fair weather and the planes, I explored the cliffs and sea coast and high tundra for long days at a time. Beyond Nash Harbor, there was no slightest sign that man had ever existed—neither a foot trail nor a wisp of smoke nor even his drifted litter on the beach. There was only the immense raw silence, accented sometimes by a bird, or a far silhouette of animals on the grass horizon. Even the airplanes, dropping down out of this immensity of space onto the great lagoon, made no more impression on that silence than dead leaves falling on a pond.

In Nunivak, fair weather rides on the north wind, which blew one day from dawn to dusk. This first bright day was the 9th of August. As the sun sank, mare's tails of wind in the high altitudes streaked the sunset, and by nightfall, the wind had backed around into the west. At dawn it came strong from the south again, with rain.

Nevertheless, the Cessna appeared during the morning, and we flew immediately on a survey of the island. Teal wanted to inspect the herds at the west cape, but the foul weather pouring in on the south wind was at its worst at Cape Mohican, as the Eskimo landmark known as Ikook has been named by federal surveyors. The heavy pall of fog shrouding the place turned us away, and we flew down along the windward coast.

The south shore of Nunivak, battered by storm winds and the rough surf of the straits, is a low coast, falling away from the high plateaus of the interior. Here a series of small rivers have cut ravines on their way down to the sea, and the river mouths form broad lagoons behind high dunes of dark sand, said to contain the tusks and bones of prehistoric animals. (Tusks and fossiliferous rocks are also found in the Mekoryuk River.) The whole structure of the south coast is extremely strange and various, a mournful landscape of odd lights and old volcanic cones vanishing upward into the mists, and dark dunes like a small mountain range stretched out along brown swathes of stormy surf, and the ravines, and two sepulchral swans like statues by a sullen pool, and dark flying silhouettes, and the dark beasts. The musk ox are common on the southeast shore, near long riverbeds of dwarf willow, which is their favorite browse. They share the region with reindeer herds of thousands, and deer trails spider everywhere across the green, like cracks in paint. There is something romantic here in this strange light, a deer park atmosphere: the hills roll softly, and streams curl gently in green meadows of bright wild flowers.

The musk ox, few and heavy and disgruntled, have more presence in this landscape than the reindeer. They appear from the air like great boulders rolling, sprung to life out of the dark clays of the land

There were few musk ox on the east coast and the north, though a few old solitary bulls gazed seaward from the cliffs, waiting for . . . what? It is these solitary habits of old bulls that in their Canadian range, at least, causes them to be cut down by wolves. On the islet where the three bulls were trapped, only two were visible, and one of these was lying down. The Eskimos say that Oomingmak will cross the channel near Cape Mendenhall and possibly the third bull has crossed over to the mainland, but more likely it is dead.

One night, at dark, a shape appeared on the hill above the settlement. Coffee in hand, we stood in silence by the cooking shed and watched it come. It stopped at last perhaps twenty yards above the camp, as if noticing the place for the first time; then it drooped its heavy beard into the grass. The head came up again when Teal made the noise of a lost calf; it turned on its knoll to face us. It was an outcast bull, and hoary sheds of qiviut trailed from its shoulders. The old coat swung like chain mail as it made its turn, and its huge neck muscle raised its hump high above the level of its brow. It considered us from its high knoll, then turned with dignity and went away, still searching for a night place to lie down.

The first capture was attempted on the fourteenth of August, and it was thwarted. The pilot of the herding plane crowded the animals too closely when they went into defense formation, thus driving them into it still more deeply. Musk ox will not only stand and face a diving airplane but the bull may actually leap upward like a giant goat, trying to gore it. The airplane could not budge either one of the two bands located within a few miles of Nash Harbor Lagoon, where the first ambush had been set up. We took time out at noon without having laid eyes on a single animal.

The ideal ambush is formed by a line of men leading inland from a peninsula or point. This line jumps up out of hiding as the animals, running down the shore, reach the base of the point, and the end of the line swings down and around, cutting them off. In theory, the herd is rushed onto the point and off the end of it before it can organize a defense formation.

In the afternoon, Teal and Spike Holden went out on foot to flare one of the bands, while the airplane patrolled back and forth at a little distance, keeping the animals headed toward the water. I was the wing man in a line extending straight uphill from the lake, over a lava ridge, and it was my job to move the line back if the animals came in from the wrong angle, and to signal the closing of the trap by running downhill once the band had passed, to cut off its retreat. In the distance, the plane was circling back and forth, doing lazy eights on the far side of the herd. The herd was coming in from the wrong angle, and the line was still fading back to allow them to enter the ambush when the musk ox surged onto the ridge above us. There they milled long enough to be headed right again, and we sprinted back to our original positions, and kept sprinting, for the animals were coming at full speed, rounding the hillside between ridge and lake and plunging headlong into the trap. Where the lava ridge tumbled down into the water, they were met by a line of yelling men, jumping up like goblins from the rocks. The animals wheeled, but the gate was closed. We ran down the hill behind, swinging the line into a semi-circle and cutting off retreat along the lake edge.

But the point at Nash Harbor Lagoon is blunt and shallow, scarcely a point at all, and the animals not only failed to plunge off this rocky nose but bolted straight up the steep slope. Sighting the two men at the top, they wheeled again, descending. At midslope, seeing themselves surrounded, they went into defense. The men on top closed in a little, bullying them gradually downhill with clods of earth tossed at their muzzles. Gathering momentum as they descended, the musk ox made a sudden break. It seemed to me that an avalanche of hair and horn was rolling down on us, and I flared my rain parka, yipping and dancing in dismay. This grotesque spectacle helped turn them back onto the lakeside, where they went again into formation. There was a cow facing uphill and another facing the lake, with a young bull and two calves pressed in the middle. From start to finish, the young bull comported himself without distinction, but the cows snorted bravely, tossing their heads, and gazing in a calculating manner from one man to another, as if to determine the weak link in the chain. Facing big animals backed up this way, like a coiled spring, is nervous business, though we had it on faith that they must give way at any second, like their Canadian relatives, and rush into the water.

Had they been given breathing room, and time to consider the hopelessness of their position, the animals might have done what was expected of them, for the opposite bank and a vista of open tundra were not far off. But we were impatient at their ignorance of musk ox ways, and finally rushed them. Thus provoked, one cow charged straight uphill, calf at her side, tearing a big hole in our line and so disrupting it that three others breached it moments later. Teal made an heroic dive for a passing calf and got his hands on it, but the three-month musk ox is the size of a ram, and fast, and extremely strong. Electrified by terror, it kicked free and away before the stunned men could rush in and pile on.

The animals flew northward toward the settlement. One cow and calf swung east across the channel; the other climbed the slope diagonally, north toward the sea cliffs. Of the young bull no more was seen or heard.

The planes caught up with the first cow as she climbed the steep butte a mile to the east of the old graveyard. The cow persevered against the planes, gaining the top of the butte. There she stood outlined against the sky as the two monstrous birds dove and roared across her path. Because she was exhausted by her brave run, the planes held her long enough for the men to ford the channel and run the mile and climb the butte and cut her off at the high cliff edge.

All this time, throughout drive, ambush, breakout, and run, the calf had been pressed tight to her side. Like the shorebirds in their swift cascades up and down the tidal flats of the lagoon, the creatures seemed to move as a single animal, with the same heart and rhythm, as if her calf were still a part of her. And invariably, she placed herself between the calf and the threat of danger, so that it was scarcely more than a wool protuberance, glimpsed as she wheeled.

The cow's tongue was white with running and her chest heaved. Our chests heaved also, and doubtless our tongues were white as well. Both parties panted and glowered. The tired cow was mean as slag; she made several rushes, hooking and snorting. She would not be forced back toward the lagoon, despite hurled sods and stones and imprecations, but fixed angry red eyes on every man in turn. Once in a while, the head of the calf would poke out from behind her flank and stare at us, reproachful. The calf looked surprised, as if to say, "Have you gone mad? What can you want with us?"

We opened the ring to give her a way out, and after a while, she took it. She turned her back on us, and the two shaggy skirts, one large, one small, moved westward. The musk ox rump is the most endearing of any in the animal world except that of the elephant, but apart from that, we were all affected by this cow. She had led the breakout and crossed the channel and run still another mile before climbing a steep tortuous butte in the very teeth of two diving airplanes, and then had held six yelling men at bay. She deserved to escape us, and she did.

Picking her way slowly along the cliff edge, the cow had looked exhausted. For the second time that afternoon, as we ambled along behind her, we imagined that man had triumphed over the musk ox. The cow was keeping a weather eye half-turned toward us and did not notice the Eskimo cairn until it sprang into her field of vision. She snorted, hooked at it viciously, and sprang away. Then, to our surprise, she kept her momentum, heading off toward the lagoon and descending the butte face at beautiful speed and streaking out along the shore like a hairy cannonball. The men below tried to head her off, but she did not mean to be stopped; when a musk ox once decides to go in this angry and resolute manner, it is folly to get in its way. The cow and calf swept past the men, past the east cabin where I lived, past the graveyard and dead village killed by flu. At the channel, she hurled herself eight feet through the air, calf still tight to her side, landed with an heroic splash and kept on going. The people on the village bank tried bravely to head her off, and they slowed her for a moment, but then she was past them, streaming up the hill onto the skyline, and away. We walked home slowly, whipped, dirty, wet, exhausted, and full of new respect for the speed, dignity, and resolution of a creature that Teal believes to be one of the most intelligent on earth.

Our multiple failures had scattered the musk ox of the Nash Harbor vicinity all over the tundra, and on the fifteenth we flew the canoe across to a lagoon on the southwest point, lashing it to the Cessna's right pontoon in a way that seemed precarious to the six present or former bomber, commercial, and/or small plane pilots in our ranks. However, the canoe did not faze our hot-shot nineteen-year-old bush pilot, who flew the Cessna so low to the ground that the horizon was invariably above eye level. His Indian partner was an older, less spectacular, and better pilot, but both flew strictly, as the fliers say, "by the seat of their pants," resorting almost never to compass or other instruments, which they held in profound mistrust. Casual fog and sea-cliff flying, a daily adventure on Nunivak, was a taste which I had not acquired yet, especially since the pilots, due to their disregard of compass bearings, were often so hopelessly lost as to seek and accept advice from their own passengers.

A herd was found at the edge of the great seacliffs that form the island's western rampart. It was perhaps four miles from a stark lagoon that had a fine, long point. Brant geese rose in strings as the planes dropped in, and the delicate kittiwake, a small oceanic gull that nests among the murres and puffins on the cliff face. Eskimo sod huts, fallen in, were scattered along a low bluff near the channel, and half-submerged at the water's edge, on the blackish beach of gravel, lay a gigantic whale jaw, like a silver tree.

Now Teal flew in from a last survey of the herd and placed his men in ambush, then set out across long sloping hills toward the Ingri Butte. I went with him. The plane was ahead of us, trying to start the animals toward the ambush point, but the dense mists hanging on the cliffs soon turned it back. It disappeared behind the gloom.

The mists crept down on us on a wet wind. The heavy surge of Etolin Strait broke far to sea, in a wide white arc curving outward to Cape Mendenhall, and the clouds and fogs and sea mists met and parted. Inland, on a sloping plain, a herd of reindeer moved downwind, like a slow cloud shadow.

Then fog surrounded us. We trudged on again, through a coarse tundra of black grassy water bog and broken tussock ground. We searched for a landmark pond seen from the air, and were fooled, in the mists, by phantom fields of Arctic cotton and white daisies. There were no ground birds or colored flowers in this pale world, only the ghostly kittiwakes drifting through the murk over our heads, and the hollow call of the red-throated loon from some pool beyond the gray.

We had gone several miles before the fog lifted once again, and water came in view. This was not the pond that we had searched for but the upper end of the lagoon that we had left: we had walked in a great circle, far off course. Again we set out toward the cliffs, taking care this time to keep the steady wind at our right cheekbones, and by the time we neared the cliffs, the plane was in the air again, circling out over the ocean beyond the animals. Somewhere on the cliff edge the musk ox had gone into defense formation, for it could not move them. Uncertain of their location, we chose a point well to the west, to be certain not to spook them in the wrong direction. At the seacliff, searching, we moved west, then east, the fog swept in again, and the airplane disappeared.

Behind the fog came a weak sun, bringing to light the colors of the cliffs, which were two hundred feet or more in height. Thousands of sea birds were in sight at once, voicing a depthless squall and shriek and din; the shuddering calls of murres rose from the roll and thunder of the boulders like dark spirit voices from beneath the sea.

The sea cliffs at the Ingri Butte extend westward to Ikuuk (The End) gaining in stature as they go. The only break occurs at the mouth of the Dooksook River, which is the loveliest place on all the island. There are dead villages on both sides of the Dooksook channel, and near these ruins are large heaps of stones—caches to protect whale meat from foxes, for the skeletons of two large whales lie on the beach, and there is a den of foxes on the slope above. The bolder of two we were watching one morning lay down in a bed of flowers by its hole, the better to observe us, and a rare sun glistened on fur that the dank cold climate has made rich and lustrous. The fox hollow had a dozen earths, and the heads and wings of fallen murres were scattered before each one. Yet foxes cannot much affect the number of sea birds, which live in their millions all along the island's western face.

Bird cliffs are an hypnotic spectacle, like fire and the sea, and I was startled, as if awakened, when we came upon the musk ox, in a grassy hollow to the eastward. They were but a few yards from the rim, a large bull, a young bull, a cow and a single calf. The large bull was awaiting us, backing the others into place. He nuzzled his shin and snorted. In the pale sunlight and sea wind, head and hump raised high and long hair blowing, he was a portrait of the ancient musk ox, regarding with fine semblance of disdain the tired men who stumbled toward him, whooping and waving.

In fact, he brought us to a sheepish halt. The bull showed not the slightest sign of giving ground, and tiredly, for want of better news, Teal notified the ambush line by walkie-talkie that the animals were now in view. Then we whopped and waved again, and the cow showed an inclination to go away, but the big bull held her. The third time, as if suspecting that the others might leave anyway, he butted them into motion, and they all humped off in that rolling canter, in which the long hair and green grass flow together like wind and grain.

Every mile or so the animals stopped, and we waved and whopped them on again, backed by the airplane which had reappeared. By making a low pass well behind them, the pilot was able to goad them forward when they slowed.

They ran on along the cliffs, stopping often for us to stay in sight of them. Their defense could be exploited whenever they veered off in the wrong direction, for then the plane could stop them short until the gasping runner could flank them once again and start them back in the right direction. The runner had to avoid coming too close, for tactical reasons as well as for reasons of safety. To the musk ox, man at a distance is a mere disagreeable presence, to be quitted as soon as possible, while a man closer is a threat, requiring defense.

Now they were headed perfectly. They rushed along the bank of the lagoon, slowing down and trotting docilely into the trap before most of the ambushers, crouched low out of the wind, knew they were there. Teal and I arrived in time to take our places in the line; we followed the animals out onto the point. In three hours we had walked twelve miles of bog and run two more, and I felt my legs stiffen as I slowed. Even the remarkable Teal with his huge stride and strength of purpose looked stunned and pale and gaunt with perspiration.

The musk ox were given time to sniff the water, and step into it, though they did not want to swim. The far bank was a half mile off, and they were tired, and the water was cold as snow. We waited. Intermittently we banged a pan and yelled, but kept our distance, trying to avoid a breakout. Finally they moved into the water.

But the bull was not thirty yards from shore when he found a submerged rock to stand on, and stand he did, proud and defiant, while his band circled desperately in the freezing water. The calf, all but submerged, seemed on the point of drowning. A barrage of stones, backed by the oncoming canoe, dislodged the bull; he plunged away toward the far shore, his exhausted band low in the water behind.

The musk ox were overtaken by the canoe and the calf snared with a long crook. A collar was placed around its neck and it was hauled speedily ashore, where it was met and overpowered by four large men. They hobbled and swathed it in towels and laid it in the soft grass with its head in Charley Bradley's lap so that it would not dash its brains out in its thrashing and bawling.

Meanwhile the bull had turned back toward the shore, and behind him trailed the young bull and the cow. But the cow's heart gave out and she stopped swimming, and we watched her drown. The young bull actually turned around and swam back as if to encourage her, but she did not respond to him. The canoe went after her and dragged her to the beach, but her eyes were already glazing over, and buckets of white fluid poured from her mouth and nostrils.

At Teal's command, we hauled the carcass up into the grass, for later its muscles and organs would be salvaged for physiological research. John Teal is a very big man with a big expressive face, and he was unashamedly upset. So were we all; the death had marred the victory of the first capture. The cow's death had come about through bullishness on the part of her own bull, but it would not have occurred in the silent days before green airplanes and yellow parkas and a blue canoe had brought their unnatural modern pastels to this muted landscape.

The next day two cows and two calves found close to the sea fjord at Kigoumiut were driven onto a rocky point within an hour after the runners started out. But the point was a poor one, wide and blunt and rocky, with a steep rock coast across the fjord to swim to, and the cows refused to lead their calves into the water. For five hours the two cows withstood loud noises, pregnant silences, bluffs, threats, rocks, and sod, during which time they retreated twenty yards, into the shelter of shore boulders. The larger cow held us at bay with frequent charges. A cold wind blew and then the rain fell, and as darkness neared, a total victory for *O. moschatus* seemed at hand. The one bright interlude of the afternoon was the performance of a long-tailed weasel (the ermine of winter), pale tawny pink and quick and pretty as a carnivore can ever be. Started up by the loud convention of big mammals where only dull rocks had lain before, it whisked from point to point, peering at man and musk ox.

Because the animals were on a shelf partly surrounded by large boulders, they could be approached within a few yards. Teal tossed out a
loop, hoping to snare a calf by neck or ankle. This task was not made
easier by the tight grouping of the animals, calves in the middle, and
we wondered just what we would do should he snare an angry cow by
neck or horn. When eventually a calf was caught around the neck, we
looked at one another, wondering who had who.

The calf could not be hauled straight in, first because all its companions were snarled in the rope, and second because any tightening of the
noose, unless we could relieve it within seconds, would leave us after
our long day with a dead calf. We could not flare the animals for the
same reason, and they did not depart of their own accord, even after
the circle around them was dissolved. And so we waited once again;
the next decision would be theirs.

The less belligerent of the two cows disengaged herself at last and
climbed the bank above the boulders, calf at her side; the old red-eyed
animal then followed. The second calf, until now philosophical about
the rope around its neck, loosed an almighty bawl, for when it sprang
after its mother, the noose tightened and yanked it down upon its side.
The others wheeled and rushed back, driving us onto the outer rocks.
The canoe was already standing by, but the sea was choppy and the
calf was choking, and I did not envy the two men who would have to
wrestle with it. Burge Smith is a lean hardy man who climbs steeples
and wins races in canoes, and Duke Watson, a mountaineer of the
Alpine Club, is an old white-water man whose exploits are of record in
national magazines, but neither looked happy about ending that long
day with an Arctic swim, a fate which seemed under the circumstances
inevitable. Teal himself was quite unnerved, bellowing at all of us what
we knew well, that this was a dangerous situation, though his chief
concern was plainly with the calf. Its tongue was starting to protrude,
and the outraged cow and her companion and even the second calf
were following the victim as he hauled it in hand over hand.

The second cow was driven off at the last moment in a hail of stones;
she too had had a long and weary afternoon, and she wheeled suddenly and departed. The herd instinct, in this moment, triumphed over

the maternal one, and the red-eyed cow, confused by the defection, rushed off, also. We leapt to relieve the noose and hogtie the young captive which, bawling with fright and outrage, departed within minutes on the first of several airplane rides that would take it eventually to Fairbanks.

The men left on the beach sat down, exhausted. A five-hour confrontation with trapped, fast, angry animals, bearing horns that can sling an eviscerated wolf or dog twenty feet into the air, had left us all rather worn out. "Once a musk ox decides to go for you," Teal observed one morning, "you've had it. He is going to get you, and you're not going to survive it. So try to avoid provoking him to go after you." This chilling remark was an unpleasant reminder that we had all signed affidavits relieving the expedition of any responsibility for our deaths. (The remark was lent weight by the subsequent news that, while we were on Nunivak, a musk ox in Norway killed a man who made the mistake of cornering it.)

Teal's words came back to me two days later at Dooksook Lake, where the third calf was taken. Teal and I were trying to start a herd toward the ambush, on upland tundra with no cover for a half mile. Instead of moving off, the biggest bull trotted straight at us. Teal was on the radio to Bob Rose and now he said, "We've gotten behind the animals, Bob, but they're moving in the wrong direction toward us." Later we laughed at this, but he had not meant it humorously at the time.

On Nunivak, despite Teal's past experience, new capturing techniques had to be evolved. The Canadian animals were far more easily flared by man and plane, and swam without hesitation when driven out onto a point. The Nunivak herds turned to face both planes and man, swam only under extreme pressure, and even then turned about and started back toward their pursuers. Probably this was due to the absence of good cover to retreat to, but whatever the reasons, they made the first captures difficult and dangerous.

On every drive after the first, the herd was brought perfectly to ambush. It was only when musk ox and man came face to face that the real troubles began. We were lucky that no one was injured in the first breakout, and Goddefroi Lippens, a fearless young Belgian naturalist who joined the expedition in mid-August, was almost run down in a second breakout, later on. An improvement on the lasso—in effect, a noose manipulated by two men which was draped over the head of the young captive—became part of the capture equipment. However, the device was only useful where large boulders or other rare conditions permitted a very close approach. Another device which considerably speeded up the work at Dooksook Lake was a burlap-and-gasoline flare hurled upwind of a stubborn herd, to move it off position. But neither noose nor burlap flare was ever used again, for an all-purpose device, already on its way, was to render both of them obsolete.

Calf Number One, called Dahloongamiut after its place of capture, proved to be a bull. Calf Number Two, Kigoumiut, was female, but her herd mate had been a bull—in that long vigil, one calf was observed to urinate as a bull should—and we were fortunate that the noose fell on the heifer, for we sought heifers in a ratio of four to one.

Dahloon and Kig, as they were known, displayed from the first the marked individuality that characterizes musk ox, large and small. Both were hogtied and flown out to Nash Harbor, and both were lugged laboriously a long half-mile uphill from the plane landing to their quarters in an old church. Then they were tagged, respectively, with a red (male) and blue (female) Number One, and given a preventive shot of Azimycin against pneumonia. Here the pattern ended. The little bull, upon release, sprang to his feet and charged. Throughout his first feedings, it required three men to hold him, one of whom was knocked flat by surprise attack; another well-wisher received cuts over the eyes from a milk can sent flying by the woolly head.

The lassoed heifer, on the other hand, panted woebegone on her bed of grass for a long time, and when she rose, moved timidly out of our way. On her first night she nibbled willows provided her, and the next morning she accepted docilely her forced-fed bottle of half concentrated milk, half water, learning quickly to suck on the nipple. (The heifers will wean themselves by choice early next spring, while bull calves, if indulged, will hanker along after the nipple for two years.) But other heifers that came in later proved as belligerent and stubborn as the males.

Except that the heifer was slightly larger, the two calves were identical. With ears and tail submerged in hair, they looked like stocky bales of bunched thick wool, with white stockings, white foreheads, and big dark reproachful eyes. And they were as dignified as their parents, and as spirited.

Marianne Moore, the *grande dame* of our poets, was fascinated by the statement, in an article by John Teal, that musk ox calves were odorless, even when wet. Having wrestled all of the first ten calves at least once each, and had my nose pressed to their wool, I can only remark that Teal's reverence of the animal must have blunted his senses. The musk ox calf, on Nunivak at least, has a faint, pleasant, unmistakable odor of manure.

As the calves came in, calf-wrassling became an expedition sport, and the best at it was Terry Hall, a strong stocky young man who will care for the young animals in Fairbanks. But in a day or two or three, depending on the individual, the forced feeding was over. Once the calves realized that no harm was meant, they tamed immediately, placing a friendly and whole-hearted trust in our safekeeping.

In early August, Teal had been in no hurry to make captures, preferring to get his camp established and all procedures running smoothly. Unweaned calves are very delicate, especially when penned up and when in transit, and he had meant to take the calves in a concentrated period, so that none of them would be confined too long in the damp church before being flown out to their corral in Fairbanks. But now the middle of the month was past, and only three calves of the twenty needed had been taken. The helicopter was ordered out from Anchorage because bad weather and the recalcitrance of the animals made this expensive measure necessary. It was nearing September, and the first snow would soon be on its way.

The helicopter, quick and angry as a dragonfly, arrived at twilight of the 21st. The bright orange machine broke the vast northern silence in a way that light planes could not, and it settled down directly on the village.

The pilot was a short, breezy man decked out in the flight jacket, dark glasses, Wellington boots, and wax moustache of the story-book flier. Good helicopter pilots are uncommon, and this was one of them: he flew his loud complex machine with a flair and skill that made it almost graceful. He had been to Nunivak before and knew a little something about musk ox ways, and he was experienced in the use of helicopters with wild animals, having handled rhinos out of India.

That day, two families of Eskimo fishermen were in camp; they had taken shelter from a gale, and the seas were still too rough to reach Mekoryuk. The Eskimos were fascinated by the helicopter, and clustered close, like children, to poke and marvel. The pilot claimed to know one older Eskimo, from his first trip to Nunivak. When the man murmured gently, "This year I lived at Nome," the pilot declared that all Eskimos looked alike. Another man, inspecting the tail rotor of the machine, was told to keep his cotton-picking hands off it. The pilot suggested that the man might steal some parts for his own boat, but the man's son said very carefully, "You can trust my Dad." The pilot said, "I can trust you, too, when I can keep an eye on you." The boy looked incredulous. "Not all natives are bad," he insisted slowly.

The pilot, finding no sympathy among his listeners, decided to say that he was only joking, but the boy did not smile back at him. The young men have gone away to school and served in the Army, and they are proud Americans. They do not like the taste of seal meat, and they are less willing than their fathers to give the white man the benefit of the doubt. And this is sensible and just.

Yet the older Eskimos, who were born in a much older time, know something that their sons may never know. They know what matters. They do not fight against new ways but neither have they lost touch with the old ones. At the loud words of the pilot, the old man had merely raised his brows and smiled.

Teal flew out immediately in the helicopter and returned delighted. The musk ox encountered had been confounded and put to rout, less by the racket than by the rush of air. Hanging directly above the animals and dipping down, the machine had broken up defense formations, cut a cow out of the herd, and even separated the mother from her calf.

Three calves were taken on the following day, not one of which got as far as the ambush line. Separated from their mothers, the calves would try to hide, and could be leapt upon. August 23rd was fog-bound, grounding the bright machine until the evening; on a late reconnoiter after supper, a fourth calf was seen and seized. On the 24th, three more were captured, making ten. Almost all of the last seven captures had been made single-handedly by Teal, who had fine big bruises to prove it.

The rout of Oomingmak was absolute and final; as musk ox hunters, our great days were done. We were now glad of those first days of running and ambush and encirclement, of the three calves that had been won in long hours of hard work. The helicopter calves were tagged and fed and cared for with the rest, and they were named, but in their numbers and faint ignominy they remained somehow anonymous, and their names were not remembered.

On the twenty-fifth, the first ten calves were transported to Mekoryuk. Five went in the cargo skiff of Peter Smith, the rest by plane. Peter was glad that the fierce musk ox were travelling in his boat; he told me simply that the people of Mekoryuk would be very proud of him. On the 26th, the calves were flown out to Fairbanks.

In the worsening weather of the week that followed, eleven more calves were taken, seven of which were set free again as excess males. By the time September storms closed down the camp, the helicopter tactic was so perfected that Teal counted on a take of six per day; he could return another time to pick up the heifers that bad weather had protected.

The musk ox were beaten, and everybody knew it; the Nunivak expedition, in the way we liked to think of it, was at an end.

Already the weather had turned colder. The golden plover were less numerous each day, and geese moved restlessly on every wind. The Eskimos said that a cow in season had called from the cliffs to the bulls trapped on the islet and prevailed upon all three to come ashore. The

Dolly Varden in the channel made way for small pink salmon, and the reindeer herds moved down off the plateaus onto the coast. One day they overflowed the high butte to the eastward, hundreds and hundreds of them, streaming first in silhouette along the skyline, then pouring downhill toward the lagoon. The mass of life was changing shape like some vast protoplasm, waxing and waning as it flowed. Catching sight of man, it milled confusedly, gathering in its streamers, and lost itself beyond the high horizon of grass and sky.

One rare day when the fog fell back, we flew to look at the west cape called Ikook. On the narrow rim of rocks beneath the cliffs lay a dead beluga whale, as pale as ivory. The cliffs themselves were white with the breasts of birds. When the plane neared, the birds swirled off their ledges in huge gusts, like wind-blown snow, plummeting down into the sea. Their shriek and din was blown away by the motor of the plane, causing a sense, in all this swarming life, of eerie silence.

Ikook itself gives shelter to few birds; even sea birds must shrink back from this high jutting hatchet blade of rock, wedged viciously into a tumult of rough tide rips. At Ikook is an automatic light, rarely visible to the occasional ship, and beside the light stands a lone wooden cross. Here, not many years ago, a man was blown backward from the cliff and fell four hundred feet to the rocks below.

The Eskimos fear the tide rips at this cape, which few have rounded. On the trip outward from Mekoryuk, Charlie Spud had announced without conviction that he had been around it once. When asked what "Ikook" meant, he stood solemnly a while, as if at a loss to understand how one could ask such a simple-minded question. "It means The End," he said, with a gesture outward toward the gray engulfing sea. "No more. The End."

In the spring past, an Eskimo hunting seals along the coast down toward The End found himself cut off from his boat by two great musk ox bulls; they lay facing him in the new grass. He yipped and waved, to scare Oomingmak, but they did not move, nor did they stir when he threw a stone and struck one. The beasts had come down to Ikook together, and together died.

DAVID BOERI

Grandfathers of Gambell, Grandsons of the Stone Age

David Boeri holds degrees from Wesleyan University and the University of Washington. With James Gibson, he authored *Tell It Good-bye, Kiddo: The Decline of the New England Offshore Fishery*. His articles have appeared in *The New York Times Magazine*, *GEO*, *Oceans*, and *Yankee*.

Awaiting the hunters' return were two old men who knew better than anyone else the dangers of being trapped offshore. Samuel Irrigoo, age eighty-eight, and Lloyd Oovi, age eighty-two, sat on a sled, binoculars in hand, and scanned the sea intently from the beach. Both were dressed in white cotton snow shirts pulled over parkas and fur-trimmed hoods that fit snugly around their faces. Irrigoo's face was lean and furrowed, and his eyes were magnified by a pair of glasses as thick as storm windows. He couldn't see or hear or walk as well as Oovi, but he could be heard from farther away. In a near-shout, he liked to boast, "I saw Oovi when he was a baby." Saying that, he would break into convulsive laughter that shook his shoulders. His cockiness was easily forgiven, for Irrigoo was the oldest villager or, as he phrased it, "I am the last man."

Oovi was a bigger, if also younger, man. Though he had the voice of a bear, he spoke softly like a storyteller, in the deep, sometimes whispering tones of a wave climbing the gravel shore. Whether among a crowd or alone on the beach, he radiated dignity and a cheerful presumption of goodwill in others. He greeted visitors and villagers alike with a marvelous smile that enveloped his round face, drew the eyelids together, and brought back memories of grandfathers at Christmas.

They would sit for hours, Irrigoo and Oovi, looking outward, occasionally interrupting the silence with which they were so comfortable to comment about the effect of currents and wind, the moon and the tides. Every so often someone would come by with news or with a walkie-talkie so they could hear for themselves the talk of captains far from land. "North and south currents real strong," Irrigoo would inform his audience as he gestured to the pack of ice cakes and bergs moving steadily along the shore. "One must learn the currents and the cake ice. It's hard, just like learning arithmetic, but when those ice cakes close behind us, we have to stay among the ice for the night."

His use of the present tense seemed to transpose Irrigoo into the past as if he were a hunter again. Yet Irrigoo and Oovi didn't seem to divide their identities into a past and present; they had been and always would be hunters. "In the springtime I never sleep," Oovi said. "It's like I am whaling again."

When they were young, both of them had spent cold and hungry nights amid the offshore ice. They had been the lucky ones, however, because they had found their way back.

There were a number of ways, all of them simple, in which the unlucky ones were lost. The shore fast ice might snap off behind them while they were hunting on foot; loose pack ice might surround their boat; or they might become lost in the fog or blinding snow and travel in the wrong direction, out to sea. The fate that befell them was drowning or freezing or, for the truly unlucky, starving on an ice floe drifting to oblivion. Those who escaped were blessed by a fickle but propitious movement of the ice.

In those days, death on the ice was a common occurrence. The dangers were greater then, not because ice conditions were more severe, but because the Eskimos weren't as well equipped as they are today. So small was the chance of rescuing anyone and so great the regularity with which the ice claimed its victims that Eskimos reacted in an often fatalistic manner when villagers were cut adrift or trapped offshore. How dramatic it must have been for Oovi and Irrigoo, when they were old men, to watch a Coast Guard helicopter rescue a crew of Gambell hunters from the ice. Grandsons of the Stone Age, they were witnessing the ascendance of the jet age.

Irrigoo and Oovi were among the last of a generation born in the nineteenth century, the grandchildren of those who had met the first whaling ships a half-century earlier. They grew up in a world already reshaped by white men, for the coming of Western tools and goods had ushered Saint Lawrence Island out of the Stone Age into an era of firearms and calico, gunpowder and sugar, iron and flour. The population of whales and walrus had already been plundered by the commercial fleet, and before Oovi was born, the first missionary had arrived to "make boot talk" and civilize "barbarous people."

Despite the abrupt and overwhelming intrusion of Western material culture, young Irrigoo and Oovi had been guided into a pattern of life substantially the same as their grandfathers', and now, long after that pattern had changed, the two old men on the beach seemed the last living connection to Eskimo antiquity. Their memory, their manners, and even their bodies bore witness to a distant culture. On their joints were two small dots that had been tattooed many years earlier, after each man had struck his first bowhead.

The remains of the past to which Oovi and Irrigoo were connected lay close to the surface of Gambell, although I did not see the extent of them until the snow melted late in the spring. On the gravel spit that extends from the base of Mount Seevookak lay four low mounds littered with thousands upon thousands of bleached-out bones from walrus, whales, and seals. These were the sites where the people of now extinct cultures lived some two thousand years ago. Underneath the mounds were buried semisubterranean sod homes called *ningloos*, the construction of which identified those who lived in them as a people of the whale, for the walls were built with whale ribs, walrus skulls, and driftwood. The floors were made out of mammals' shoulder blades, and the sod roofs were held up by jawbone beams.

Oovi and Irrigoo's fathers had grown up in the same sort of ningloos, but like the rest of the villagers they had abandoned them in favor of loaf-shaped houses that were built aboveground. The new dwellings had walrus-skin roofs and floors; and inside, like a house within a house, was an inner room made out of walrus and reindeer skins, where the families cooked, slept, and worked in the wintertime. "They were nice and warm, not like today's houses," Irrigoo said of the dwellings he and Oovi grew up in. Pointing to the light switch in his new prefabricated home, he alluded to the modern world's abject dependence on the constancy of electric power. "When the lights go out, it gets cold." (About the white men's-style houses, an old mainlander was even more unhappy. "Before the missionaries came," he lamented, "we lived underground in sod houses and laid our dead out on the tundra. Now we live aboveground and bury the dead, and I haven't been warm since.")

Not only were houses built with sea mammals, they were heated and lit by them as well. Women filled long, shallow clay bowls with oil rendered from seal, walrus, and whale blubber, and they tended low flames from the wicks of moss they had collected on the tundra. In the soft, warm light of the seal-oil lamps, Irrigoo and Oovi had watched as hunters fed wooden idols by rubbing fat on them in hope the animal-shaped figures would bring good fortune.

When Irrigoo and Oovi were still young, the universe was full of spirits and souls at whose mercy the Eskimos lived each day. Judging by the amazing array of taboos that governed an Eskimo from waking to sleeping, the chances of offending these spirits were many. Yet the occasions for honoring them were just as common. Elaborate rituals had evolved to conciliate the spirits and souls whose beneficence Eskimos so desperately needed if they were going to survive.

When a hunter killed a seal, for instance, he would melt ice in his mouth and give it a drink of fresh water to placate its thirst—which he knew must be great because seals live in salt water. After its meat had been eaten, the seal's skull and bones were returned to the sea to further appease its soul so that it would return again as a seal to give itself up to the hunters once more.

Before Aghvook approached them in springtime, whalers worshipped the Moon, because it was he who ruled over the animals, especially the whale, around whom the greatest ceremonies revolved. Oovi's father made his sacrificial offering to the April moon. His crew cut up meat from whale and young walrus they had killed the previous spring and left it in a certain place to "give it back to God, to the Moon," Oovi recalled.

It was to honor the spirit of Aghvook that the islanders performed so many rituals and respected so many taboos. When a crew came upon a whale, for instance, reverence dictated that the harpooner strike the animal only once with his weapon. Then, if they captured it, the men sang ceremonial songs while they paddled homeward using oars decorated with whales' tails painted on with lamp soot and eye fluid from a previous whale catch. Once ashore, the hunters prayed and chanted secret songs in their homes for several days in thanksgiving for the honor and for the tons of food, heat, and building materials that had been bestowed upon them.

Cutting little pieces of meat from the whale, Irrigoo's people would string them together to wear around their throats. Returning home, they would hang the meat to dry and, later, put the necklaces into their charm bags along with such things as dried whale eyes, pieces of the fluke, parts of the sex organs, and rocks that might be shaped like Aghvook. So sacred were the charms that nobody else might open a hunter's bag. So sacred was Aghvook that even the bag's owner might open it only after killing the whale or if someone in his family were sick.

It was after striking their first whales that both Irrigoo and Oovi had been tattooed with a long thread and needle and a mixture of urine, soot, and whale oil. "Oh, it hurt!" Oovi grinned when he thought back on it. Unlike Irrigoo, he had been given a second set of tattoos, in the corners of his mouth and chin, to commemorate his surviving an incredible event in which a whale fell on top of his boat.

He had been out at the point of Mount Seevookak one summer day when it happened. A whale surfaced close to a boat containing him and a couple of others. "I turn and watch for where it comes up again," whispered Oovi—he was reenacting the event with his voice and hands. "Coming, coming. Ooh, big thing. Oh, it covered the sun when it jumped out of the water. Sky got dark and the whale came over us. When it tumbled back, its flukes tore the boat in three pieces. We went into the water. I tried to swim. Another boat came to the rescue, but one man died. Smashed in half. The whale was gone. Later that day, my sister tattooed me. I don't know why my father tell her to do it."

It was in front of the seal-oil lamps that Irrigoo and Oovi were instructed in the ways of their people, if not always in the reasons why. As the oblong ring of flames cast dancing shadows on walrus and reindeer walls of their skin houses, they listened to the elders talk about the ice, the animals, and "the men" who had lived *I-you-me-rooh-lak*, "long, long ago."

You know that little camp the other side of Tapphook? One of our people from there knew of the white men's coming long before they came here. Long, long ago, he made an igloo that looked like a two-masted schooner. He cut up a spotted sealskin, then toothed 'em up, toothed 'em up to make it soft, and formed the masts and made a leather flag. Our people had never seen such a thing before the white men come here.

When he hoist up that leather flag, he sang this song:

Eye-stow EE-eye-o
Oy-*kan*-a EE-a-low
Bowhead.

Another one, maybe when he lowered that flag:

AA-AA-coooy AA-AA-coy
An-kan-ning kan-ning new *kat*-zi kan-ning
Va-va-cat-tin tem-pa-kal-y
Va-cas va-cat-tin tem-pa kal-y, ta-cooy coy.

Irrigoo sang it for me when we were alone. The melody rose and fell softly like a walk across the tundra. He finished with childlike laughter, and I asked him what the lyrics meant.

"I don't know," he said. "Maybe that man did. I don't know none of them. Must be Chinese." His shoulders jumped up and down before he stopped laughing to add, "That's a *true* story. Not a fairy tale."

Inside the skin houses where Irrigoo had heard such stories as a boy, the seal-oil lamps and crowded bodies made the air so warm that the Eskimos wore loincloths or nothing at all. There was a strong practicality to many Eskimo ways that most missionaries and teachers never accepted. In each home, for instance, families kept a urine tub whose collected contents were used as soap for tanning hides and for bathing, because uric acid breaks down the animal fats that smeared clothes, skin, and hair. "Effective grease cutters" is how modern admen might have described urine, but to missionaries like Vene Gambell, after whom the village of Seevookak was renamed, the odors of both his namesake's homes and their inhabitants were "unspeakable." (With the advent of real soap, however, the urine tubs were relegated to the status of chamber pots.) "When I was your age I used to wash in urine," Irrigoo informed me. He paused to reflect. "I don't care for that way now," he added, a statement that set him and an assembly of grandchildren to fitful giggling.

Intent on civilizing the likes of young Irrigoo and Oovi, the missionaries instituted conventions that gave Gambell's people the form if not the substance of Christianity. At birth, Irrigoo and Oovi had one name apiece. But the missionaries named them Samuel and Lloyd and made their Eskimo names surnames, a practice that may have flattered the Natives, who liked giving and getting names, but caused endless confusion for the white men who came here. It was the missionaries, too, who decided how old Irrigoo and Oovi were. "They just picked a day, any day, and tell us, 'That's your birthday,'" Irrigoo said, laughing.

Although they had proper names and birthdays, young Irrigoo and Oovi hardly passed for the Hardy boys. Their hair was cut like a friar's —bald on the crown—and as boys, they wore sealskin pants, boots, and socks. Their parkas were made with reindeer skins or bird skins of auklets, cormorants, murres, puffins, and ducks. In the wintertime, they wore inner clothes also made from reindeer skins obtained from Siberian tribesmen, who had been the islanders' sole trading partners until the arrival of *Laluremka*, the white men.

For perhaps as long as Saint Lawrence was an island, an island with neither caribou nor reindeer, Siberians had supplied it with deerskins; for as long as a thousand years, Siberians had supplied small amounts of iron; and even before the islanders ever met Europeans, Siberians were trafficking in tobacco.

From Asia had also come waves of emigrants to coexist or conquer. Within the reach of oral history, Oovi's mother's clan, the Aymaaramkas, had come from Siberia, as had Lilly Apangalook's forefathers. Well into the twentieth century, families were still arriving. With the Siberians of the Chukchi peninsula the islanders shared both an ancestry and a language that were foreign to Alaska's mainland Eskimos. Indeed, the people of Saint Lawrence had had little contact with the eastern continent until this century. By blood and economy, their ties were to Siberia. Even their wars, of which there was a long history, had been with Siberians. And in times of peace, they sailed their skin boats westward every spring, to trade, visit, and hold games after whale and walrus hunting were over.

"Nearly every year when I was young," said Irrigoo, "I went to Siberia. Good people. Hospitality people. You see that end of the Siberian mountains? On the other side of that place I went to wrestle. They never beat me. I beat them all." Laughing, he repeated the last line.

Looking westward many years later, Oovi could still see the Siberian mountains, silhouetted on clear spring sunsets by a brilliant crimson curtain. But Irrigoo had grown poor-sighted and both had grown old since last traveling there. Today Siberia is a world apart. Wrestling matches, trade, and travel ended during the last world war when the Soviets closed the borders, thereby culminating a hundred-year-long shift of the island's orientation from Asia to America. Though Saint Lawrence was an island in between, the economic and cultural bridge traveled only eastward now.

It was from the coast of those Siberian mountains that the European explorers had first come to Saint Lawrence. In search of the geographical relationship between Siberia and America, Vitus Bering sighted the island in a bank of fog and rain in the summer of 1728, on the feast of Saint Lawrence. How bitterly ironic, I thought on so many bone-chilling hunting trips with the Eskimos, that their island was named for a martyr the Romans had roasted over a slow-burning fire.

Although Bering observed "a few huts," his crew found no one ashore, perhaps because the Natives chose not to be seen. (Stories are told of people hiding in the mountains after sighting "a great angyag with sails.") Bering's ship sailed onward in what proved an unsuccessful mission to find an eastern continent, and almost a century passed —during which other explorers like Cook sighted the island—before Europeans apparently made their first contact with the islanders. Even if they had not yet seen them, the islanders must have known about Laluremka already, from the Siberian traders who brought them such exotic goods as tobacco and metals that had come far from the west, from Russia. In an account of his voyage, Russian explorer Otto von Kotzebue described the encounter and the culture he found.

> We were met by a [skin boat], with ten islanders, who approached us without fear, calling aloud to us, and . . . holding fox-skins in the air, with which they eagerly beckoned us. . . . After some salutations . . . their first word was Tobacco!
> We observed several European utensils of iron and copper. Every islander is armed with a knife [two feet long] . . . adorned with large blue and white glass beads. . . .
> They do not appear ever to have seen any European, to judge by the amazement with which they beheld us. Nothing attracted their attention so much

as my telescope; and when I showed them its properties, and they really saw quite distant objects close before their eyes, they were seized with the most extravagant joy.

Dramatic though it may have been, there was little in Kotzebue's encounter to arouse European economic interest. Poor in commercially valuable furs, the island remained isolated until the middle of the nineteenth century, when another resource, the world's last unhunted stock of bowheads, was discovered by American whalemen amidst the ice-strewn waters of the Bering Strait.

Because the bowhead swam slowly, was easily pursued in open water, and tended to float after being killed, it made a ready catch for Yankee whalemen. They valued it for two anatomical features: its thick coat of blubber and the two rows of tall, fringed mouthplates—called baleen—that hang from its upper jaw. The blubber of one whale might fill a hundred barrels with lighting oil and the jawbone could yield fifteen hundred or more pounds of fiberglasslike baleen that was proving increasingly valuable as a raw material in the manufacture of carriage wheels and springs, upholstery, umbrellas, and especially women's undergarments. When the trend in women's fashions turned to tight waists and hourglass figures in the latter half of the nineteenth century, its use in corset stays and skirt hoops drove the price of baleen skyward, to the point where an average bowhead fetched over $10,000, enough to pay for the expense of a ship's entire whaling season. Excited by reports of large catches in the Bering Strait, a wave of whaling ships sailed northward after 1848, and for the next sixty years the waters of the western Arctic would sustain America's most profitable whaling industry.

Between 1848 and 1885, over three thousand voyages were made. Many of them brought the ships into regular contact with Irrigoo and Oovi's parents and grandparents. Sailing to the Arctic from Hawaii in springtime, the whaling ships worked their way through the ice pack north of the Aleutian Islands, following leads of open water that generally channeled them toward the western coast of Saint Lawrence or mainland Siberia, on the opposite shore. While waiting for an open

passage to the Bering Strait, they hunted whales at the edge of the retreating ice front, and when the whales migrated farther into the ice—
where ships couldn't follow until June or July—they spent their time
hunting walrus and trading with the Natives for valuable baleen, walrus ivory, and fur clothing.

Whaling ships were greeted eagerly whenever they arrived. It was
toward the schooners, anchored offshore or still under sail, that a
flotilla of skin boats would stream, their Native paddlers anxious to
trade for Winchester rifles, whaling guns, shotguns, fixed ammunition,
primers, powder and shot, tobacco, pipes, hard bread, beads, matches,
molasses, and whiskey. The firearms and matches were revolutionary.
So was the whiskey, for the Natives had never distilled their own form
of alcohol.

In recent years, we have come to view all past dealings with Native
Americans as unfair, but it is interesting that Irrigoo remembered just
how advantageous the trading sessions with whalemen had proved for
his people. For the Eskimos' pragmatic adoption of white men's tools
and goods made hunting, and life in general, easier and safer. Certainly
the Eskimos must have thought as much, since they were the ones who
initiated almost all the trading sessions with white men.

Along with the technological genius of Western civilization, however, came the effects of its commercial application. Thousands of
whales were slaughtered, at first for both blubber and baleen. Then,
after the market for whale oil fell, even the blubber was discarded and
the headless carcass cut adrift once the whale's upper jawbone was
hacked out with axes. That they were destroying tons of meat, organs,
and blubber that would otherwise be used so resourcefully by Eskimo
hunters did not seem to bother most Yankee whalemen.

With fewer and fewer whales to hunt at the edge of the ice pack in
springtime, the waiting ships turned their attention to herds of lumber-
ing walrus for their blubber and ivory tusks. From 1860 to 1880, ships'
riflemen may have gunned down 200,000 walrus, a staggering number
from a herd that harpoon-carrying Eskimos were becoming increasingly
dependent upon for food in the wake of the whale herd's decimation.

Destruction of the Eskimos' sea mammals was matched by another kind of turmoil that was engendered not by bread and guns, but by whiskey, disease, and a plague of bad ice. Eskimos "drank excessively from the first sip of liquor," writes historian Dorothy Jean Ray; they chose to use it as both a stimulant and a temporary escape from behavioral restrictions within Native society. The results were often disastrous. Yet despite the refusal of many captains to traffic in it, large quantities were traded by the rest of the fleet.

The bouts of drunkenness always ended after the whalemen sailed away for the year and the supply of whiskey ran out. Disease and famine did not go away as readily, however, and they proved devastating. By 1880, they had decimated the island's population, according to that year's report of Alaska's first census-taker. Speaking of events in his own lifetime, Oovi said, "All winter we didn't get nothing, but whenever ships came in springtime, the men bring fever, flu, measles, other things." During the whaling era, "other things" included syphilis, which was spread by Yankee whalemen who exploited Eskimo attitudes toward sex and often used trade goods and money to induce Native husbands to lend them their wives.

The Eskimos never counted or recorded the deaths that might have dramatized events for later historians. It was white missionaries and anthropologists who compiled the statistics that documented for outsiders, far too late, what had happened. When an outbreak of flu hit Gambell in 1916, for instance, white men reported that it killed 10 percent of the population. But an outbreak of measles a generation earlier, when no white men were there to count, may have been far deadlier, to judge from a report of gold prospectors turned away from the village, who then traveled to Siberia to find half a village killed off by the same disease.

Worse than disease was famine. It followed in the wake of the whaling ships, with equal effect on both sides of the Bering and Chukchi seas. Twelve years before Irrigoo was born, famine had wiped out seven of the eight villages on Saint Lawrence Island in what became known as the Great Starvation.

As children, Oovi and Irrigoo knew occasional days of hunger, times when summer tents made of walrus skin were boiled for food. Hunger came with extraordinarily high and persistent winds from the north or the south, winds that either blocked the hunting grounds with ice or pushed them too far out to sea. When the seas were open and whipped with wind, the hunters could not launch their boats. When the ice was piled against the shore, they could not reach the main ice pack. And being unable to find or reach sea mammals or even fish, most of the islanders starved to death in the two winters between 1878 and the spring of 1880, a time when bad winds seemed unrelenting.

Some survivors and later villagers said the famine was caused by no more than bad winds and ice. If they were right, then weather conditions must have been unprecedented that year, for the island has no evidence of earlier famines like this one. To the contrary, earlier islanders enjoyed a luxuriant supply of fresh meat, to judge from rubbish heaps piled nearly thirty feet high with walrus and whale bones and some old village sites. A famine that could kill off two-thirds of the population seems such an aberration as to suggest that more than just bad weather was to blame. Indeed, the evidence points in other directions as well.

In the late summer and fall of 1878, Yankee ships traded barrels and barrels of whiskey along the coast of Saint Lawrence. According to some Eskimos who talked with white men who came to investigate afterward, islanders drank to the point of oblivion. They gave no thought to hunting, and by the time they recovered, it was too late. Bad winds were upon them, and in their frenzy for whiskey, many Eskimos had traded away the very nets with which they might have caught enough seals to tide them over until hunting conditions improved.

Widespread drunkenness in the fall undoubtedly aggravated the disaster that came in the winter. But afterward, many white men sensationalized its role and made it the only cause, which it was not. Crusading missionaries, for example, saw the disaster as an object lesson in the evils of liquor, and at least one popular writer describes it as an example of how Eskimos "were cheated and misused and debauched with whiskey."

Even whaling captains found in the disaster a confirmation of their own prejudice. Shrugging off responsibility they or other captains bore for trading the whiskey, some of them blamed the disaster on Eskimos' improvidence. One captain criticized that improvidence as reaching "the point of often failing, through . . . sheer laziness, to provide sufficient food for their winter consumption." But the islanders' drunkenness or alleged improvidence hardly absolved commercial whalers of depopulating the herds that served as their source of food. Had the industry not killed so many whales and walrus, the hungry Eskimos might have found more food during the Great Starvation. Instead, the extraordinary years of bad ice coincided with the end of a twenty-year-long slaughter of walrus and thirty years of whaling.

Plagued by bad ice, short on food, and weakened by drunkenness, the islanders must have been even more susceptible to the outbreak of diseases they apparently contracted from white men that same year of 1878 (according to several ships' logs). But in the end, establishing the relative importance of this and all other possible causes is no more than conjecture among white men. The only clear thing about the sequence of events leading up to the famine is its result. At Kialegak, on the island's southeast cape, there were no survivors to tell what happened: just skeletons that still lie about like parts of a rock garden in the grass that they and countless other bones have kept green on an otherwise drab and dun-colored tundra. At Kookoolik, 250 skeletons were found where the villagers had been laid, first on the burial grounds, then atop rubbish heaps, then outside ningloos as the survivors weakened, inside the sod houses where they were piled like logs, and finally, under furs on the sleeping platforms where death overtook those who had attended the other victims.

For food the people of Kookoolik had boiled not only the skin roofs of their houses but skin dog harnesses and skin rope as well. There were no dogs left, so the only way to get food was to walk across the mountains to Gambell and pull the meat back on a little sled. After a while the visitors stopped coming. Returning home from the coast near Kookoolik, two Gambell hunters found out why. Irrigoo explained: "The people of Kookoolik all lay down dead."

Perhaps accelerated by the sharing of meat with Kookoolik, famine overtook Gambell as well. A man came from a village in the east with his dogs, only to find that people were hungry here, too. They ate his dogs. Giant breakers and gales made hunting impossible, and the ice did not come until late in the winter.

When animals were killed, the hunters were too weak to carry full loads of meat back home. Some died from exposure and exhaustion, and in the desperate attempt to get food, others fell through thin ice and froze to death while retrieving walrus. Still more providers were swept away.

In the village, they too boiled skin roofs and "gut" raincoats made of dried walrus and seal intestines. "I heard of one woman who fed her husband with her breast when there was no more food," Irrigoo recalled. Even after enough walruses were caught and butchered to sustain life, people still died . . . from gorging themselves on food their shrunken stomachs could not assimilate.

Gradually, animals appeared in greater abundance on safer ice, closer to shore, where they were killed by crews made up of women and boys, for so many men had died. And in the spring, the famine ended when a large bowhead whale was harpooned and brought to shore with its tons of meat, skin, and blubber. This single event may best exemplify what Aghvook meant to the Eskimos.

Only three hundred islanders were left when Irrigoo was born in 1890, there had been as many as twenty-five hundred when the white men came a half century earlier. Kookoolik and Kialegak were desolated; the southwest cape would soon be abandoned; and Seevookak, later to be renamed Gambell, was the only major settlement that remained. Neither Irrigoo's family nor Oovi's were true Seevookakmet, "people of Seevookak." Irrigoo's father was from Nungoopugahk, to the east of the mountain; and Oovi's father was from Puwughileq, near the island's southwest cape. Like almost all the famine's survivors, they had come to Seevookak.

Growing up there, Irrigoo and Oovi saw the last of the whaling fleet. The diligence with which it pursued the whale had led the industry to the historical fate of all commercial whalers. Out of a population that once may have numbered thirty-thousand bowheads, probably no more than three-thousand remained. Most ships could not catch enough to make a profit. Indeed, the scarcity of whales drove the price of baleen so high that a cheap substitute—steel spring—was developed and the market for whales collapsed altogether. Foiled by their own proficiency and overzealous hunting, the whalers abandoned the Arctic by 1914, leaving behind them a new technology for killing that might enable the Eskimos to finish off the slaughter the Yankees had begun.

From the sailing ships' first arrival it was probably inevitable that Eskimo culture would be transformed, but the offshore commercial whalemen didn't cause that transformation. Although they traded with the islanders aboard ship, they seldom went ashore, and stayed only when shipwrecked. When the whalemen left for good, the islanders were still engaged in an ancient way of life. Even though Eskimos had adopted guns, the pattern of hunting remained the same, and their religious rituals endured for a long time after.

What cut far deeper than the whaling industry ever could were Western institutions that came ashore to stay. Christianity and white men's education, trading posts, and the economic system they represented changed values, customs, and people's relationship to the world around them. Among the villagers of Gambell, Irrigoo was the only one left who had been alive when the second era began. It started with the ringing of a church mission's school bell, first rung by V. C. Gambell, that brought the whole village running.

I came to Gambell eighty-three years later, expecting to find a village that had last existed in Irrigoo's youth. Of that village, however, there remained little more than Samuel Irrigoo, Lloyd Oovi, and the hunt for whales. And like others who came here, I wondered if Aghvook too would die, like the two old men who looked out eagerly for whales and boats on the ocean where their people had hunted for as long as there had been Eskimos.

ANNE MORROW LINDBERGH

The King Islanders

Anne Morrow Lindbergh was born
in 1906 in Englewood, New Jersey,
and was educated at Miss Chapin's
School and Smith College. The author
of several books including *North to
the Orient*, *Listen! the Wind*, *The
Waves of the Future*, *Steep Ascent*,
Gift From the Sea, *The Unicorn*, and
Dearly Beloved, she holds honorary
degrees from Amherst College and
the University of Rochester, and in
1934 she received the Hubbard Medal
from the National Geographic Society.
A pilot and licensed radio operator, she accompanied her husband,
Charles, on many continental and
transcontinental flights.

ESKIMO SPORTS
Tomorrow Afternoon at 4 P.M.
At Barracks Sq. and Water Front
ESKIMO "WOLF DANCE" IN COSTUME
At Arctic Brotherhood Hall 8 P.M.
Public Invited
LINDBERGHS' BE GUESTS OF HONOR

The Nugget, Nome's daily telegraph bulletin, lay on the table, its front page announcing the day's entertainment. We had arrived in this old Alaskan mining town after a short flight from Shishmaref Inlet. The night mists had melted when we woke the morning after our adventure with the duck hunters. In front of us glistened a promised land. This was the Alaska we had read of. Snow-capped mountains climbed ahead of us instead of flat wastes. Green valleys cut the morning light. And the sea, the Bering Sea, rising in the gap between two hills as we approached, burned brilliant blue. We followed the beach, a gleaming white line, toward Safety Harbor. A second white line ran parallel to the shore, like foam or scattered flowers. As we came nearer I saw it to be a tangled trail of driftwood, polished white by the surf after its long journey down the Yukon River, out into Norton Sound, and up the coast to Nome. Pounding, dancing, tossing, all the way they had come, these white arms, these branches from an alien forest, to flower on a bare coast that had never known a tree. They were as startling to see here as the waxen stems of Indian pipe in the heart of green woods, ghostly visitors from another world.

No trees yet. We had come far south from Barrow, but there were still no trees on these green hills falling to the water's edge. A broad trail cut its way over the slope, rippling up and down, like a whip cracking in the air. An Eskimo trail, I supposed, until I saw a black beetle crawl around the corner. A car! A road! We had not seen a road for so long that I hardly recognized one.

A little later we were bumping along the same road on our way into town. It had been a trail in the Gold Rush days. Old roadhouses were stationed along the side, a day's dog-team journey apart over winter snow; we had already passed the second one in forty minutes. Dilapidated shingled buildings they were, fast becoming useless; for the airplane on skiis is replacing the dog team. It is cheaper per pound to fly.

Nome has changed since the Gold Rush days when in the 1890s the precious metal was discovered in creeks and on the coast, and the great trail of prospectors swarmed over the mountains to that far cape of Alaska; when all the beach for miles—that white line we had seen from the air—was black with men sifting gold from the sand; when banks, hotels, theaters, and shops sprang up overnight and busy crowds thronged up and down the plank streets. Twenty thousand people once filled the town; now there are hardly more than a thousand.

But there were still signs of the old life. We passed a deserted mining shack by a stream. Fireweed, yarrow, and monkshood sprawled over the rusted machinery. On the beach two men were shoveling sand down long wooden sluice boxes, "washing" gold.

"Just about manage a day's wage that way," explained our host as we passed. Ahead was a gold dredge in action; the water pipes or "points" plunged deep into the ground to thaw it out before dredging.

The banks, the hotels, the shops, were still there as we rattled over the plank streets of Nome. Empty shells of buildings, many of them, gray, weather-beaten, sagging like an old stage set, tattered banners of a better day. But Nome was still busy. Besides a number of stores selling drugs and provisions, there were little shops showing maccaism and ivory work. One large window was a mass of climbing nasturtiums grown from a window box. There were boats coming in, trade and tourists. There was the loading and unloading of lighters in the harbor. That was what brought the King Islanders.

This Eskimo tribe from King Island in the north came to Nome in the summer to get what work they could as longshoremen and, perhaps, selling trinkets to tourists. They paddled eighty miles down the coast in huge "umiaks," walrus-skin boats holding twenty-five or thirty people. When they put to shore they tipped their boats upside down and made tents of them. Here under a curved roof they sat—those of the tribe who were not working in the harbor—and filed away at walrus-tusk ivory, making bracelets and cigarette holders.

Not today though. Today they were all down at the wharf, as we were, to see their Chief win the kayak race. For, of course, he would win. That was why he was Chief. He was taller and stronger and stood better and danced better and hunted better than anyone else in the tribe. When he ceased to excel, he would cease to be Chief. I wondered, looking at him, if he had to be browner than the rest of them too. He stood quite near us on the dock, shaking his head and sturdy shoulders into a kind of raincoat, a hooded parka made of the gut of seals. His head emerging from the opening showed a streak of white across the dark crop of hair, and, looking at his face, one was shocked to see the same splash of white on the side of brow and cheek, as though the usual Eskimo brown were rubbing off. It was not a birthmark, they told me, but some strange disease which was slowly changing the color of his skin. Would it detract from his superiority or increase it? He seemed quite invincible as he stood there, his broad shoulders thrown back, his head well set. Even his features were stronger than those of his men; firmer mouth, more pronounced cheekbones, unusually deepset eyes. He belonged to those born rulers of the earth.

The three men who were to race squeezed into their kayaks (a native boat entirely sealskin-covered except for a hole where the man sits). Each one then tied the skirt of his parka around the wooden rim of the opening so that no water could enter. Man and boat were one, like Greek centaurs. Then they were launched. A cold rain was driving in our faces and the bay was choppy, but the three kayaks, far more delicately balanced than canoes, rode through the waves like porpoises. It was difficult to follow the race. Sometimes the waves hid a boat from view, or breaking over one, covered it with spray. But the Chief won, of course. The crowd on the beach shouted. He did not come in; merely shook the water from his face and started to turn his kayak over in a side somersault. A little flip with the paddle and he was upside down. "That's how easily they turn over," I thought. For one horrible second the boat bobbed there in the surf, bottom up, like one of those annoying come-back toys with the weight stuck in the wrong end. A gasp from the crowd. Then, "A-a-ah!" everyone sighed with relief. He flipped right side up, smiled, shook the water off his face. What was he thinking as he shoved in to shore after that triumph? He had won. He had turned a complete somersault in rough water. No one else could do it as well. He was Chief of the King Islanders.

We saw him again at night. The bare raftered hall was jammed with the Eskimo and white inhabitants of Nome. Around the walls, as in an old-fashioned dancing school, sat a row of Eskimo mothers. Leaning over their calico skirts they peered at the audience and at the same time kept watch of their black-eyed children who sprawled in and out among the slat chairs. There was much giggling and rustling of paper programs. As the curtain rose one noticed first the back wall hung with furs, one huge white bearskin in the center. The stage itself was empty except for a long box, like a large birdhouse, in which were five portholes. On top of the box over each hole squatted an Eskimo in everyday dress: skin trousers, boots, and parka. Out of the holes suddenly popped five wolves' heads. Ears erect, fangs bared, yellow eyes gleaming, the heads nodded at us. Nodded, nodded, nodded, insanely like a dream, this way and that, to the rhythmic beat of a drum. For now in the background of the stage sat some Eskimo women and a few old men chanting and pounding out the rhythm of those heads. Every little while when a head became awry, the Eskimo on top leaned over and jerked it straight by pulling at an ear. The snarling heads began to look childish. Weren't those squatting figures just like the nurses in Central Park? "Tony! Anne! Christopher! Come here—what have you done to your coat? Look where your hat is! There now go along." They apparently had no part in the drama, these nurses. Like the black-hooded figures who run in and out on the Japanese stage, they were, I assumed, supposed to be invisible, and only there for convenience.

Pound, pound, pound—out of the holes leaped the wolves (who were dressed in long white woolen underwear below their fierce heads). On all fours they stared at us. Pound, pound, pound—they nodded this way, that way, this way, that way, unceasingly, like a child who is entranced with a new trick and cannot shake himself free of it, but repeats it again and again, a refrain to his life. Pound, pound, pound —they were on their feet and shaking their bangled gauntlets this way and that. The wolf in the center tossed his head and glared at us— the Chief of the King Islanders. Pound, pound, pound, the nodding went on and on. Pound, pound, pound, their movements were sudden and elastic, like animals. There was more repose in their movement than in their stillness, which was that of a crouching panther, or a taut bow. One waited, tense, for the inevitable spring. Action was relief. Pound, pound, pound—legs in the air and a backward leap. They had all popped into the holes, disappeared completely. The crosslegged nurses merely nodded approval. And the curtain fell.

The Chief of the King Islanders came out from a door to the left of the stage. The wolf's head lay limp in his hand. Sweat ran down his face. He stood a head above the rest of the group and had that air of being looked at which is quite free from any self-consciousness, as though stares could reflect themselves on the face of the person beheld even when he is unconscious of them. The Chief did not notice the eyes turned toward him, for he was watching the sports now beginning in the hall.

Chairs pushed back, the Eskimo boys were kicking, with both feet together, at a large ball suspended from the rafters. Their toes often higher than their heads, they doubled up in a marvelously precise fashion like a jackknife. Now the girls' competition. The ball was lowered from the ceiling to meet their height. A thin strip of a girl was running down the aisle, her black braids tossing arrogantly. Stop, leap, and kick —the ball shot into the air and spun dizzily. That was an easy one. "The Chief's daughter," someone whispered to me. The ball was raised; the contestants fell out; one fat girl tried and sat down on the floor; everyone laughed.

There were only two left now. A run, a jump, and a leap—the ball floated serenely out of reach. Three times and out. Only the Chief's daughter left. A run, a jump, and a leap—the ball gleamed untouched. She missed it. She ran back shaking her braids. The ball was still. Several people coughed, rustled their programs. I saw her sullen little face as she turned. A run, a jump, and a leap. We could not see her touch it but the ball quivered slightly and began to spin. She had grazed it. "Hi! Hi!" shouted the Eskimos, and the crowd clapped. Her expression did not change as she wriggled back into her seat. But the Chief of the King Islanders was smiling, an easy, arrogant smile.

The next morning we walked down the plank streets of Nome to the King Islanders' camp. The town was quiet after the excitement of the night before. Life in camp was going on as usual. In the shade of their long curved "umiaks" sat whole families, mothers nursing their babies, old men filing at ivory tusks, while near by were young men curing fish, hanging long lines of them up to dry in the sun. We stopped and talked to one of the ivory filers. He had a half-finished match box in his hand. A pile of white dust lay at his feet. He was, we were to discover, the Chief's brother.

"That was a wonderful dance of yours last night." A broad smile accentuated his high cheekbones. Then gravely he looked up at us.

"My," he said simply.

" 'My,' " we echoed. "What do you mean?"

"*My*," he repeated with emphasis, putting down his file, "*my* brother, my son, my nephews—" He took a long breath. "*My*."

That was it, I thought, as we walked back. That was what the Chief of the King Islanders felt, shaking the water from his face after the somersault. That was what he thought tossing his wolf's head. That was what he meant by that smile when his daughter made the ball quiver—simply, "*My*."

ROBERT COLES

Distances

Physician and child-psychiatrist
Robert Coles is the author of several
books, most notably the five-volume
Pulitzer Prize–winning *Children of
Crisis*. Other books include *Walker
Percy: An American Search* and *The
Last and First Eskimos*. A teacher at
Harvard, Mr. Coles lives in Concord,
Massachusetts.

The Arctic coastal plain is flat, sandy, blessed with a network of lakes. The water is shallow. Sandbars and islands run parallel to a substantial stretch of the shore. Inland, the tundra seems limitless. The eyes are stopped only by an occasional clump of hemlocks, a burst of caribou, fast moving and soon enough out of sight. At about six or seven, certain Eskimo children ask their parents or schoolteachers whether the tundra ever ends. They are told about rivers that have their origins in mountain streams, about valleys that cut their way through rugged, uneven terrain. But they smile in disbelief—most of those stories Eskimo boys and girls only gradually come to accept as "true," or as eminently suggestive as well as entertaining, intriguing. In the summer those children, and their parents, too, become preoccupied with what is near at hand: the thaw, which turns glacial gravels and permafrost into a lacework of turbid puddles; the wild flowers, in all sizes and colors; the profusion of grasses, thick and sometimes deep; the carpet of mosses and lichens, deep green or white or brown. But all of that, close by and for a while arresting, is no real match for the commanding presence of the sea, the tundra, the sky—the mystery of space, of distances.

An Eskimo youth, a young woman of fourteen who once spent half a year in Fairbanks, comments on the village life she lives, and the life she saw in the city, as well as the life she knows millions of her fellow American citizens take for granted: "I remember waking up in the house we had in Fairbanks; I went to the window, and I saw—another house. I bent my neck and looked, and there was the sky, a small piece of it—the size of fish or meat we have in the middle of the winter, not fish or meat we eat in the summer! Everywhere we went there were houses or stores. We kept looking at walls. I couldn't see beyond a street; there were always cars and buildings. The sky was not the same sky I knew. There was no ocean. At school there was a playground, but across the street there were stores. My mother said she felt a lot of the time as if she wasn't getting enough air inside her. My father ended up in the bars at night, drinking. He didn't see anything except the beer inside a bottle.

"One day he came home and said he wanted to go back to our village; he wanted to stand near the ocean and look at the water, not drown in beer. We left the next day. My uncle has been in Fairbanks for a long time, but my father couldn't stay, and I'm glad we're back here. As soon as we got home, my grandmother told me to go say hello to the ocean, and to the ponds, and to take a walk through the grass, and to watch for foxes and say hello to them. And not to forget the sky; she never does—she's always looking at the sky and watching the clouds, and she can tell if the weather will change by the way the clouds go across the sky. She won't tell me her secret. She says I'll learn it by looking long enough myself!"

She does that; she looks and looks. She looks closely at flowers nearby, the short stems, the heavy blossoms. She looks closely at the snow—soft and clumpy, or crusty, or shimmering in its subtle lines, currents, and crosscurrents. She gazes—a mix of attention directed outward and a meditative mood. She scans the horizon, or the flocks of ducks, geese, birds: whither and with what dispatch and how many? She stares fixedly—the movements of a dog, a fox, a bird hold her in apparent thralldom, as she herself seems to realize: "I can't take my eyes off a duck sometimes. I pick one, and I follow it, until it lets me go—by flying far enough away. Then I am free to go away myself: I'm back looking at the clouds, and trying to see if they are running or walking, and if they bring summer rain or just themselves, with the sun melting them every once in a while.

"If you look far enough away you see the point where the sky and the land join; that is where I would like to go. My father says you can never get there, because there is always a point, far away, where the sky and the land join! Maybe that is why the caribou herds keep running all over; they are trying to find that place! They must be looking for something; otherwise, they would stay still more, or only move when they see us. But I've watched them when they haven't seen me, and they keep going, going. I'm sure they are looking for a home—and it must be at that place where the sky and the land touch each other; then there wouldn't be anyplace farther to go. As long as there is more land to see, and a sky to look at, the caribou decide to keep moving. They must get tired every once in a while. They must close their eyes and stop staring out at the land and the sky."

She constantly refers to vision, to the subtleties of sight; and in so doing, she indicates what obtains her interest—the vast landscape, part of which she stands on, part of which she stands under, and part of which, she knows, enables her and others to stay alive. That last, the sea, is nourishing to her, but mystifying, too. She runs to the sea when she is unhappy—only, at times, to run away, toward land, because she is not quite soothed, and maybe made troubled afresh. Her life is a matter of balancing horizons—that of the water, that of the land, that of the air. She has been told since she was a young girl that she would have to learn to do so. She was told through stories, whose moral or instructional implications were not missed by her and the other grandchildren who listened: "My grandmother used to tell us we must all come listen to her. So, we did. She would point to the ocean, and tell us we must never forget its seals and fish and whales—our food. She would point to the land, and tell us that we are, all the time, guests of the land. We walk on it, and sit on it, and run on it, and our houses are on it, and our food—the caribou—are also its guests. She would point to the sky, and remind us that the sky brings us water, and brings us air, and the light of the summer.

"She would tell us how our people have kept alive all these years: we haven't forgotten the sky and the land and the ocean. My grandmother bows to the ocean, and to the sky and to the land every morning. She doesn't like bowing to the cross in church; she says the church is too small, and the cross is too big. She asked the priest why we don't pray outside in the summer. He said a church is a place you go inside—to speak with God. My grandmother says God is in the ocean, and in the sky, and under the ground. We can never see Him, but He is there, way off in the distance. You should look, she said, very hard—because He'll know you're trying to see Him, and when you go to sleep and die He'll remember you were thinking of Him."

She remembers times when she thinks she may have elicited a pre-burial day response from Him. She has found herself taking walks, or simply standing on a slight turn upward of the land, when, all of a sudden, the world around her seems responsive to her. She does not, afterward, say that such was the case. She never moves from the tentative to the convinced. But she has felt herself in the presence of a watchful, heedful universe, and the result has been a touch of awe, a moment of perplexed acquiescence—as if she can't quite believe what she has seen or heard and found so significant. She makes, finally, no effort to "resolve" her mystical side and her practical side, her Eskimo side and her American-educated side. She simply recalls how it went for her: "I walked to the ocean because I felt sick. My mother sends us to the ocean when we get sick. I had a pain in my belly. The teachers tell you to have a Coke, or milk. My mother says to take a walk, and look at the water, and way off, the ice. I did. I forgot about the pain. I got lost —in the ice. I pictured myself riding on a moving pack of ice. The next thing I knew, the wind came up; I felt it right on my face, strong. I guess I was brought back to shore by the wind!

"When I look way out, across the water, I am sure there is somebody there who sees me. God? I don't know. Maybe my grandmother was wrong. Maybe no one is there! Sometimes I stare at the sky, and watch the clouds in the summer, and suddenly they all scatter, and the sun is staring back at me! I don't just look away. I lower my head, then I turn toward the ocean. Maybe the sun doesn't like me trying to figure out what the weather will be. The teacher says in the lower forty-eight they have machines to predict the weather. In the naval station they have those machines—down the coast. But the sun fools them, and the clouds.

"I'll be running, and I kick up some land. I keep running. I kick up more land. Then I fall—a hole in the ground. I always feel I've been punished. The teachers send you out of the classroom; my grandmother warns you with a story; the land decides to trick you and make you stumble. I can swear I see a shadow, way off in the distance, when I get up. I can swear there is a reason for my falling; my grandmother says there is a reason. The soil has been kicked by my feet. I'll get in trouble. I can feel the 'ouch' coming from the ground. I might stop and try to put everything back in its place, or I might run even faster. Either way, I'll catch it later; I'll usually stumble. Or I'll see darkness ahead— a black cloud so far off it seems to be coming out of the land, not down from the sky. Then it's time to turn around and go home."

When she is back home she turns around again, looks again. She has an intent, wandering, searching pair of eyes. She seems to be wondering whether someone, something, has been following her—spirits, ghosts, one of those saints the priest talks about, maybe God Almighty Himself. They are all off there, in the distance—so she believes. The world ends—or begins—a step or two outside of the settlement she belongs to, a rather finite and circumscribed collection of houses, with a small store and a small school. There is nothing, really, between her community and any others in Alaska—no roads or railroad tracks or even pathways to connect one group of people to another. She and her cousins and friends don't make reference to other places, even neighboring villages—meaning a place fifty miles or one hundred miles away. Life is directed at survival from day to day—though a plane once a week does bring in mail and provisions.

Children as well as old people (the latter remember a time when no plane came, and when it was successful hunting and fishing, or starvation) regard the settlement as a spot in a stretch of infinity, a lone star in a sky whose mysteries are very much beyond everyone's reach, though (as always) there are plenty of explanations and theories around. Teachers have their maps, with mileages; the priest, his Bible and conviction that God is, to say the least, immanent and transcendent both—not unmindful of anyone, anywhere. But the girl looks up or straight outward—and feels removed in space (and, maybe, time) from just about everyone and everything. She also feels, has been taught to feel, vulnerable as well as self-reliant: "A strong wind, and we suffer. We have to be prepared to be alone all winter. The plane may not come for weeks and weeks. It is us against the sea and the sky and the land; they send snow and wind and the worst cold against us, and we have to be strong. When I was small I remember asking my mother why the weather came from someplace—and there was probably trouble there, and that's why we get trouble here. But she wasn't sure what kind of trouble. My grandfather said he knew—the fights our ancestors had with other people keep going on, and they cause the storms we get here."

She remembers as a younger child standing beside her grandfather.

He held her hand tightly. He told her to stare out across the tundra, not to blink, not to look away. If she did so, bowed her head or closed her eyes for any noticeable length of time, he told her why it was important for her to stand fast—with her head, her eyes, as well as her body. There are spirits waiting, watching, or alas, venting their spleens, way over "there"—across the frozen soil and across the ice-covered sea, or across the water temporarily unlocked from winter's bondage, or beyond the visible sky. There is only one way Eskimos have learned to endure; they know to face up to extreme danger, to face down nature's unpredictable assaults. If a child is going to become, one day, a sturdy, tough-minded, inventive, and persevering hunter or fisherman, or a mother who gives hope to children in the face of the fiercest, most unyielding storms, then there is no better way to learn than on the shore's edge when a strong gust comes up, or amid the grasses of the tundra when the clouds gather ominously and the temperature falls, falls, and the snow begins to come down with a thickness and speed—all of which indicates that the summer is over, the light will slowly go away, and (as some Eskimos believe) the distant horizon will disappear.

The young woman explains how that last phenomenon happens, and why: "During the summer we have been allowed to look far, far away. There is light all the time, and we can see over to the islands and beyond them, and way inland, past several ponds. And there are no clouds a lot of the time, and we see the entire sky and the sun. Then winter comes, and we get to see very little. There is nothing far away to see. We are lucky to be able to walk to a friend's house and get there in the dark—against the heavy snow. The sea gets covered, and so does the land, and so does the sky: ice, snow, and clouds. In the winter my grandfather used to tell me it's all right to close your eyes and not even try to look outside. The harder you try to see, the less you do see because your eyes begin to go blind with fear!"

That said, she closes her eyes for a moment—even though it is now midsummer. But they are soon enough open, and she is looking across the bay at her favorite sight, place, spot: a cone-shaped rock that juts out of the water—a resting place for sea gulls. Those gulls have always meant a lot to her, maybe too much, she says. Her mother once told her to stop paying so much attention to sea gulls. She obeyed—or seemed to. She became a more covert observer of them. She came to believe that she had in her a sea gull's temperament, if not "spirit." She has spent minutes watching them, perched on that rock, watch the world. She observes them observing the Arctic coast from the air. She envies them for the grace of their carriage while flying. But she especially pays attention to them when they land on the rock. Then, for her, they are kindred souls. Then, for her, the distance between that rock and the shore becomes inconsequential.

She has them meditating as she does—thinking about the various Arctic scenes and trying to make some sense of things: "I wonder if the sea gulls see me. I've tried moving, to see if they would move. But they know the difference between near and far! If they were on the shore, here, and saw me move, they would fly away. Even here, they keep an eye on you, and if you're not too near, they'll stay on their feet, but watch you all the time. It's got so that I know if I take one more step, they'll fly off. The teacher says I should figure out the exact distance and keep testing the gulls, and then I'd be a scientist, and I'd have my proof—so many yards, and the birds take off! But I don't want to know how many yards. I want to play games, I guess! I can see them playing games with me; and they always win.

"Once, a gull let me come closer than ever before. I couldn't believe it! I thought I'd be able to touch it. I thought it was in trouble—the wings didn't work. I kept moving, nearer and nearer. All of a sudden the gull took off. I can hear its wings going, right now, in my ears! I'll never forget the noise—like waves, hitting the rocks. The gull didn't fly away; it flew right over me, back and forth. I saw its eyes, and it saw mine! I think it was trying to figure out what kind of Eskimo I am! It kept circling me. I decided to walk. The gull followed me. I was sure it was trying to be friendly. Then it landed, way up the shore. I ran toward it, and it flew away, out toward the rock. I think I scared it when I ran.

"My father always tells me that the distance between us and an animal or a bird or a fish is very important. If you're going to catch something, you have to figure out how near you can come. You have to know how far the bullet will go, and how far the line will stretch. You can't chase a bird; you can creep up on it, but you have to be very slow and patient. When you run, you're wasting your time. I've chased sea gulls, but that's having fun with them. If I want to get close to them, I take a step, and count to ten, and then another. But I've never got as close to a sea gull as I did that one time. My grandmother says the gull might 'know' me. Maybe an Eskimo's spirit is in the gull!"

At other times she leaves the shore, walks inland, kneels down and admires the summer flowers—a poppy, some Arctic cotton. She especially likes to look at the land when the snow has first fallen, or when it has melted down, but not disappeared. She notices patterns, designs, lines and circles of white that cover the tundra. She likes to make her own lines and circles, too—sketches of sorts on the snow. Her ears are as sensitive as her eyes. She listens to the gulls, hears the wind working its way through shrubs, plants, man-made nets or lines. She walks up to the drying salmon in the late summer and smells the fish, touches the fish, steps back and watches a beam of sun on the pink-red of the fish. She moves back, savors the fish again, now from a small distance; she reminds herself how full her stomach is, how relatively empty it will be in midwinter, when severe and repeated storms can jeopardize even a carefully stocked supply of provisions. She sits and watches the sun, falling late at night over the ocean—the strange pink color against the distant ice floes, the uncanny mixture of light and dark. And in winter she notices the blue color of the air: enough light to take the edge off the blackness, but not enough to let the color of things really stand out.

In the summer she has stood transfixed, it seems, by the sight of a boat out in the ocean. She hopes the boat will move in closer, but knows it will not. It is on its way to a harbor farther up the coast. Yet, for some reason, it has stopped, is biding its time. She wonders why —wonders whether the Eskimos would be alive today were it not for boats like that, and the planes that fly overhead, and the canned goods she has come to accept as inevitable, as helpful indeed. She has put the question to her grandparents, and heard their answer: "My grandfather said that we were here long before the white people had their planes and ships. My grandmother took me to the fish she has stored. She took me to the skins, hanging. She showed me the meat. She said I am going to school, and that's my trouble! She's not against the Eskimo's going to school; she just wants us to remember that the teachers should come see us, and take lessons from us. They spend a lot of time making sure they're all right until the next plane lands. We don't have to worry about the next plane."

It is a distance from her house to the school. She goes back and forth, literally and spiritually. She admires the tough, independent, self-sufficient ways of her parents and grandparents, yet has not failed to notice that they have stoves, pots and pans, canned goods—and recently, a snowmobile. She remembers when that last phenomenon first arrived in her community. She was excited by the machine—the strong, assertive noise, the colors, the complicated machinery, and not least, the effortless speed. The dogs were jealous, she was convinced. She was jealous—such an immediate and gratifying capacity to overcome distance, "destroy the space." That is what she said one day about the snowmobile: "It gets you from here to anywhere in a few seconds. There's no space left; you just get inside, and the machine goes, and you sit there and watch the land go by, and there's nothing left between you and any place. You destroy the space."

She treasures that space, those distances she has come to find so much a part of her life. She has not stopped taking rides on the snowmobile; has not ceased enjoying herself, feeling the thrill one might expect a person of her age, especially, to acknowledge. But she can get out, after laughing, even shrieking with apparent joy, and look gratefully across the tundra, or out toward the sea. No matter how fast that snowmobile goes, and no matter how promptly she gets taken in it from this place to that one, there are still farther distances—to the point, she knows, that the immense, boundless Arctic is more than a match for those roaring, cocky motors that belong to those boastfully painted metal bodies.

Acknowledgments

"The Last and First Eskimos," photographs reprinted by permission. Copyright © Alex Harris, 1977, 1978.

"Alaskan Wilderness" reprinted from *Runes of the North* by Sigurd F. Olson. Copyright © 1963 by Sigurd F. Olson. Reprinted by permission of Alfred A. Knopf, Inc.

"In Camp at Glacier Bay" reprinted from *Travels in Alaska* by John Muir. Copyright © 1979 by Houghton Mifflin Co.

From *The Klondike Fever* by Pierre Berton. Copyright © 1958 by Pierre Berton. Reprinted by permission of Alfred A. Knopf, Inc.

Reprinted by permission from *Jack London Reports* edited by King Hendricks and Irving Shepard. Copyright © 1970, Doubleday & Co., Inc.

"The Forest of Eyes" reprinted by permission of Richard Nelson.

"Going Down in Valdeez" originally appearing in *Playboy*, by Harry Crews from *Blood and Grits*. Copyright © 1979 by Harry Crews. Reprinted by permission of Harper & Row, Publishers, Inc.

"With Dogs Around Denali" reprinted by permission from *Journeys to the Far North* by Olaus Murie. Copyright © 1973 by Crown Publishing Co.

"Ice" reprinted by permission from *Stories We Listened To* by John Haines. Copyright © 1981 by John Haines. Published by The Bench Press, 1986.

"Riding the Boom Extension" from *Table of Contents* by John McPhee. Copyright © 1980, 1981, 1982, 1983, 1984, 1985 by John McPhee. Reprinted by permission of Farrar, Straus and Giroux, Inc.

"Brooks Range" reprinted by permission from *My Wilderness: The Pacific West*. Copyright © 1960 by William O. Douglas, published by Doubleday & Co., Inc. Reprinted by permission of William Morris Agency, Inc.

"Toward Doonerak" reprinted by permission from Robert Marshall, *Alaska Wilderness, 2nd ed.*. Copyright © 1956, 1970 by Regents of the University of California, published by the University of California Press.

Selections from *Four Seasons North* reprinted by permission. Copyright © 1973 by Billie Wright, published by Harper & Row, Publishers.

"Geese" reprinted by permission from *Two in the Far North*. Copyright © Margaret Murie 1957, 1962, 1978, published by the Alaska Northwest Publishing Co.

Barry Lopez, "Borders" from *Crossing Open Ground*. Copyright © 1988 Barry Holstun Lopez. First appeared in *Country Journal*, 9/81. Reprinted with the permission of Charles Scribner's Sons, an imprint of Macmillan Publishing Company.

"Alone With Death on the Tundra," copyright © 1983 by Alalie Fosso Johnson. Reprinted with author's permission.

"Letter from Wales (Alaska)" first appeared in *The North American Review*. Copyright © 1980 by John Morgan. Reprinted with author's permission.

"Fables" reprinted from *Reading the River: A Voyage Down the Yukon* by John Hildebrand. Copyright © 1988 by John Hildebrand. Reprinted by permission of Houghton Mifflin Company.

"Tundra of the Emperors" from *Wild America* by Roger Tory Peterson and James Maxwell McConnell Fisher. Copyright © 1955 by Roger Tory Peterson and James M. McConnell Fisher. Copyright © renewed 1983 by Roger Tory Peterson and Crispin Fisher. Reprinted by permission of Houghton Mifflin Company.

Oomingmak reprinted by permission. Copyright © 1967 by Peter Matthiessen, published by Hastings House.

"Grandfathers of Gambell, Grandsons of the Stone Age" from *People of the Ice Whale* by David Boeri. Copyright © 1984 by David Boeri. Reprinted by permission of the publisher, E. P. Dutton, a division of NAL Penguin Inc.

"The King Islanders" from *North to the Orient*, copyright © 1935, 1963 by Anne Morrow Lindbergh. Reprinted by permission of Harcourt Brace Jovanovich, Inc.

"Distances" reprinted by permission from *The Last and First Eskimos*, copyright © 1977, 1978 by Robert Coles. Published by New York Graphic Society.

The editors would like to thank Wake Forest University for providing funds which helped make this book possible and Karen Bennett for her help in the preparation of the manuscript.

The Editors

Robert Hedin was born and raised in Minnesota and holds degrees from Luther College and the University of Alaska. His books include *Snow Country, At the Home-Altar, County O*, and *In the Dreamlight: Twenty-One Alaskan Writers*, which he co-edited. Mr. Hedin has taught at Sheldon Jackson College, the Anchorage and Fairbanks campuses of the University of Alaska, and has been the poet-in-residence at Wake Forest University in Winston-Salem, North Carolina, since 1980.

Gary Holthaus was born in Dubuque, Iowa, and holds degrees from Cornell College, Boston University, and Western Montana University. He taught school in Naknek for a number of years and later at Alaska Methodist University in Anchorage. The author of *Unexpected Manna* and *Circling Back*, Mr. Holthaus has been the Executive Director of the Alaska Humanities Forum, a statewide program of the National Endowment for the Humanities, since 1972.